Through his encounter with St. Francis of Assisi, Gerry Straub came to love Christ and the poor. That encounter transformed his life. Here in this beautiful gem of a book he traces the footsteps of St. Francis—in Francis' age and our own—showing a way of prayer and compassion with the power to transform our hearts, and thereby transform the world.

❈ **ROBERT ELLSBERG**, AUTHOR OF THE SAINTS' GUIDE TO HAPPINESS

Straub not only knows the life of Saint Francis well but has lived a Franciscan life through his commitment to the poor. This is a book that rings with authenticity. Highly recommended.

❈ **LAWRENCE S. CUNNINGHAM**, JOHN A. O'BRIEN PROFESSOR OF THEOLOGY (EMERITUS), THE UNIVERSITY OF NOTRE DAME

Gerard Straub gives us a St. Francis of and for the poor: the materially poor and those who are poor in spirit. Here is a humble, mellow pen "trying to fall in love with Francis again" and in the process finding words to reveal the depths of a St. Francis who speaks to the poverty of our own loneliness and longing in the twenty-first century.

❈ **FR. MURRAY BODO, OFM**, AUTHOR OF FRANCIS AND JESUS

In this bold tale, Gerry Straub puts his finger on the desire that is within us all to live simply and sustainably, with holy wisdom and a strong sense of the beauty around us. Bringing together his own journey with that of St Francis of Assisi, he provides a common, universal language that helps us all see the Creator with new eyes.

❈ **BILL HUEBSCH** AUTHOR OF THE SPIRITUAL WISDOM OF ST JOHN XXIII

A Franciscan nun once told me that part of her work was to rescue Saint Francis from the birdbaths in which so often he is held captive. Gerry Straub's book does just that. If you are willing to meet a rag-dressed beggar who has changed the world, this book opens the door.

❈ **JIM FOREST**, AUTHOR OF ALL IS GRACE: A BIOGRAPHY OF DOROTHY DAY

Forged in the fiery smithy of the author's own soul, this beautiful book is urgent, passionate, and compelling. Its unique power springs from the fusion of Straub's personal involvement in today's most shocking scenes of human poverty, his sense of the extreme, essential soul of St Francis, and his intense awareness of his own vulnerability and demons. In this fire a spiritual masterpiece is born.

❋ **DANIEL O'LEARY,** AUTHOR OF ALREADY WITHIN: DIVING THE HIDDEN SPRING

Many of us speak of biblical paradox. Gerry Straub lives it. Through his art and commitment we have a deeper understanding of this difficult matter of richness in poverty. He has wrestled with that reality at great length and, through the struggle, gained unique insights into the person of St. Francis.

❋ **TOM ROBERTS,** EDITOR AT LARGE, NATIONAL CATHOLIC REPORTER

Gerard Thomas Straub has devoted his life to shining the light of the gospel into what Pope Francis has called the "existential peripheries" of our time. Through film, photography, and writing he has highlighted the urgent need for a compassionate response to chronic poverty. I am privileged to call him a friend and brother.

❋ **HUGH MCKENNA, OFM,** MINISTER PROVINCIAL, FRANCISCAN FRIARS, PROVINCE OF IRELAND

An atmosphere of prayer pervades Gerard Thomas Straub's prose. This is an engagingly contemplative book.

❋ **JONATHAN MONTALDO,** EDITOR, DIALOGUES WITH SILENCE: THOMAS MERTON'S PRAYERS & DRAWINGS

Taking us through the stages of Francis' life, Gerald Straub makes connections with contemporary events and with his own life. "St. Francis of Brooklyn" (page 218) is a good illustration of the originality of this book."

❋ **JEAN-FRANÇOIS GODET-CALOGERAS,** PROFESSOR OF FRANCISCAN STUDIES, ST. BONAVENTURE UNIVERSITY

The LONELINESS *and* LONGING *of* SAINT FRANCIS

Gerard Thomas Straub

A HOLLYWOOD FILMMAKER, A MEDIEVAL SAINT,
AND A LIFE-CHANGING SPIRITUALITY FOR TODAY

TWENTY
THIRD 23rd
PUBLICATIONS
www.23rdpublications.com

Cover Art

ST. FRANCIS OF ASSISI

Painted by Paolo Grimaldi

tempera, oil and gold leaf on panel

website: www.paologrimaldi.it

e-mail: pernaalessandro@tiscali.it

Second printing 2014

TWENTY-THIRD PUBLICATIONS

1 Montauk Avenue, Suite 200, New London, CT 06320

(860) 437-3012 » (800) 321-0411 » www.23rdpublications.com

ISBN: 978-1-62785-025-4

Library of Congress Catalog Card Number: 2014935253

Francis wished that everything should
sing pilgrimage and exile.

❊ **THOMAS OF CELANO**

St. Francis singing canticles to field and flower, conversing
with Sister Bird, reasoning with Brother Wolf, saving
from his heel the brief insignificant life of Brother Worm,
is concerned only with uniting his soul in the charity
of Christ with all created matter. He is listening to
God. Every being to St. Francis has a word from God.

❊ **CLARE BOOTHE LUCE**, *Saints for Now*

He [Francis] dared to let the eternal truth in him conquer
all; which is simply to say that he dared to let the surging
love in him determine his every movement and thought.
And if a man does this, he must stir up drama like dust
at every step. It is what every saint does, of course; but
Francis did it more impressively, more graciously, and
more amusingly than any other. A born artist, a natural,
unconscious dramatist, a wit, he showed forth this greatest
of all dramas, the clash of the Eternal on the things of
Time, in a life story so stirring in its ascent to an awful
climax that the world has been able to match it only with
that played by his Master twelve hundred years before.

❊ **ERNEST RAYMOND**, *In the Steps of St. Francis*

Inconsistencies did not bother him; he did not notice them. He was a contradiction, a paradox. Unbound by custom or tradition, he could act as if he were the first man in the world. Think of his originalities—the concept of total imitation of Christ, and that of systematic poverty as a way of life in the world, his intimacy with birds and animals and all nature, his bearing the stigmata, his enactment of the Christmas crib, the foundation of three novel, enduring orders, clerical and lay, the fathering of Italian poetic literature. Abhorring the pretensions of intellect, he was one of the great innovators of intellectual history. His originalities have become our commonplace. But he himself does not become commonplace; rather, as we seek to pin him down, he flees and escapes us. He is the saint of the poor, the simple, the unlettered. But he is also the saint of the subtle, the fastidious thinkers. He is the saint of the devout, who love the Lord, and the saint of the rebellious, who would reject society, success, civilization. He is the saint of nature lovers and the dwellers in foul ghettos. And chiefly he is the saint of those who need no saint, those who have sensed in him the sweetness of God's perfume. These bow to him not the devotion accorded to Saint Francis, but love for Francis, the Little Poor Man of Assisi.

❊ **MORRIS BISHOP**, *St. Francis of Assisi*

Contents

Would I might wake Saint Francis in you all,
Brother of birds and trees,
God's Troubadour,
Blinded with weeping for the sad and the poor:
Our wealth undone, all strict Franciscan men,
Come, let us chant the canticle again
Of mother earth and the enduring sun.
God make each soul
The lowly leper's slave:
God make us saints, and brave.

■ **VACHEL LINDSAY**

Why?

I t is Christmas morning, 2013. The sun has not yet risen on this day when we celebrate the birth of the Son of God. Wrapping gifts is easy. Wrapping your mind around the unfathomable mystery of the Incarnation, God assuming human flesh while still maintaining the essence of divinity, is far from easy. My mind for the past two weeks has been intensely focused on the life of one person whose sole goal was to imitate Jesus as fully as possible, a man who came closer to attaining that lofty goal than any other person in recorded history. This one man, a poor, simple man from medieval Italy, is as hard to understand and imitate as is Christ. He was, of course, Francis of Assisi. I have twelve days to deliver my manuscript about the saint to the publisher. It is my second book on St. Francis.

Suddenly on this most festive day of the liturgical year, I was thrust into a dark cave of doubt about my book—this book. Why am I writing it? The easy answer is simple, and it has nothing to do with a desire to have the book published. I'm writing this book in order to fall in love with Francis again. St. Francis has animated my life for nearly twenty years. Everything I have done over that span has been inspired by my understanding of the saint and my wish to emulate his spirit in my own unique way. I'm a different person today than I was when I wrote the first book. My admiration for St. Francis has deepened; my understanding of him has broadened. My first book on St. Francis caused me to change the direction of my life. Writing it sent me on a journey into the depths of poverty around the world, where I witnessed unimaginable suffering. Published just over a dozen years ago, the book was far too long—just over six hundred pages. The new realities of publishing no longer allow such long books. As I struggled to boil down the complex story of this simple man, I needed to get to the core of his message and vision. While the external historical life of Francis is very important, I wanted to enter more fully into the internal spiritual life of the saint, and in as few pages as is possible.

My sudden doubts this morning were triggered by something I read. I was standing in front of a bookcase in my library glancing at the titles of the more than one hundred twenty-five books on Francis that I own. Francis, of course, eschewed all forms of ownership, including books. He even gave away his only copy of the Bible. I was very familiar with all of the books I saw. But one title failed to spark my memory. I pulled it off the shelf. Clearly, I had not read it, as none of the text had been highlighted and there were no marginal notes. Folded up inside was a review of the book that had been published in *Commonweal* magazine in 2009. It was written by my friend Professor Lawrence

Cunningham of the University of Notre Dame. Larry had written a very gracious blurb for the back cover of my first book on St. Francis. He also invited me to Notre Dame to screen one of my early documentary films on poverty, which was narrated by Martin Sheen. We also spent time together in Italy attending a conference on theology. In his review of the book in question, Professor Cunningham basically said it wasn't a bad book, but that it had missed the mark in its interpretation of the facts of Francis' life. Cunningham mused about how hard it is to write about a historical figure who was "both a model of orthodoxy and a charismatic innovator." He goes on to say how different authors present Francis through their own prism of interest. He gave a few examples of very well-known books on Francis. One presented the saint as a Protestant, another as a religious zealot, another as a medieval hippie, and another as a precursor to liberation theology. Cunningham adds that "many, many biographers have viewed him through the rose-colored glasses of pop romanticism."

The rest of the day, I was haunted by two questions: What would the erudite professor, who has written extensively on St. Francis, make of this book? Through what prism am I writing this book?

I have no idea what Professor Cunningham will think of this book. But after thinking about that less-than-enthusiastic book review, I realized this: I wrote this book through the prism of the two ingredients that made Francis special: poverty and prayer. The saint had two great loves: the poor and solitude. He enriched himself in solitude, and he shared the wealth of his spirit with the poor and the rejected, the desperate people living on the margins of his rapidly changing society. Pope Francis chose his name because he wanted to focus the Church on poverty and prayer. Like St. Francis, Pope Francis wants to rebuild a Church that has been torn apart by scandal, a Church weakened by clericalism and dogmatism. Pope Francis wants the poor to be the center of the Church.

In these humble pages, I want to share with you the Francis who never ceases to inspire and motivate me. I'm not a historian or a theologian. I'm an artist who was touched by the saint in a profound way. Francis changed my life. This is the story of the saint and his impact on a thoroughly modern guy who dropped his skepticism and tried to embrace, albeit poorly, the mystical way of the little poor man from Assisi.

St. Francis' love of poverty will be mentioned frequently in this book. I want to make it clear at the outset that the poverty embraced by St. Francis was voluntary poverty, which is vastly different from the involuntary poverty that millions of people who are thrust into a prison of immoral, chronic poverty experience every day. Francis, like Christ, wanted to free people from the bondage of the degrading poverty that causes hunger, illness, and isolation. There is a huge difference between giving up all for Christ through voluntary poverty as espoused by St. Francis and the wretched state of poverty inflicted on people by injustice. The latter form of poverty was hated and denounced by the Jewish prophets before Christ, and has nothing to do with Franciscan poverty.

An Empty Church *and an* Empty Man

"It is a good belief that our life is a pilgrim's progress—that we are strangers on the earth...our life is a long walk or journey from earth to heaven." ❋ **VINCENT VAN GOGH**

Assisi is a fairly small, inconsequential medieval town clinging to the side of a mountain in central Italy. It would seem not to have much to offer a modern, skeptical person whose spirit and temperament were molded by the frenetic and egocentric world of television production in Hollywood and New

York. Yet in a plot twist that even Hollywood would reject as too implausible, in 1995 Assisi melted my heart, renewed my spirit, and changed my life. My encounter with the town's most famous son—St. Francis of Assisi—dramatically altered the course of my life. Goodbye, Hollywood and show biz. Hello, poverty and prayer.

In 1206, St. Francis of Assisi was alone in an abandoned and dilapidated church not far outside the wall surrounding Assisi. At the time, Francis was far from being a saint. He was confused and disillusioned about life and his future. The fun-loving playboy turned soldier had been captured in a bloody battle with a neighboring city and spent nearly a year as a prisoner of war, enduring the brutal conditions of a medieval jail where he became very sick. After his father negotiated his release, Francis was free to resume his privileged life as a son of a wealthy cloth merchant; but Francis was unable to do so. He was a prisoner of doubt and uncertainty. This isolated and broken-down man entered the secluded and decaying church of San Damiano to seek God's will for his life. Light flooded in through the partially collapsed roof as Francis humbly knelt in prayer in front of a large, painted Byzantine cross that hung above the altar. In this moment of weakness, Francis felt the strength of God—and everything changed. During what must have been a long, intense period of prayer, Francis heard a "voice" address him. It was Christ speaking; and he said, "Francis, go repair my house which, as you see, is falling completely to ruin."

Francis would respond to the directive with every fiber of his being. During that numinous moment of transformation before the San Damiano cross, his own private, self-made world came to an end. A new world appeared within him and around him—a world where the impossible became an everyday experience. Despite his own weakness, Francis began to rebuild himself. He tore down his own inner fortress and rebuilt it in the image of Christ. His heart, which had been hardened by vanity and lust for money, fame, and glory, was slowly being transformed. Kneeling before the crucifix in the rubble of San Damiano, Francis didn't have one stone fixed upon another in his own life. Yet the more he surrendered to God, the more God visited him with consolations and help. After restoring San Damiano and other small chapels, Francis began the progressively more difficult tasks of restoring the universal Church and restoring himself.

Francis' mission was clear: help people find reconciliation with themselves, others, and God. He did this stone by stone, rebuilding individual lives, communities, and the world. Touched by God, filled by God, Francis burned with a desire to help others open themselves to receiving God's grace. Even today, he invites us to rebuild our lives according to the design given by Christ; Francis whispers in our ears, ever so gently, "God is simply waiting for your response."

St. Francis of Assisi, by God's unmerited grace, transformed my life. My encounter with the saint took me from the glitz of Hollywood to the misery of the worst slums on earth. By the time I was thirty-eight years old, I had already produced popular soap operas on all three major television networks. Despite my glamorous, high-paying job and unquestioned success, I was very unhappy. I had so much, yet I felt something was missing. I had an unexplainable emptiness inside me, which I tried to fill with all kinds of things, mostly bad things. The money and glamour were hollow rewards. I was an empty man, spiritually bankrupt, alone and lost.

I had this inner longing for God, even though I doubted God's very existence. Yet at the same time, because of my power, prestige, and money, I felt no need for God. I had no clue that only God could fill the emptiness I felt inside of me. I left the world of network television and went looking for myself, exploring my own tormented inner world, searching for answers to what went wrong in the life of the teenage boy who wanted to be a missionary priest and had entered a Vincentian minor seminary but ended up being a television producer and an atheist. It was a long, lonely search that followed the most unpredictable route imaginable, including a detour through an Orthodox monastery in a remote village in upstate New York, before winding its way to an empty church in Rome and a dramatic, unexpected encounter with the Source of Life. My story is really about how a saint from medieval Italy walked into the life of a modern, skeptical American and turned it upside down. Or more correctly, turned it right-side up.

In March 1995, I found myself seated in an empty Franciscan church in Rome. I had no idea that an empty church and an empty man were about to become a meeting place of grace. The four-hundred-year-old church was silent. It had been a dozen years since the last time I had spoken to God, and I wasn't about to break the silence. I was merely resting. But something highly unexpected happened. God broke through the silence. And everything changed. Without warning, I felt the overwhelming presence of God. I didn't see any images or hear any words. What I felt was beyond images and words. I felt immersed in a sea of love. Within the space of a fleeting moment, I knew—not intellectually, but experientially—that God was real, that God loved me, and that the hunger and thirst I had felt for so long could be satisfied only by God. It was as if the thin veil separating earth and paradise had been lifted and the division between here and there had momentarily vanished. In that liminal flash of revelation, which was at least a dozen years in the making, I went from being an atheist to being a pilgrim. I went from denying God to searching for God, wanting more than anything else to experience more and more of God. And I went from being a Hollywood television producer to a documentary filmmaker whose lens was focused exclusively on chronic poverty not only in the United States but all around the world.

I adopted St. Francis as my spiritual guide. Day by day, this medieval saint showed a modern skeptic how to enter the heart of God. Over the years, the hillside town of Assisi became my spiritual home and opened the mystical windows of my soul. In the span of a few days, in a place far from home, the direction of my life changed. Over the course of the next five years, I devoted virtually all my time and energy to writing a book about St. Francis of Assisi. During that time, I spent a total of about nine months in Assisi and other places in Italy that played a significant role in the life of the saint.

As I was writing *The Sun & Moon Over Assisi*, the hardest thing for me to understand was the saint's love not only for the poor but for poverty itself. It made no sense to me. I had lived such a pampered life that I didn't even know any poor people. St. Francis may have chased after Lady Poverty, but I chased after Sister Mercedes. For St. Francis, voluntary poverty was a way for him to always be dependent upon God for everything. I could perhaps understand that on a theoretical level, but it was very difficult to grasp on a practical level, especially in our culture, which insistently promotes personal strength and independence.

In order to better understand, I lived for a month with Franciscan friars serving at St. Francis Inn in Philadelphia. It was another transformational experience. Every conception I had about the homeless and the addicted turned out to be a misconception. I met real people, people just like me in so many ways. It's easy to label a homeless person as lazy, or an alcoholic or drug addict as weak. The labels removed my obligation to do anything because it's their fault they are homeless; it's their fault they are addicted. Christ didn't label or judge people. He reached out to them; he excluded no one. The people that I blithely dismissed as worthless, and those who were dedicating their lives to serving them, moved me to want to make a film about the St. Francis Inn. I persuaded some of my TV friends to volunteer, and we made a simple film that surprisingly ended up airing on about 70% of the PBS stations across the country. People who saw the film donated more than $225,000, and the Franciscans were able to build a new soup kitchen to better serve the poor. Moreover, they added a second-floor chapel so that the homeless had a place to experience God for themselves.

My life's mission became instantly clear: I wanted to put the power of film at the service of the poor. So I left Hollywood and show business and devoted myself fully to making films about the wonderful people who embody the self-emptying love of Christ by dedicating their lives to the poor. Between my former ministry and Pax et Bonum Communications, I've made eighteen films in the worst slums on earth. Making those films has brought me face-to-face with gut-wrenching, chronic, unjust poverty and unimaginable and preventable suffering.

I'm still haunted by memories of the massive slums of India, Kenya, and Jamaica, and by the mountain of garbage in the Philippines that is home to tens of thousands of people who scavenge for a living while enduring a nauseating, noxious stench that I could only withstand for short periods of time. Following St. Francis led me to a leper colony in the Amazon region of Brazil and to the home of a saintly American doctor who cares for seriously ill kids in Lima, Peru. I've lived among the homeless in Los Angeles, Detroit, and Philadelphia, meeting scores upon scores of people who bravely faced unthinkable indignities every day, people who constantly confronted the plague of anger, resentment, rejection, despair, crime, addiction, and mental illness. I've traveled the long, hard road north with undocumented migrants from Mexico and El Salvador, many of whom die trying to cross the blazingly hot desert in order to find a job no one else wants in America.

I was in Uganda for eleven days in May 2006, and again in July for nineteen days, and once more in January 2007 for eight days. I was working on a film titled *The Fragrant Spirit of Life.* All of my time was spent in the massive slums of Kampala and in the IDP (internally displaced persons) camps in the north in an area that had been ravaged by a twenty-year-long civil war. Making *The Fragrant Spirit of Life* left me emotionally exhausted. My three grueling trips to Uganda broke my heart more than any other place I had been. (Of course, I had no idea that a far, far worse place, namely, Haiti immediately after the earthquake, was in my future.) Uganda's vast slums were nothing short of a nightmare. The horror of the internally displaced persons camps in the north, where more than 1.5 million people lived without water, electricity, or enough food for survival, was beyond comprehension. On my second trip to Uganda, I became very sick with malaria. For nearly a year after my time in Uganda, I struggled with bouts of post-traumatic stress disorder.

My eight-year journey with the poor up to that point

had been an intense immersion into a hidden world of suffering. Over and over again, I saw Christ nailed to the cross
by our inexplicable indifference and apathy. But as I walked
down poverty road, I slowly learned about the kind of radical
dependency on God that St. Francis of Assisi relied upon.
Yet after Uganda, I felt I could not see any more suffering
and dying, could not see any more starving children with
bloated bellies. I needed a break from the suffering I had
witnessed. I needed a time of renewal. For the sake of my
soul, I needed to see beauty. My heart longed to return to
Assisi, longed to go home, longed to return to the one place
where I could find spiritual refreshment and renewal. And
so, in September 2008, I headed for Assisi for a month-long
pilgrimage in hopes of renewing my spirit and rededicating
my life to God and the poor.

I wrote many of the reflections contained in this book
during that pilgrimage. My dream was to have them form
the basis for a film on the life of St. Francis. That dream was
interrupted by the nightmare of the earthquake that struck
Haiti in January 2010, killing over 300,000 people, reducing
most of Port-au-Prince to endless piles of rubble, and leaving over a million people homeless. I was filming in Haiti
just weeks before the earthquake, and I returned just days
after the earthquake to document the unimaginable carnage
and death. (The full story of my time in Haiti can be found
in my book *Hidden in the Rubble: A Haitian Pilgrimage
to Compassion and Resurrection*, which was published by
Orbis Books.) The suffering and death I witnessed in Haiti
left me with a severe case of post-traumatic stress disorder, which in turn caused me to take a six-month sabbatical
from my full-time ministry. I desperately needed time to sit
in silence, to pray and to ponder all I had seen in my eight

years of filming extreme poverty all over the world and to try to better understand St. Francis' love of poverty, because Franciscan spirituality shimmers through all my films. Many of the reflections in this book emerged from that time of stillness and silence.

The 2008 pilgrimage was my third pilgrimage to the Franciscan shrines that are sprinkled throughout Italy. Since 1995, I've made nine trips to Italy. In the spring of 1997, as I was writing *The Sun & Moon Over Assisi*, I was handed a once-in-a-lifetime opportunity: to participate in a month-long study pilgrimage to Assisi with a group of Franciscan friars and sisters. The pilgrimage was to be a time of spiritual renewal as modern-day followers of St. Francis from six nations traveled to the origins of the Franciscan way of life and reconnected themselves to their spiritual heritage and deepened their journey with Christ as they walked, slowly and prayerfully, through all the places that played a key role in the life of St. Francis. I made the very same month-long study pilgrimage again in 2008. In 2004, I made a similar but shorter (ten days) pilgrimage. On the remaining six trips, I traveled alone. Over all those years, Assisi became my spiritual home. As I walked in the footsteps of St. Francis, I often paused to jot down my reactions to the places and events that I had come to love so much.

In Lent 2013, moments after Cardinal Jorge Mario Bergoglio of Buenos Aires, Argentina, was unexpectedly elected pope, Franciscan Cardinal Cláudio Hummes, archbishop emeritus of São Paulo, Brazil, who was a strong supporter of liberation theology, whispered in his ear, "Don't forget the poor." Instantly the new pope, who was known for his simple lifestyle and dedication to social justice, knew he would take the name Francis in honor of the saint from

Assisi who loved the poor and all of creation and who was a man of peace. It was a bold and daring choice. Days later, Pope Francis said, "How I would love a Church that is poor and for the poor." In the first few weeks of his papacy, the world was drawn to the new pope's humility and simplicity. He paid his own bill and picked up his own bags at the hotel where he stayed during the conclave. He opted out of wearing extravagant, ermine-trimmed papal attire or traveling in the papal limousine. Instead of a gold pectoral cross, the new pope wore a simple, silver cross. What Pope Francis wore—and didn't wear—spoke volumes. He decided not to live in the papal apartment or sit on magnificent thrones. He not only washed the feet of a Muslim woman prisoner on Holy Thursday, he also kissed them. He held a handicapped child in his arms and kissed him. These were all symbols and signs that a new day had dawned at the Vatican. Cardinal Bergoglio's audacious choice to use the name Francis signaled that he would be resetting the Church's priorities, away from divisive dogmatic assertions and closer to the poor.

The spirit of St. Francis was suddenly alive. The story of the saint's life is an authentically human drama with universal appeal, a story of an ordinary man who accomplished extraordinary things while transcending his time and place on his way to becoming a true saint of incarnation. The life of St. Francis exudes a spirit of unaffected simplicity and deep piety. The saint was repulsed by the ecclesiastical corruption of the thirteenth-century Church; he resisted the temptation of clerical privilege and sparked sweeping church reform. His life was a visible manifestation of the conversion process that was going on inside of him. His life was his sermon. And his sermon still has something important to say to us today. St. Francis of Assisi belongs to all humanity, and this book hopes to reintroduce the saint's spirituality to a world sorely in need of his insights—insights garnered from a life of prayer and poverty. St. Francis had only one desire: the reconciliation of humanity with God, itself, and nature. *The Loneliness and Longing of St. Francis* will take you on a prayerful pilgrimage to the heart of Francis so that you may share in his dream and his vision.

Each of us is, ultimately, alone on our journey through life. Each of us longs for something beyond what can be found on earth. Within each of us there is a loneliness and a longing. Following St. Francis into the depths of unjust poverty has been a long, lonely journey, during which I've struggled with periods of intense spiritual dryness. And far too often, sadly, my longing for God has waned and I've thirsted for things beyond God, and I have sought relief for my loneliness in unhealthy behavior that diverted me from God. The heart of Franciscan spirituality—which understands that while finding God in the world, in pain and suffering, is essential—stresses that we must always remember that social action needs to be tempered and nurtured by contemplation, even as we struggle with prayer and periods of spiritual drought.

In my book *The Sun & Moon Over Assisi*, I presented a fairly detailed account of the life of St. Francis, which is why the book topped six hundred pages. In this book, I'm more interested in the spirituality of St. Francis than the historical details of his life. Nonetheless, I'll present abbreviated sketches of the most important events in the life of St. Francis. More biographies have been written on the life of St. Francis than any other saint, a fact that clearly supports the oft-repeated claim that he is "everybody's favorite saint." Entire libraries are dedicated just to him. A collection of the numerous accounts of his life written within a hundred years of his death fills up more than two thousand printed pages. The smallest details of his life have been carefully examined and hotly debated by scholars. Year after year, still more books appear, each author presenting another dimension of the charismatic saint. Francis of Assisi has the longest single bibliography of any person in history. Even Marvel Comics has published a best-selling version of his life, entitled *Francis, Brother of the Universe*. Moreover, within a century of his death, Francis was the subject of thousands of works of art; in Italy alone, more than 150 paintings of the saint survive from the thirteenth and early fourteenth centuries. Today, people from a wide variety of religious backgrounds, who are concerned with such issues as ecumenism, interfaith relations, the sanctity of creation, and animal rights, all point to Francis as an example and spiritual focus. Eight centuries after his death, Francis still has the power to inspire people.

Paul Sabatier, in his introduction to his *Life of St. Francis*, writes: "One must not ask too much of history. The more beautiful a sunrise is, the more difficult it is to describe it." Sabatier's book was published in 1892 and was the first modern biography of the saint. Paul Sabatier, a learned and skeptical man, claimed he had a hard time preserving a comprehensive viewpoint regarding Francis' life; for instance, he came to accept the authenticity of the saint's stigmata, while rejecting many of the miracles attributed to Francis. Sabatier accentuated Francis' charm and downplayed the supernatural elements found in the early Franciscan sources. The complexity of St. Francis' life opens it to all kinds of speculation and interpretations...and distortions. His story, crammed with drama and pathos, has the inevitability of myth; separating fact from legend alone would require the patience of a saint. During the past 750 years, much of St. Francis' life has been embellished to such a degree that the real Francis is almost totally obscured, making it all the more difficult to distinguish between the mass of truth and apocrypha about the saint. Most people are shocked to learn that the saint actually did not write the famous Prayer of St. Francis.

The Loneliness and Longing of St. Francis of Assisi is primarily concerned with applying the lessons learned from the life of the saint to our modern, skeptical lives. St. Francis still has tremendous relevance for my life, and he helps me focus my life more intensely on Christ. My ongoing journey with St. Francis helps me to grow in understanding of my life, my faith, and the life of Jesus. St. Francis is still my teacher and guide, and following him has taken me to the extreme margins of society in the poorest nations on earth; in these pages I'll share some of my experiences in those places.

In the midst of our fast-paced, noisy, overstimulated secular culture, where money, power, and fame are worshiped, people are hungering for something deeper, something more meaningful and real. For Francis, prayer was the breath of life. Prayer was the simplest, most direct way for the saint to acknowledge his dependency on God for everything. Prayer enabled Francis to become more aware of God's presence, a presence that was at once far beyond him and deep within him. Prayer is communion with God. Prayer was Francis' safest haven, and he devoted himself to long periods of intense prayer, sometimes lasting throughout the night. He sought out solitary places where he could enter into communion with God. For Francis, silence was the language of God; and he knew the importance of being still and resting in God. Fully half his converted life was spent in contemplation and prayer. Prayer was part of the fabric of his life, and everything he did began with and grew out of prayer. Francis spent hours on his knees before the crucifix; adoration was the oxygen of his spiritual life. And he breathed deeply the pure divine glory of life itself. Francis sacrificed everything in order to enter deeply into a life of prayer. For Francis, prayer was reality, and it became the center of his life. He peppered his life with periods of solitude. It was in remote hermitages and caves, often atop a mountain far from the noise of commerce and idle chatter, where Francis encountered his Creator in uninterrupted silence and solitude. In prayer, Francis learned about the richness of poverty of spirit and humility, and he heard the vibrant, pulsating sound of the great choir of silence singing harmoniously between humanity and God. In the recesses of his heart, Francis renounced his own ideas and the wisdom of the world, and with stunning tenacity he clung to God and God alone, wanting nothing but the consolation of God.

St. Francis was a spiritual innovator; like all who have created something original, he must have endured a great lonesomeness, despite his numerous followers and companions. On Easter Sunday 2009, during a liturgy at the Ermeo di Carceri, high above Assisi, a favorite place of solitude for St. Francis, it dawned on me that the loneliness and longing within each of us is a very basic way for each of us to connect with the saint who did not forget the poor. In reality, we are all poor, all in need of God's tender love and endless mercy. Days after his election, Pope Francis said, "Mercy is the Lord's most powerful message." St. Francis knew that every act of mercy and kindness brings us closer to the reality of God.

GERRY STRAUB

January 5, 2014
The Feast of the Epiphany of the Lord

PART I

The Setting

A VERY LONELY ROAD

In the galaxy of Christian saints, the star of St. Francis burns brightest, a saint whose appeal is universal and timeless, a saint who is cherished by people of all faiths and is even admired by people who don't believe in God. In the fall of 1926, *The New York Times* published an account of preparations in Assisi for the commemoration of the 700th anniversary of the death of St. Francis. The headline read: "Simple Homage Paid to Saint Francis." The story claimed: "No saint in the roster of Rome has as many admirers outside the circles of orthodoxy as the saint who went his way singing not in the official language of the Church but in the language of the plain people. By writers of every nation, representing every shade of religious belief, the husband of Lady Poverty has been proclaimed as an apostle of humanity, and one of the possessions common to all mankind." Nearly ninety years later, St. Francis' popularity continues to increase. He seems to be not only a saint for all people, but for all seasons as well. Yet Francis is truly a product of his time and place. He lived eight centuries ago in a small city that sits on the side of a mountain overlooking a lush valley located in the heart of Italy. However, this man, who chose poverty for his bride, managed to transcend the thirteenth century and his small city and is still able to attract followers and admirers from all around the world.

In the fall of 1992, a special edition of *Time* magazine dedicated to a look at the coming new millennium selected St. Francis of Assisi as one of the top ten major figures of that fading millennium. The list included Galileo, Columbus, Michelangelo, Gutenberg, Shakespeare, Jefferson, Mozart, and Einstein. For a man who didn't discover any galaxies or continents, who didn't create any great works of art or write any literary masterpieces or compose any enduring music, who didn't invent anything or solve any of the mysteries of the universe, and who instead chose a life of prayer and poverty, Francis ranked in some very impressive company.

Rembrandt painted him, Zeffirelli filmed him, Chesterton eulogized him, Merton admired him, Gandhi studied him, Lenin died with his name on his lips, Toynbee compared him to Jesus and Buddha, Kerouac picked him as the patron of the 'Beat' generation, and Sir Kenneth Clark called him Europe's greatest religious genius. Even such literary luminaries as Nikos Kazantzakis, Oscar Wilde, and Albert Camus wrote glowingly of him, as did poets Henry Wadsworth Longfellow and Alfred, Lord Tennyson. Francis touches and inspires a wide range of people, people with an infinite variety of outlooks on life.

Still, it's far easier to admire Francis than to understand him. He can charm us with his gentleness or chill us with his unfathomable asceticism and long fasts; he can be seen as a nature lover, a social worker, a humanist, a lyric poet, a rebel, a radical, a drop-out, and an extremist. Especially an extremist. He was, in fact, the saint of excesses: excess in sacrifice, excess in love. And then there is the perplexing matter of the stigmata. Francis can be many different things to many different people. The Francis I've come to love and admire isn't a pious, plastic saint, or a simple man who tamed wolves and preached to birds and loved nature, but a complex man who was demanding and uncompromising, yet who above all else loved God with his entire being. Francis is a human saint, a saint who could laugh and make mistakes, including misunderstanding what he thought God was telling him.

Professor Lawrence Cunningham said that "when one goes beyond the usual romantic clichés about Saint Francis, one discovers a person who, for all his transparent attractiveness, is complex to the point of enigma." He was a living sermon to the people of Assisi in his day and to the world of today. His very being was a rebuke to the un-Christ-like behavior within the Church and society. The truth of his humble life stood in stark contrast to the brutality of the Crusades, as well as the unbridled thirst for power and possessions. His faith was strong and his spirit gentle. The beauty of his life still burns brightly.

Francis did not dominate anyone, not people, not animals, not creation; he wanted to be *with* everyone and not *over* anyone. He had no interest in power. To be poor, for him, was to be free, free to be open to everyone and everything that crossed his path. For Francis, poverty was a path to humility, and humility was an essential characteristic of God. God was so humble he emptied himself and hid within all of creation. Through his deepening humility and growing appreciation of the Incarnation, Francis was able to lovingly accept people as they were. He did not judge or try to change anyone. He simply wanted to be "good news" to everyone.

Francis is an unlikely hero of the Church. He wasn't a bishop or an abbot or a theologian; *he wasn't even a priest!* Francis had no theological training, and he remained a deacon, either out of humility or because he simply did not find himself so moved by the Spirit to pursue priestly ordination. After his conversion, Francis never set out to be a religious. He never intended to form or head a new religious order, and he never imagined writing a rule of life for others to follow; all these things were done only when Francis was asked to do them by the pope in order to provide structure and direction for the thousands who chose to follow his radical, full-gospel way of life. Moreover, Francis wasn't well-versed in the Bible or the lives of the saints, and he had no interest in scholarly pursuits.

Francis wasn't at home in high, ornate pulpits; he preferred to speak directly to the peasants he encountered along the road. But when he did stand behind a pulpit, he didn't preach, he conversed. He didn't concern himself with complicated reasoning or developing a theme; he merely said, simply and directly, what came into his mind. He lacked any real oratorical style, and his sermons were devoid of dogmatism, theological quotations, or pompous phrases. Francis' words came freely from the inspiration of the moment. Having lived, loved, and suffered, Francis knew about life and had not forgotten its trials and sorrows—or its joys. He spoke and acted from the heart, and above all else he was profoundly human, and a man who gloried in his own commonness. His love of simplicity grew out of his desire to avoid all forms of pretentiousness. Francis' life took on heroic proportions because he became the *Poverello*—God's poor little one. He knew true and lasting joy is never found in possessing.

St. Francis, the one true follower of the naked, crucified Christ, was devoted to poverty and embraced it as if it were his bride. He believed that what Jesus said was true: "Blessed are the poor in spirit, for theirs is the kingdom of heaven." Because he loved God, Francis became detached, both in mind and heart, from all worldly possessions. During his life he grew systematically poorer, while finding true joy in penance and self-deprivation. He wanted none of the excesses of wealth. He didn't merely reject wealth; but, more important, he rejected its sufficiency. Francis believed voluntary poverty was quintessential to a holy life; for him, God alone was sufficient. He took Christ's words literally, and Christ said it would be as difficult for the rich to enter heaven as it would be for a camel to squeeze through the eye of a needle.

Over time Francis grew to realize that poverty was his highest wealth. He harbored no aspirations beyond Christ. He became poor in order to possess some of the richness of God and to lavish it in love on all creation and every creature whom God allowed to cross his path. His weightless wings of poverty allowed his soul to fly into the sunshine of true freedom. Francis, having nothing anywhere, found God everywhere. He was completely indifferent to temporal things. Yet his material poverty paled in comparison to his poverty of spirit. Nothing distracted him from prayer, and nothing diverted his love from God. His detachment was so great that his heart was completely emptied, leaving it undivided and available for God alone. In the state of emptiness, Francis was better able to encounter the fullness of God.

St. Francis of Assisi longed for God beyond all measure. His intense longing took him to places few had traveled to, places deep within himself and places far from Assisi. On his journey to God he traveled down a very lonely road. His soul longed for God even in the night; from early morning and throughout the day, with the sweet affection of Mary, he kept watch, looking and longing for God and God alone. To long for God is already to experience, albeit faintly, the presence of God. And to experience more and more of God was all Francis wanted.

To come to Assisi and to walk in the footsteps of St. Francis is, ultimately, to walk in the footsteps of Christ. During my first visit to Assisi, I found myself being drawn to Francis' radical interpretation of the message of Christ and how that message transformed Assisi and the legions of Francis' followers down through the centuries. In his own time and for all time, St. Francis is the tireless messenger of love, continuously singing incarnation's song. St. Francis is a towering figure because of his simplicity, which reduced the entire Christian faith to one word: Love. As he neared the end of his earthly pilgrimage, St. Francis of Assisi did not judge, reject, hate, or condemn anyone or anything; he merely loved all, equally, passionately.

"Merely"...as if it were that simple.

St. Francis was a spiritual artist in the sense that great artists are really simplifiers. Vincent van Gogh thought Christ was the greatest artist of all time. Francis, I believe, finished a close second. He did not paint or sculpt; Francis was an artist whose medium was life itself. His story is a human drama with universal appeal, a story of an ordinary man who accomplished extraordinary things while transcending his time and place on his way to becoming the brightest burning star in the galaxy of Christian saints.

AN AGE OF CONFLICT AND CONTRADICTION

Francis was born in 1182, smack in the middle of an era of heated hostility and confrontation. The second half of the twelfth century was a turbulent and tense period for Europe and the Western Church. A great schism had rocked the Church. Heresies sprouted and spread like weeds. Monasticism was on the decline. Critics of the rich and powerful clergy expressed open hostility toward the Church hierarchy. The laity was demanding a more active role in the Church. Meanwhile, the Church set out to conquer and convert the pagans of the Moslem east. It was the era of the Crusades, when violence was employed by the Church as an instrument of the kingdom of God. The Inquisition was soon to bring terror to the homes of many in Christendom. Carlo Carretto, writing in the first person as St. Francis in his inspirational book *I, Francis*, wrote:

> Religion in my day was badly lived. Parishes were only half alive, and were for the most part cults rather than life. Priests in their sermons sought to terrify people with the usual discourses on eternal punishment, while the Gospel was buried in a heavy and inexorably clerical tradition. There was no room for the laity, married people, country folk. Only the religious counted. Above all, joy was missing. To be a Christian meant to be sad— especially for women, who stifled their femininity in a thousand fears.

21

After centuries of governing every aspect of social life, the land-rooted feudal system, solidly structured from top to bottom and ruled by a small number of powerful lords, was on the verge of collapse, and a new, more mobile society of merchants and craftsmen was slowly emerging. An economic revolution was brewing. The emerging market system gave rise to an unprecedented desire for wealth, goods, and power. Additionally, there was a dramatic population explosion that created a doubling of the population between the years 1000 and 1200 and gave birth to a powerful trend toward urbanization. It was a time of profound social upheaval and transformation. People and ideas were on the move, and new cities were being formed.

But change did not come easily. By the thirteenth century, gruesome urban riots were sweeping across Europe. Economic conflict erupted in the towns, pitting apprentice against master. Peasant violence spread like wildfire in the countryside. Barter slowly disappeared as the Crusades sparked an unprecedented increase in commercial trade in the West. Money became a part of everyday life as banks set up exchange branches in all the major cities throughout Europe. Merchants, bankers, and shipbuilders accumulated enough money, prestige, and power to rival aristocratic nobles, and a new class of "haves" emerged. The entire social order was being overturned. It was an age of conflict and contradiction. In his book on St. Lutgarde of Aywieres, a Cistercian nun and mystic born in the same year as St. Francis, Thomas Merton said the thirteenth century "was a century of great saints and great sinners, great greed and great charity, great mercy and great cruelty."

At the close of the twelfth century, Assisi had its own specific troubles: it was caught in the vise grip of an intense international power struggle for control of the entire Italian peninsula. Southern Italy was controlled by the Normans, who wished to push north. Northern Italy was controlled by the Germans, who were determined to expand to the south. In the middle were the Papal States, who wanted to push their domain north and south, to seize as much control as they could and prevent a united Italy, ruled by either the Normans or the Germans, from forming. The lush Spoleto Valley below the mountainside town of Assisi in central Italy was a geographical prize cherished by all. Besides these external political pressures, Assisi itself was a community awash in conflicts between the newly rich merchants and the old aristocracy, and between the rich and the poor, as long-existing economic structures began to crumble. It was a city where the extremes of greed and misery lived side by side; social inequality was tearing the city apart.

In this extremely volatile religious and political environment, Francis grew into an apostle of peace and justice, preaching reconciliation and restitution and the joy of holy poverty. In his early twenties, Francis began to experience two sensations that have caused countless mystics to take the first step along the road to illumination: self-loathing and a dissatisfaction with life. During the torturous agony mystics call the "dark night of the soul," a psychic transformation occurred, and Francis, following the gospel admonition, turned his back on life, left his family, even stripped himself of the clothes his father had given him, and went off to lead the demanding life of a hermit and beggar. At first, he was ridiculed by the people of Assisi; even his friends called him mad. To the worldly, the saint always appears mad; and to the spiritual, worldly values seem insane.

TICKTOCK

Near the end of the twelfth century, just a half dozen years after Francis was born, the citizens of a small town in Belgium asked the king for permission to set up a clock in a public square and strike the hours in order to regulate business hours. Before then, knowing the correct time was not important. Besides, church bells already divided the day into three periods of prayer (morning, afternoon, and evening) and that was sufficient. But now people felt a need to divide the day into shorter intervals, which created more deadlines. Beat the clock was the new game in town. In the beginning of the fourteenth century, the world's first public mechanical clock was installed in Milan, not all that far from Assisi. The clock marked the beginning of a new age: "modern times."

Francis saw it coming and rejected modern times and its unquenchable thirst for progress that eventually led to atom bombs and computers and our own explosive times that are measured by milliseconds. Francis wanted no part of modernity; he wanted people to look back and refocus on the life of Christ and follow him because Francis believed Christ was the true way to progress. And Francis, an idealist who put his ideals into practice, followed Christ the way Scripture suggests: in complete poverty, giving up all and trusting fully in the Lord. He didn't want to own anything except the bare essential minimum of clothing, which amounted to a hooded robe fastened about the waist with a rope. Francis had no books; in fact, he was skeptical of the printed word, except for the word of God. He did not wish to feed his spirit on anything apart from God. Pondering Francis' total focus upon God, I'm struck by how many ungodly and unholy things upon which I fed my spirit over the course of my life. It has taken a lot of time to clean up all that toxic waste—and I'm far from done.

Francis had only one desire: the reconciliation of humanity with God, itself, and nature. Of all those who have responded to Christ's plea to sell all they own and give the proceeds to the poor, Francis was the most literal, the most ardent, and the most successful. Francis wanted to own absolutely nothing but the rags he wore. Mystics have always seen poverty as a key to spiritual wealth, because without resources one must rely totally upon God. Francis was so aware of this principle that he once threw away his belt buckle, considering it too grand a thing to own, and used instead a piece of rope.

Machiavelli said, "Christianity was dying; St. Francis resurrected it." Francis rediscovered Christianity, which had lost its luster as it deteriorated into a lifeless formula. Yet, in that dead formula, Francis saw life itself. Staring at the face of a painted Christ on a cross, he experienced the revelation of the Passion, a revelation that gave birth to completely new forms of sensibility. For Francis, an ounce of transcendence was worth more than a ton of reasoning. In stark contrast, for most of my adult life "reason" was my God, and the transcendental was a temptation to be assiduously avoided.

Francis enjoyed life. As a young man, Francis was full of vitality and enthusiasm; he loved clothes, splendid feasts, and music. He was, in short, a playboy who always had a smile on his face. Even after his conversion and new path of asceticism, he truly delighted in life and began singing the praises of God and nature. But in his day, religion was serious, God was a stern judge, and life was violent, and so when people encountered anyone as happy as Francis, they assumed that the happy person must be sinning. But Francis

25

was filled with a holy joy, a joy that infected all who came in contact with him.

St. Francis' spirit renewed everything around him; as Dante wrote in *Paradiso* (Canto XI), "Like the sun that rises behind the mountain of Assisi," Francis made Italian art, poetry, and even drama flourish. His mission was simple, yet profound: to humanize the divine. For the people of Assisi, God was in heaven and had nothing to do with their miserable lives. Francis boldly preached a joyful God willing to be born into a messy world. This idea slowly infiltrated religious art, which began to reflect the radiant aspects of Christianity: goodness, gentleness, and love. The effulgence of Christ could be seen on the faces of the saints portrayed on the walls of the cathedrals. Art and literature before Francis had become stiff and formal; forms of convention stifled inspiration. But that changed with Francis. Poor Francis was a rich source of inspiration for artists such as Cimabue, Giotto, and Dante. The glorious, unfettered spirit of the Renaissance can be traced back to the soaring spirit of a humble saint clothed in rags.

Charity and love, the essence of Christianity and the secret of the gospels, were never better expressed—either before or after—than they were during the thirteenth century. Biblical scenes were suddenly populated by knights and common folks doing ordinary things...and God was in the picture! Francis and his followers began singing the praises of God and his saints—the "lauds"—in the vernacular. Little by little, Italian was substituted for Latin in the chanting and hymns. The mobile new friars, wandering from town to town preaching in Italian, managed to reach more people than the great monastic orders, secluded and stationary, ever did.

A SMALL, CROWDED TOWN

Francis was born in the Imperial period, when Assisi was often threatened by the neighboring towns of Perugia, Urbino, and Milano. The large fortress that overlooks the city was built by German feudal rulers; it was later enlarged by the popes and was once the home of Emperor Frederick II. When Francis was a young man, the fortress was the site of some fierce battles between the aristocrats and the common people. Francis even fought in some of the battles. Life in the city pretty much revolved around war and an orgy of violence; periods of peace were a rarity. Because Assisi is situated high on the slope of a mountain, it held a great strategic importance in the Middle Ages: its position controlled the roads that led from Foligno to Perugia.

Assisi was a small, crowded town in Francis' day. Life was shrouded in mysteries, and many daily events, everything from marriages to funerals to common tasks to journeys, were performed under the rubrics of countless civil and religious formalities and ceremonies. Few people living there could read, and even fewer could deal with abstract concepts; the people of Assisi were walled off from the world of ideas. They had full confidence in the Church's answers to the few questions they asked. They believed in supernatural powers and the power of prayer. Angels and saints protected them; evil and natural disasters were the handiwork of the devil. The clergy were the elite members of society as well as the most educated; the Church was corrupt and riddled with simony and debauchery.

The physical reality of life in the Middle Ages is an important part of Francis' story. Everything in those days was marked by stark contrasts, the likes of which the modern mind can hardly imagine. In Francis' time, when it was night, it was night: pitch black; and when it was silent, it was so silent that even a distant cry in the night was startling. The difference between suffering and joy, between illness and health, between misfortune and happiness, between town and country, was also more sharp and striking. Back then, the cold and darkness of winter were so severe they were experienced as real evils. Nature was a cruel tyrant whose whim could make every aspect of life utterly miserable.

Then there was the unspeakable physical misery and suffering. Many of the people living in the city were deformed from birth or horribly disfigured by war and accidents; some had lost teeth due to poor diets. Because of a lack of medical treatment, most illnesses and injuries impacted people for their entire lives. Outside the walls of the city people encountered lepers whose open, festering sores filled the air with the most repulsive odor. In short, life was hard—more brutal, more exciting, more dangerous, more mysterious, more glorious, more ritualistic than anything we can envision. Each day presented new battles requiring fresh heroism. I would have lasted about a week.

Today, Assisi, with its ancient gateways, narrow medieval streets, and stone houses with shuttered windows, is an endearing and charming little town, rising in a series of shelves or terraces on the mountainside. It's truly a magical place. Assisi feels like an Eternal Shrine honoring not only Francis, but also the mirror of his love, Christ. Christ, through Francis, hovers over this enchanted, saintly city. Its twisting, climbing streets seem to lead straight to heaven. Grace and hope are in the air. Assisi soothes the soul and stirs the spirit. God's smile can be seen even on a cloudy day.

Assisi lies roughly halfway between Florence and Rome, in the center of Umbria, the only Italian province that lacks either a coastline or border with a foreign nation. The dark, wooded Mount Subasio looms behind Assisi like a massive hump, 4,900 feet high; the vast Valley of Spoleto lies below Assisi, a lush, green carpet thirty miles long and five miles wide, covered with meadows, vineyards, fields of wheat and maize, groves of olive trees, and stands of cypress and oak trees. The natural beauty of the mountain and valley easily enticed the sensitive young Francis to fall in love with nature and instilled in him a joy of life. St. Francis sang the praises of the verdant valley and smiling hills of Assisi all his life. He said, "I've seen nothing lovelier than my Valley of Spoleto." For Francis, the beauty of the valley and hills and sky—indeed, the wonders of all of nature—made a fitting altar for the worship of the Infinite.

On my first visit to Assisi, I was captivated by the brilliance of the golden Umbrian sunlight as it bathed the valley and the mountain, creating a halo above the entire scene. The stone walls of the ancient churches and homes glimmered in the sunlight air that vibrated with freshness and purity; in the glow of sunset, the soft light danced gently on the dark forms of cypresses standing erectly on the hillside, like knights protecting the holy shrines. During the day, the landscape below the calm azure sky spoke as loudly as the church sanctuaries and the frescoes. It was easy to see how Francis saw God's life-giving radiance and flame of divine love in the face of Brother Sun as it rose over Assisi.

The entire landscape—the humped mountain, the walled city, the wooded hillside, and the fertile plain—seems to shout a joyful hymn of praise to the Creator. Harmony and communion abound in Assisi; it can be seen in nature and art, towers and churches, trees and shrubs, hills and fields. Peace is in the air, a peace you can almost touch, a peace that

transcends the intellect. In Assisi, the Franciscan motto—
Pace e Bene (Peace and Blessing)—fits like a glove. Francis
is so real here, you expect him to pass under some archway
or poke his head out of some alley.

Life in Assisi is still measured by the sounds of church
bells, some ringing mightily, others brightly. Added to the
peace and charm that grace the town is something easy to
overlook: the flowers. Flowers enliven the town on every side.
They bloom in window boxes and in pots; they cascade from
balconies and are hung in festoons from ancient walls and
archways, giving an air of festivity to Assisi. The olive trees
that cover the slopes of the hills below Assisi are considered
to be the oldest in Italy; for centuries upon centuries their
silvery leaves have shimmered under the bright sun. Fields of
giant, bright yellow sunflowers dot the valley below; they all
seem to be smiling at the city kissed by God. In Assisi, there
is a synthesis between poetry and prayer, between sanctity
and song, between asceticism and aestheticism. Assisi taught
me that simplicity, serenity, sincerity, silence, and song are
the heart of the Franciscan spirit. Assisi is an eternal shrine
in which Francis' candle still burns brilliantly.

IN THE BEGINNING

Francis was born into a relatively wealthy family. His father,
Pietro Bernardone, was a hard-working cloth merchant and
shrewd businessman who had reached the highest level of
the city's mercantile class. His shop in Assisi sold precious
fabrics, which Bernardone acquired during his many trips to
France. He was strongly attached to his money and goods.
He owned a number of homes in Assisi, and even to this
day, it cannot be determined with absolute certainty exactly
which one was the house in which the saint was born.

Very little is known about Francis' mother, whose name was Pica (although there is even some doubt about that). It seems probable that she was born in France, perhaps in Provence, where Pietro often traveled in search of fine cloth. Francis' early biographers bathed her in the gentlest of lights, illuminating a devout, quiet woman who worried about her son's future and frail health. Pietro was in France when his son was born. He was traveling with a long train of heavily baled pack horses and mules to a distant fair. Trips to France might have lasted for a couple of months. While he was away, Pica named the child John, in honor of John the Baptist. Upon his return to Assisi, Pietro promptly changed his son's name to Francis—or, Francesco—perhaps to celebrate his good fortune on the expedition to France or simply to honor his wife's native land. Whatever the reason for the name change, the nickname stuck, even though, as the saint's first biographer points out, the name was rare—"singular and unusual"—at the time. The young Francis would grow to become singular and unusual in his own time.

There is precious little recorded information about Francis' early childhood or cultural formation. Most of the biographical sketches show Francis as a lively child, prone to playing pranks on neighbors and friends. Everyone seemed to like the affable young boy. By all accounts, he had a sweet temperament and was well-mannered. He was likeable and gregarious. St. Bonaventure, who was just a young boy when Francis died and who eventually became the minister general of the Order, writes in his *Major Life*: "His gentleness, his refined manners, his patience, his super-human affability, his generosity beyond his means, marked him as a young man of flourishing natural disposition."

His education was modest at best, but more than adequate to the needs of a future cloth merchant. He attended school at the Church of San Giorgio, where he learned to read and write. Decades later, Francis was provisionally buried in the very same church. Today, the Chapel of the Blessed Sacrament in the Basilica di Santa Chiara is located on the very spot where Francis learned to read the psalms in Latin and began his religious education. Francis' knowledge of the Bible appears to have been gleaned from his active participation in the liturgical life of the Church rather than any systematic biblical study. Despite his regular church attendance, Francis was not considered especially pious.

We can assume that Francis, thanks to his father's social status, had an enjoyable and sheltered youth. As a teenager, he relished drinking and singing with his friends. In fact, Thomas of Celano, in his *First Life* of the saint, writes that the young Francis lived "in sin with the zeal of youthful passion and was driven by the feverish impulse of his age to satisfy all his youthful desires as he pleased, since he did not know moderation he was easily driven to evil...."

Burning with cupidity, the teenage Francis lived closer to the state of debauchery than to the state of grace. In his book *The Last Grain of Wheat*, Hans Urs von Balthasar, SJ, wrote: "It is difficult to make young people understand the real mystery of Christ, because the mystery of weakness runs counter to the impulses of youth." Perhaps this was true for Francis. All we really know is that as a young man the spirited and jovial Francis loved the songs of the troubadours. He wore expensive clothing and used his parents' hard-earned money to fund lavish feasts and drinking bouts. He dreamed of romance and becoming a soldier. And like his mother, Francis also loved poetry. His childhood gave no hints of his future sainthood.

BEAUTY AND THE FACE OF GOD

The youthful Francis loved life and lived it to the fullest. He loved to party, to have a good time in everything he did. His being pulsated with life; he eagerly greeted each new day with overflowing exuberance. And while those early years gave no hint of his looming total dedication to God, there was something different about him, something that clearly separated him from his fellow revelers. In his youthful coarseness, there was a hidden gift: the capacity to see beauty in all its purity. In time as he grew closer to God, Francis became a wordless poet, easily intoxicated by a sunflower, ready to fly to the moon on the wings of a dove. He heard birds speak and saw stars sparkle. For Francis, beauty led to contemplation. In time his love for the beauty of nature was transformed into a love of the beauty of God. God was beauty and made everything beautiful. Francis began to see beauty even in ugliness. And Francis' response to beauty was wonder and worship, and the growing knowledge that the earth was sanctified by the very fact of its creation. For him, creation became the revelation and manifestation of God. In his eyes, the sun became the face of God. Within him, the poet became the saint.

I've always loved the beauty of nature. Watching the sunset over the Pacific Ocean has never failed to fill me with wonder and awe. And peace. But beauty speaks to me in a hushed whisper compared to the way it spoke to Francis. Perhaps I'm too busy to hear it speak any louder than a murmur. We rush past beauty, giving it little chance to sink in and touch us. Ever since that day in an empty church in Rome when for a fleeting fraction of a second I caught a veiled glimpse of the reality of God, the natural world has been more beautiful than ever. Still, I'm more often than not overwhelmed by the ugliness of life. Ours is a coarse age. I need to cultivate the poet within me, to enlarge the sphere and capacities of my heart, so I too can see the face of God in the ugly ghetto of my daily life and experiences. Beauty and cruelty are a painful paradox that we each must learn to reconcile.

THE CALL TO HOLINESS

Studying the lives of the saints arouses within us a response, a desire to imitate real examples of holiness. The good news is we don't have to be another St. Francis. We simply need to become the saints we were uniquely created to be. Somewhere deep inside of each of us, there is, I believe, a desire to be holy. We can quibble about what being holy means, but essentially it means being really, really good—even when no one is watching. For a Christian, the essential meaning of holiness is more precise: it means being like Christ. But the manifest goodness on full display in the lives of the saints grows out of love. Their love of God is so strong, so deep, that their lives pulsate with God's love and goodness.

Francis discovered his unique and authentic self by his willingness to pay the high price of debunking all the illusions he had accepted as true, especially the misconception that he was different or separate from all of creation. Like all of us, Francis had to do more unlearning than learning. His ongoing illumination was much more than simply saying "yes" to Jesus; it required a life of constant changing as he dug deeper into the unfathomable depths of God. We live in a constant state of genesis, always changing, always evolving, always being born anew. Today we begin again. This very moment is pregnant with new possibilities for growing in God, with God, through God. Today is a new creation. We were made for growth and creativity. The Creator designed us to be creators. What are we creating? Conflict and war? Justice and peace? Those are our basic choices. We are all called to participate in the sanctification of the world we are privileged to inhabit. Each of us is called to become a saint in our own quiet way.

It was his willingness to be "grasped" by God that made Francis unique. He approached each day with a simple, very child-like attitude: God, what do you have in store for me today! This outlook released him from the burden of self-groundedness and into the freedom of being grounded in God, thus allowing himself to experience a realignment of his passion, and a complete recentering of his affections. For Francis, conversion was a liberating experience, freeing him from the prison of self-rule. Francis never underestimated the importance of relationships; he clearly saw how interdependent we are and how much we need each other.

The call to holiness is an invitation to enter fully into a committed relationship with God. As we respond, God graciously nurtures growth in the relationship by using events, circumstances, and people in our lives as instruments to hasten a contemplative outlook on life. Prayer becomes a vital part of our day; and, in prayer, we encounter more fully the author of our life. This personal encounter with the Creator slowly transforms us into a divine likeness, as it gently erases all traces of the un-God-like substance within us. In prayer, we unlock the vault to our deepest self and allow light to shine on God who is already abiding at the very core of our being, a tangible presence hidden from us yet patiently waiting for us.

In time, St. Francis came to understand that a cluttered heart is a deaf heart. God can't pour love into a vessel that is already full. Poverty of spirit is a manger of gentle receptivity that allows the divine to be born within us. To be wholly present to God, with all of our heart, mind, and soul, we must be poor in spirit. Poverty of spirit is far more than material poverty. While material poverty may help to facilitate poverty of spirit, it is nonetheless important to realize that a person without possessions can still be possessed by a craving for things. It is the craving that makes us restless, distracting our hearts and minds from being present to God alone. Poverty of spirit frees us from being divided by false idols and uncurbed passions. Sex, power, fame, and money are not enough to still the longing within us. Only God is enough. Poverty of spirit is a means of maintaining a continual attitude of dying to self without succumbing to self-hatred or causing a lack of self-esteem. Like Francis, we need to die to self because it is the only way to be fully alive to God. Without self-denial and sacrifice, my prayer life will wither on the vine. When your emotions and desires are moderate, it is easier to reach a state of harmony within yourself and with others. St. Francis has helped me see—and know—that God loves me because I am weak and powerless, not in spite of those qualities. I am poor and needy, and God lifts me up.

Nonetheless, periods of anguish, doubt, and confusion are part of the life of faith, because faith is not a static or unchanging force; faith has ups and downs, peaks and valleys. Even Mother Teresa of Calcutta experienced long, tortured periods of great darkness, even years of it. In that darkness, she wrote in her private diary: "I am told God loves me—and yet the reality of darkness and coldness and emptiness is so great that nothing touches my soul." Darkness, at times, surrounds all of us. It is impossible to calculate the amount of suffering that is endured each day. So often, everything seems hopeless. Despair often shadows our days. We cling to a hope that things will change, that we'll catch a break. Mystical hope does not look for miracles; it does not depend upon external circumstances. Mystical hope wells up from within; it springs from a deep sense of presence and intimate communion. Not tied to good fortune, mystical hope can smile in the face of the harshest of hardships. We, on our own, cannot generate mystical hope even though it comes from within us rather than from outside of us. To look deeply into the darkness of your own imperfect life is the surest way to be transformed by the hopeful light that springs forth from the mercy of God.

Still, there are going to be days when our faith lacks any sense of presence, when faith seems to be out to lunch or, worse, on a prolonged hiatus. But the very desire to feel or sense our faith points to the reality of our faith—that it exists and is real. If our faith is alive, it is always growing, changing, and maturing, or else it is slowly dying. Prayer is the oxygen of faith. Mother Teresa continued to pray through the darkness, and she continued to see the beauty within the lost and lowly who were sleeping in the gutters of Calcutta.

Francis was about to enter the dark furnace of transformation.

PART II

The Conversion

IN HIS FATHER'S FOOTSTEPS

When Francis was five years old, Jerusalem fell to Islamic forces under the leadership of Saladin, setting off the Crusades, an enormous enterprise that would directly influence Francis' life. When he was sixteen, a civil war erupted in Assisi as members of the rising merchant class, which included Francis' family, revolted against members of the old nobility. The opening of new trade routes gave common people access to wealth and pitted them against the ruling nobility. In a nutshell, the conflict in Assisi could be boiled down to "old money" vs. "new money."

At fourteen years of age, Francis followed in his father's

footsteps and became a member of the merchants' guild, which marked his formal entrance into the civic life of Assisi. Within two years, he was deeply involved in the revolt of the bourgeoisie of the city against the established nobility. The conflict turned violent and culminated in 1198 with the destruction of the Rocca Maggiore fortress, which overlooked the city. In 1202, when Francis was twenty, Assisi went to war with its archenemy, the city of Perugia, its neighbor across the valley. The violent brutality of the battles left many of the combatants with horribly mangled bodies and missing limbs. As a knight fighting on horseback, Francis participated in the opening battle at Ponte San Giovanni (St. John's Bridge) between the two cities, where he endured the humiliation of being taken prisoner. Assisi was conquered.

Life in the insalubrious prison was hard. During his year-long imprisonment in Perugia, Francis suffered a series of illnesses and grew weaker and weaker. While the harsh, filthy conditions in prison took their toll on his body, Francis' indomitable spirit remained strong. He took it upon himself to keep morale high among his fellow prisoners. He laughed at his chains and rejoiced in the Lord. But eventually his delicate health crumbled under the privations of prison, and he became very ill with malaria, often called paludal fever. Suddenly, the frail youth was in a battle for his very life. Fortunately, his father came to his rescue. Pietro Bernardone paid the ransom required to release seriously ill prisoners and liberated his son, who was still in the grips of a high fever. Francis returned home to Assisi, a sick and defeated young man. And the effects of his illness plagued him in the form of quatrain fever, now associated with malaria, until his death.

Francis' imprisonment and subsequent illness brought him face-to-face with his own personal limits and forced him to take a deeper look at himself and the meaning of life. During this time, St. Bonaventure says, "the hand of God weighed heavily on him." Back in Assisi, while convalescing, Francis felt deep sadness for the first time in his life; not even the sight of the broad, shimmering valley and vineyards, or the olive trees and the poppies in the wheat fields below the city could lift his heavy-heartedness. Francis had become disenchanted with worldly affairs and began to withdraw from society. He realized that worldly possessions and fame were worthless trophies that did not have the power to fill the void within him. Memories of the past assailed him. His former ambitions seemed ridiculous. His inner world was being transformed. The beauty of the natural world had lost its charm. The external world was no longer enough. Francis was at a loss as to how to explain his inner anguish, his changed attitude, or why a sense of restive yearning began to well up within him. He was beginning the long, hard process of transformation. The poet in him seemed to be dying; the saint was not yet ready to be born. Francis was depressed, uneasy, and anxious. He even became irritated at a beggar asking alms in the name of Christ, and he turned him away. It was an empty time of transition for Francis, a time of increased isolation and loneliness. Francis saw and felt the emptiness of life. He felt alone and terrified. For the first time in his life, Francis knew failure and suffering, and as a result, he began to see things differently.

When we realize the emptiness of all material things, we are free to encounter God. All that is "self" must be abandoned if we are to follow Jesus. The road Jesus travels is the road of self-emptying. And soon Francis would begin to take his first timid steps down that lonely road. Grace was at work in Francis' life, but for now he would run from it and chase after his dream of knightly glory.

DREAMS OF KNIGHTLY GLORY

By 1204, Francis was fully recovered and set out for the south of Italy on another military expedition. This was no petty, intercity skirmish, but a big-time battle in which Francis could at last achieve knightly glory. The forces of Emperor Frederick II and of Pope Innocent III were at war over the mastery of Sicily. A local count was raising a force to serve under the pope's general; the count was so impressed by Francis' fiery spirit that he ignored his less-than-robust physical appearance and accepted Francis as a squire, with the promise of knighthood should Francis prove worthy on the battlefield. Francis saw the expedition as a heaven-sent chance for glory. He wanted big things for himself, a slice of fame and renown. He bought the brightest and best armor his father's money could buy and headed south. But Francis didn't get far—only to Spoleto, just down the valley, where he had a dream that dramatically altered his personal dream of knightly glory.

On the road to Spoleto, Francis encountered a brave, but very poor knight who was dressed in shabby clothes and wearing dented armor. Francis was ashamed that a seasoned warrior should have such poor accoutrements while he, a frail, untested combatant, should be outfitted in the best that money could buy. Francis gave the knight not only his armor, but also his horse, in exchange for the knight's horse and armor. When word of this absurd incident reached Francis' father, it must have truly irritated him. But this was just the beginning...

The next night, Francis had the first of two dreams that would change the course of his life. In the dream, Francis saw himself in his father's warehouse, but instead of bales and bolts of cloth, the warehouse was filled with military equipment, saddles, swords, lances, and shields emblazoned with crosses. Gradually the warehouse faded away and was replaced by a large, magnificent castle. Inside the castle was a beautiful bride. A voice told Francis the castle and the bride were his, and the munitions of war he had just seen were also his to furnish the knights under his command. Francis awoke, convinced the expedition to Apulia near the heel of the Italian boot was going to bring him more glory than he ever imagined. St. Bonaventure writes:

> ...he judged the strange vision to be an indication that he would have great prosperity; for he had no experience in interpreting divine mysteries nor did he know how to pass through visible images to grasp the invisible truth beyond.

When the expedition reached Spoleto, Francis had a second dream. Actually, it wasn't really a dream. In the shadowy state of half-sleep between dream and waking, Francis heard a voice ask, "Do you wish to go to war in Apulia?" Francis responded by saying that was his whole purpose. Again the voice spoke, this time asking, "Is it better to serve the lord or the servant?" Francis responded, "The lord, of course." The voice replied, "Then why do you serve the servant?"

Francis suddenly awoke and cried out, "Lord what would you have me do?" The voice told him to return to Assisi and then he would be told what to do. At dawn, though dazed and perhaps disappointed, Francis nonetheless got up and joyfully returned to Assisi, even though that very act would make him look like a coward. His father was appalled; the townspeople were shocked. In answering that last question, the carefree, self-indulgent son of a wealthy businessman began to search for a radically different way to fulfill his dreams of knightly glory.

LIGHT AND DARKNESS

The crucified flesh of God on the cross sends a difficult and demanding message, namely, that weakness is really strength, wisdom is really foolishness, death is really life, matter is really spirit, religion is often slavery, and sin itself, when recognized, is actually the path to salvation and authentic holiness. Of course, because of our need for the appearance of power and a firm conviction that we are right, we don't want to hear any of this paradoxical stuff.

Like Francis, each of us is a mixture of light and darkness. Each of us is temporal and eternal. Truth requires holding opposites together and allowing the natural tensions to coexist without affirming one side over the other. Faith understands and affirms both death and resurrection. Faith allows us to be humble and confident at the same time. Holiness grows out of embracing and forgiving the contradictions within us. Recognizing our inner contradictions eventually brings us to a fork in the road: one path allows us to evade God, the other, to meet God. Our inner contradictions can bring us to a place where God alone makes sense, to a place of total surrender. As Francis made his pilgrimage back to God, surrender would become his most constant companion. Without clinging to anything, he patiently stood before God with open hands.

In August 2012, I was robbed in Haiti. The thief got everything: my passport, my credit cards, and all my money. I was thrown to the ground and felt totally helpless. The traumatic incident drove home the point that faith grows in darkness, in a place of weakness where, according to the apostle Paul, we "fall into the hands of the living God."

In his darkness and weakness, Francis realized more fully that God, not Francis, was in control. When I am in control, there is no need for God. Faith requires the ability to see our true powerlessness and vulnerability. Of course, our culture teaches us to be strong and independent and to eliminate all paradoxes—which is why we see so little evidence of a living faith.

Faith grows out of a profound loneliness and desperate longing. Faith allows us to clearly see the emptiness of our perishable lives. Faith intuitively knows we were created for union and communion with God, our true selves, and each other. Faith is more than clinging to a belief or a dogma; faith is an endless exodus to the heart—our own heart and the heart of God, which in reality beat in unison. Faith takes us deep within our souls to a safe place where we can accept paradox with humility.

Faith is an ever-deepening desire to taste God more fully, which, as St. Francis discovered, primarily happens in the stillness and silence of prayer. Faith moves us beyond the superficial and trivial into the depths of the reality of a living mystery. Faith is a journey of discovery and transformation. Faith gives us the ability to become a light in the darkness of the world, a world darkened by sin of self-centeredness. Francis' ever-deepening faith gave him the eyes to see the interconnectedness of all of creation.

God is not hiding in the corner of an empty church. God is hidden in the endless stream of busy, messy, mundane moments of everyday life. And God is also hidden in the many tragedies that dot the vast landscape of humanity. God is not beyond the clouds; God is on the ground, down in the gutter with us. At the heart of every life there is a deep, mysterious pain. No one can avoid it or cure it. My faith tells me that God loves me in my brokenness. And that God loves me fully and unconditionally, without a hint of reservation, even in my darkest, most sinful, most unloving moments. God does not demand perfection; God gives love. The essence of faith is trust—trusting in God's undivided, unmerited love. No matter how much good you do or how much bad you do, God's love for you goes unchanged. You can't make God love you any more, nor can you make God love you any less.

TIME ALONE

Back in Assisi, Francis spent a great deal of time alone, seeking refuge in solitary places in order to understand and nourish his spiritual conversion. He gradually withdrew from his circle of fun-loving friends. He was seeking a spiritual perfection that he assumed required the abnegation of most of his former life. His friends feared he had gone mad, a fear that was confirmed when Francis told them that he no longer wanted to be "The Master of the Revels" (or "Lord of the Feasts") during their nightlong parties known as *serenatas*, which were wild affairs filled with loud singing and jubilant dancing. In June 1205, Francis attended his last *serenata*. He was now isolated and completely on his own. Francis only wanted his heart to be filled with the sweetness of the Lord. He was experiencing an inner desire to move past temporal and earthly things so he could more fully embrace God.

Such a movement toward aloneness is hard for us to understand. We live in a whirlwind of noise. Our homes and cars have elaborate entertainment centers. Cell phones allow us to talk while driving or walking in the woods. Cable and satellite TV serves up news, sports, and movies twenty-four hours a day. Computers link us to the Internet and chat rooms and websites featuring hardcore pornography. And, of course, crass commercialism is always screaming something at us. Finding silence is harder than finding a needle in a haystack. Our culture is so riddled with turmoil and confusion that it is easy to seek refuge in the noise of idle entertainment, channel surfing through endless hours of tedious programs. So much of life distracts us from Life. Francis knew he needed time alone in order to be present to God. He needed a desert experience. Francis would urge us to punctuate our busy days with thoughts of God, recalling God's unselfish, self-giving love for us. He would remind us that God only asks for our empty hands.

IN THE DESERT
Abraham Joshua Heschel said, "To become aware of the ineffable is to part company with words." When I look back on my journey since that momentous day in Rome when, within the silence of an empty church, my life changed, I often feel that words fail me when I try to describe what was happening within me during those first few years as I transitioned from a denier of Christ to a follower of Christ. One of the things that confronted and confounded me was my own sinfulness. I really didn't like the word sin, which seemed primarily concerned with sex. I was turned off by St. Francis' obsession with his sins and his harsh ascetical practices to conquer his normal and very human bodily urges. I was tired of hearing preachers tell everyone they were sinners and going to hell—especially homosexuals. As I read the gospels, it seemed to me that Christianity was not a moral code; it was a love affair. I slowly began to see that "sin" was simply a failure to love. And on those rare occasions when I

was truly still and silent enough to honestly look within my own heart, I saw how often I failed.

"This day is yours, Lord," I would say each day upon rising. Yet before I even finished my first cup of coffee, the day had become mine. The word "mine" is not in love's vocabulary. As I slowly entered more deeply into my own heart, God revealed my sinfulness to me, not to make me feel guilty but to offer me forgiveness and freedom from the bondage of sin. Redemption isn't a ticket to heaven; it simply means a soul has been redeemed—set free—from self-interest.

It all sounds so easy but it truly isn't. It's like crossing a desert on foot without water. But the Promised Land is on the other side of the desert.

At some point, God calls each of us into the desert. The desert is a place of discipline, which we need but don't want, and so we avoid it. In the desert, under the blazing sun, all our weaknesses are made clear. We look around and see the vastness of nothing. We do not know which way to go. In the desert, our need for God is also made clear. In the desert, we grow weary; we lose hope. We can't quench our own thirst; we know no pleasure. All around us is only a void that stretches out beyond our sight. The day turns to night. The arid, parched landscape can only be watered by God. God's water is sweet; God's manna is tasty. In the desert, God's love is our only comfort. In the desert, God's spirit transcends the bleakness in the depths of our souls, and we can see beauty and tenderness. In the desert, ideas about God give way to God.

Instead of the desert, we prefer action. We want "quick fixes"—instant redemption and salvation. It doesn't work that way; not even for Francis. Change is evolutionary, often so utterly slow you hardly notice the process. In the early days of my own conversion process, I began to set time aside each day for prayer. At first, it was not easy. Moreover, I hardly noticed any difference it made in my life. But slowly, by God's grace, the time spent in prayer began to yield fruit. I became aware of the habitual nature of a certain sin that I found hard to resist. I caught a distant glimpse of the fact that the essence of sin was saying "no" to God's perpetual invitation for us to partake fully in the reality of his love and to reach our full potential as human beings. I saw how, when I sinned, I settled for mediocrity, denying myself the chance to reach my full potential, which can only be realized by living in unity with God. Gradually the dichotomy between my prayer and my life began to narrow. Years later, I still have a long way to go. But every little bit of growth increases my capacity to respond to God's call to go further.

For Francis, the way to go was by way of poverty and humility. He emptied himself in order to encounter a liberating God who freed him from his slavery to himself. St. Francis said, "Poverty is the root of all sanctity." When his interior was liberated from interests, ownership, and desires, Francis could more easily feel God's presence. He understood that when our inner self is engaged with selfishness and egotism, then there is no room for God, because that sacred space within has become occupied territory. All God wants is a surrendered heart. St. John of the Cross summed it up best: "The soul must empty itself of all that is not God in order to go to God."

In all that he did, Francis was motivated by an intense desire to live for God. He was constantly brushing back the temptation to temper that desire. Temptations show us what we, in our weakness, are capable of becoming. They are invitations to virtue. Specific sins invite us to develop specific virtues to overcome the sinful inclinations. Temptations give us a chance to turn to God. For repentance to be real and true, it must be more than a fleeting twinge of remorse. Genuine repentance must lead to a transformation of our lives. Repentance involves two steps: stop doing something bad; start doing something good. Contrition should evolve into acts of goodness. St. Francis wrote: "I consider you more a servant and friend of God and I love you more, the more you are attacked by temptations. Truly I tell you that no one should consider himself a perfect friend of God until he has passed through many temptations and tribulations."

During a meeting with the heads of religious orders held in the Vatican in November 2013, Pope Francis said: "Life is complicated; it consists of grace and sin. He who does not sin is not human. We all make mistakes and we need to recognize our weaknesses. A religious who recognizes himself as weak and a sinner does not negate the witness that he is called to give; rather, it reinforces it, and this is good for everyone." The pope exhorted the priests, brothers, and sisters to "wake up the world" by being a "real witness" to a countercultural way of life that relies on generosity and self-forgetfulness. I can imagine St. Francis nodding his head in approval of the pope's words.

St. Francis managed to reach a point in his spiritual journey that few have ever reached, a place where severe asceticism was matched by intense joy. The awareness of his complete dependence on God filled him with overflowing joy. His poverty and fasting were living signs of God's supreme power. His songs of praise echoed the beauty of creation and the majesty of the Creator.

PILGRIM'S PROGRESS

In the spring of 1206, during the early days of his conversion process, St. Francis traveled to Rome as a pilgrim. Rome is where the apostle Peter preached and was martyred. The tomb of St. Peter was a magnet that drew pilgrims from all over the world. Francis went straight to St. Peter's Basilica. He knelt at the tomb of St. Peter and asked the apostle to help him discover the treasure of gospel poverty. As he was leaving the church, Francis noticed other pilgrims making small donations of a few coins, which disappointed him, and, in one generous gesture, he threw all the money he had into the donation box. But then outside the church he was confronted with the sight of beggars clutching the clothing of those entering and leaving the church, begging for a few coins out of love for God.

Francis was struck by the turmoil of the bustling crowd, which he found unsavory. There were an incredible number of poor people, pleading with outstretched hands as they muttered prayers. Some of them suffered from the most hideous conditions, such as monstrous sores, maimed and crippled bodies, blindness, and paralysis. Francis found their poverty to be abhorrent. He doubted he could ever stand to be so poor. As if to resist this thought, in a dramatic decision, he exchanged his tailored clothes for the rags of a beggar and panhandled for alms in front of St. Peter's. In time and in his own unique way, Francis would turn his back on what the world valued in order to follow the gospel more perfectly. Francis had known the poverty of riches, and he was about to learn the riches of poverty.

As I made my films on global and domestic poverty, I slowly learned to see the poor and the marginalized, the alcoholic and the drug addict, the mentally ill and the homeless, not as objects of pity and charity, but as brothers and sisters with whom I'm intimately related. The longer I walk with the poor—and with Jesus—the more I see the need to put to death the idea of my own self-sufficiency. To think of myself as separate from God and all of creation, including the poor, is an illusion.

Francis understood we all are the human face of Jesus; he knew that all of humanity comprises the divine face. God assumed flesh and was born into a world of oppression and persecution. Can we ever grasp the reality of the divine presence dwelling in a depraved humanity and that subsequently every man, woman, and child is uniquely precious, equal, and blessed, all brothers and sisters?

Jesus is hungry and naked. We build and decorate elaborate churches in his name but do not feed or clothe him. Every day, God comes to us in a distressing disguise, clothed in the rags of a tormented and neglected poor person, in hopes that the encounter will provide a place for healing and hurt to meet, for grace to embrace sin, for beauty to be restored. It took a great love—and many deaths—for Francis to transform the eyes of his soul so as to see God's face in every face.

We live in a time of global anxiety. Everyone feels threatened and concerned about the future, which looks more and more bleak for more and more people. Loneliness, fear, and a sense of emptiness have reached epidemic proportions. There are times in my work among the chronically poor of the world that I'm left with a feeling of hopelessness. The only way for me to chase away the hopelessness is to spend time in prayer every day.

Prayer is a lifeline to hope. And a pilgrimage can be a lifeline to prayer.

Francis went to Rome on a pilgrimage. The first step any pilgrim takes is a step in faith, a moving from the known to the unknown, from the security and comfort of his or her home to the unfamiliar terrain and language of a foreign land. The pilgrim strips himself or herself of everything familiar in hopes of experiencing something new, something deeper. Pilgrims go knocking on God's door. The pilgrim seeks new ways of seeing and understanding; ever restless, one combs the unknown land for new information and insights. Francis left Assisi and traveled to Rome in search of answers to the questions that burned within him. He was not running away from something—he was running *to* something. Francis was on fire with desire to proclaim the "good news," and he went to Rome seeking direction from the Lord—through the inspiration of St. Peter—on how best to do so.

The exterior, geographical journey, as Thomas Merton suggested, is symbolic of an interior journey. A pilgrimage is a time of transition. From before his birth, Christ was a pilgrim journeying from divinity to humanity, from richness to poverty. In the early days of the Church, the followers of Christ were simply known as the followers of the Way. And so the theme of "journey" has always been part of our Christian identity. We are called to walk the "holy road," going from holy ground to holy ground, one little step at a time.

A pilgrimage is a fitting simile for the spiritual life. Spirituality is essentially a journey in which we move from what we are to what we are called to be. Francis was just beginning to learn that life is a journey to weakness. We truly learn to live when we begin to explore our weaknesses. Every experience of weakness is an opportunity for growth and renewed life. Weaknesses transformed by the reality of Christ become life-giving virtues.

The emptiness we often feel stems from not realizing we are made for communion with God, made to live in union with God. Thomas Merton said it best: "We all exist solely for this—to be the human place God has chosen for his presence, his manifestation, his epiphany." St. Catherine of Genoa expressed the same stunning idea by saying: "My deepest me is God."

If we are not growing toward unity with God, then we are growing apart from God. Francis would learn that he had to be still in order to move into a greater union with Christ. In stillness he could enter into a dialogue with the Savior. We need to bring to Christ what we are so that in time we become what he is. Francis would learn this lesson. But not quickly. There would be years of growth, years filled to overflowing with pain and struggle. Christianity leads to the cross, and it doesn't offer an easy way around it. To become a true disciple of Jesus means accepting a spirituality of the cross and renouncing a spirituality of glory.

The cost of following Jesus is nothing less than everything: one must abandon self in order to imitate the self-transcendence of the cross and resurrection. The cross symbolizes the extremity of helplessness more than the extremity of suffering. The cross rejects power and accepts surrender. When we have little or no worldly power to rely on, we are able to offer unambiguous love and service.

A KISS OF A LEPER

Back in Assisi after his trip to Rome, Francis was drawn deeper and deeper into solitude as he struggled to figure how he could best serve God. He spent lots of time in prayer, praying in isolated woods and empty churches. One day he was praying for guidance in the small church of St. Mary of the Angels, a decaying shrine hidden in the woods. Deep within his heart, Francis heard an inaudible voice say: "Francis, all those things that you have loved after the flesh, and desired to have, you must now despise and hate, if you would do my will. Then the things that before seemed sweet and delightful shall become unbearable to you and bitter, and from those that you once loathed you shall drink sweetness and delight without measure."

Francis left the church, got on his horse, and headed back to Assisi. As he came out of the Porziuncula woods, the countryside became completely open, not even a hedge or boulder or a bush on either side of the dusty road...nothing in sight except a leper, dragging himself along, coming slowly toward Francis. Immediately, out of sheer habit, Francis began to feel horror and disgust. He lifted his arm toward his nose to block out the stench that he would soon encounter. Then a thought dashed across his mind: "You are not a knight of Christ if you are unable to conquer yourself."

Francis had a great fear of lepers and was fastidious in his avoidance of any contact with this deadly and most loathsome of diseases. He would go as far as two miles out of his way to avoid contact with a leper, and even at that distance he held his nose to avoid even a hint of their stench, even though the faint and disagreeable smell emitted by lepers does not in fact carry very far. He was physically repulsed and horrified by the very sight of a leper. But he was about to conquer this horror, set himself free from his past, and become totally open to a new future. This was a great moment, the crisis of a battle; Francis did not back down, but bravely faced it. Francis, led by the Spirit, was about to embark on a radically new kind of life.

Early in Matthew's gospel we read about a leper who approached Jesus, knelt before him, and pleaded: "If you wish, you can make me clean." Jesus was so moved by the leper that he stretched out his hand in pity, touched him, and said,

"I will do it. Be made clean." And in that instant, the leprosy vanished from the man's body. In Jesus' time and culture, lepers were considered "unclean." And the term "leprosy" was not merely restricted to what we know as Hansen's disease. Back then, leprosy included any serious skin eruptions. Lepers were outcasts. Because they were "unclean," they were not permitted to enter the temple. Moreover, according to Jewish custom, if you touched someone "unclean" you became "unclean" and therefore you could not enter the temple. This is important because in the gospel story Jesus heals the leper by touching him. Jesus certainly could have healed the leper without touching him. The gospels contain evidence of such healings without a physical touch from Jesus. In touching the leper, Jesus deliberately defiled himself according to Jewish custom. In touching the leper, Jesus is symbolically telling us that God is willing to get down in the gutter, down in the ditch, where we are.

We do not have to be clean to go to God. God comes to us in our uncleanliness.

To put Francis' fear of lepers into historical context, in those times, lepers represented the height of hopelessness. There were about 19,000 leper hospitals in Europe, doing their best to look after these unfortunate souls, who were actually regarded as legally dead. Even the Church contributed to their misery by citing lepers as an image of sin. In 1179, the Third Lateran Council issued a decree demanding that lepers be forced to live outside city walls; their exclusion from the rest of society bordered on being absolute. Those lepers who were permitted to come near a village were required to wear distinctive clothing and to beat a clapper to warn people of their approach.

Instead of avoiding the leper, Francis nudged his horse

into a full gallop, rushing toward the leper. He heard the clapper and watched the leper draw to the side of the road to give him room to pass without contamination. Disgust surely must have seized him as the putrefying stench filled the air. Francis dismounted and walked toward the leper. The leper's face was half eaten away and swollen. In an impulsive and courageous act, Francis embraced the astonished leper. Then he kissed the leper's hands, which had only stumps of fingers, before putting money into them. Finally, in a supremely bold gesture, Francis kissed the leper on the mouth.

This was a moment of true grace for Francis...and the leper.

Imagine what must have gone through the leper's mind when Francis embraced him. Moments before, the leper must have felt nothing but contempt and hatred for Francis, because the cloth merchant's son represented all the pampered, middle-class people who had rejected him and forced him to live in lonely exile—until that moment, until that embrace in which both men felt the love of God.

With the kiss of the leper, Francis began to learn that he and the leper were one and the same, and that there was no difference between them. He lived the truth of that realization. Francis responded to grace the moment he got off the horse. He got back on the horse a new man, for he had embraced God. It was a transcendent moment, a true turning point in Francis' life. He was now truly free, for he had relinquished his own ego by embracing the Other. There was no turning back now; he was on the road to glory, a glory beyond his wildest imagination. Years later, Francis summarized his life before his dramatic encounter with the leper in four words: "I was in sin." And with a kiss of a leper he embarked upon a "life of penance."

Francis was now beginning to have some sense of the presence of God in all of God's creatures. He was beginning to feel a kind of brotherhood with all created things, including lepers and lambs and flowers. More and more, he saw the image of Christ in the poor and the afflicted. It was as though in looking at a leper Francis saw the broken and bleeding body of Christ his brother. Francis would never again be able to treat another human being, no matter how lowly or disfigured, with indifference or contempt.

Francis understood that we need each other to become whole. Human convergence comes through love. Love unites what has become fragmented and isolated. And in our unity we still keep our individuality, with each gift of life creating a beautiful particle that helps form the whole of life, the full body of Christ. God is unity. God pulls us out of our isolation by showering us with the grace to see that our lives and gifts must be put to the service of others and all of creation— through acts of sharing and serving that shall move toward union. In reaching out to others, we are reaching out to God.

As he grew in relationship with God during prolonged periods of solitude and prayer, Francis' growing awareness of God's presence within himself gave him a new way to look at the world around him and helped him see God's presence within others. For St. Francis, prayers were not an escape from the world, but an entrance into it. Because he had been touched and embraced by God's diffusive and self-giving love, Francis himself had no choice but to become more loving to everyone he encountered.

In time, St. Francis came to see the poor and the outcasts of his society as icons or manifestations of God's goodness. The growing awareness of God's presence within all creation, especially within all humanity, reached its apex when the saint embraced and kissed a leper. The self-humbling kiss symbolized God's union with humanity in Christ when the Word became flesh. For Francis, the Incarnation gave birth to compassion, which enabled him to see in the rotting flesh of a leper the self-giving love of God.

INTERSECTING LIFELINES

The encounter with the leper was the most critical moment of Francis' life. His attitude and expectations were turned upside down the moment he accepted God's role in the event. Before, he was unable to include the leper—a lowly, ugly outcast—in his understanding of the cosmic love of God. It was Francis who did the excluding. God, he would learn, excludes no one.

Francis would claim everybody is worthy of the love of God. I don't always agree with that idea; I would have no trouble making a list of people I would consider unworthy of God's love. Sadly, I do a lot of excluding. The leper story illustrates the importance of searching for the infinite in the finite. By embracing the flawed and the finite, Francis discovered perfection and the infinite. He met the Lord, and that changed his life. He discovered true freedom. The story also shows the role of ongoing conversion in Francis' life. Growth came through pain, conflict, and confrontation... and chance meetings

At first blush this most critical event in the saint's life seems to be the product of chance. Was Francis and the leper's crossing paths a coincidence? Or is there a reason for everything? The questions make me look at my own life, and force me to look carefully at the endless parade of "coincidences" that led me to crossing paths with Francis in the ancient city of Assisi, half a world away from my home in California. Before 1995, I would have answered the first question with an unqualified and resounding "yes"—for back then I fully believed all of life was ruled by nothing more than a random mass of chaos, and there was absolutely no reason for anything; it was all chance.

The story of Francis and the leper caused me to spend time reflecting on the twisting road that I followed to Assisi. Reflection allows time for perspective to emerge, and it gives us an opportunity to see things in a different light. It is so easy for me to forget about how my life has intersected with so many other lives, each encounter playing a role leading me out of the desert of unbelief into the garden of faith. Reflection gives me the chance to stop, pause, and see the interconnectedness of everything. God leads us to people we never expected to meet and to places we never expected to go. Today I believe there is no such thing as coincidence; every encounter is charged with meaning and possibility and grace. Without the leper, Assisi would not have become known as the home of a great saint, but would be just another charming Umbrian town handsomely sitting on a hill.

Just as the leper was isolated from society, I too was fragmented in my relationship with myself, with other people, with the world, and with God. The isolation and dividedness are ugly and painful. For so very long, I was torn apart by my inner conflicts and contradictions. They hurt me, and they caused me to hurt others. The leper reminds me of my brokenness and my divided self. I've begun to mend the wounds, but the past is still very much present. I'm still in need of healing, still looking for wholeness. Wholeness isn't easy; it doesn't come in a flash. The cross offered no shortcuts to Christ. There are no simple answers, no perfect healing. We carry our wounds and anguishes with us. We must learn to live with the pain and use it as a gateway for growth.

With the kiss of a leper, St. Francis was on the verge of learning that Christ accepts us as we are, with all our weaknesses and confusions. The healing begins when we look at ourselves honestly and open ourselves up to the transforming love of God. It is the love of God that makes all things possible and allows us to move toward a healing.

BECOMING MARGINALIZED

After the incident with the leper, Francis made frequent visits to a nearby leper colony, bringing alms and love. He wiped their sores, washed them, and bandaged them as best he could, even though the lepers railed obscenities that cursed heaven for damning them to such an unbearable hell. Francis' compassionate heart and poet's imagination understood their anger and ingratitude. He also understood that it was here, among the rejected, that God was most present. The face of the impoverished leper became the face of the humiliated Christ.

For Francis, Christ the crucified became Christ the leper. And the lepers became his brothers.

Francis was now beginning to have some sense of the presence of God in all God's creatures. He was beginning to feel a sense of brotherhood with all created things, including lepers and lambs and flowers. More and more, he saw the image of Christ in the poor and the afflicted. It was as though in looking at a leper he saw the broken and bleeding body of Christ his brother. And Francis would never again be able to treat another human being, no matter how lowly or disfigured, with indifference or contempt. His interior and exterior lives were becoming more harmonious.

As Francis—and later, his brothers—toiled among the

lepers on the outskirts of Assisi, one thing soon became clear: work with the marginalized, and you too will become marginalized. The brothers felt this, and, quite frankly, some did not like it, and they told Francis so. Francis' response to their concern was simple and direct: this is where Christ is. We are living in Christ's world.

Francis had no choice but to leave Assisi, because all facets of the society within the walls were striving for something he was no longer interested in. He left and found himself among the poor, among the lepers.

When I first read about Francis and his involvement with lepers, I never imagined that one day I would actually encounter a leper. If fact, I had erroneously thought that leprosy had long ago been eradicated. But while making my poverty films, I encountered leprosy in India and Jamaica. But the few lepers I met didn't have active leprosy. The spread of the disease had been halted, but not before the disease had eaten away their hands or feet or faces, leaving them horribly disfigured.

In 2003 I traveled to Manaus, Brazil, deep in the heart of the Amazon, where I spent time in a leprosarium and a leper colony. During one visit to the leprosarium, I was led to an isolated room of a man with active leprosy. I was truly horrified by the sight and the stench. The smell of his rotting flesh is impossible to describe. Suddenly, St. Francis' fear of lepers became very understandable. I was too frightened to enter the room. I initially filmed the man from the doorway. I will never forget the horrific smell. After taking a few baby steps into the room, I thought about St. Francis getting off his horse and not only embracing the leper, but also kissing him. In the few minutes I spent with the man, I realized the courage it took for Francis to embrace and kiss the leper, and how profound his faith was to do what he felt God was asking him to do.

In the leprosarium in Manaus, Brazil, I came to see that lepers suffer a pain that was perhaps worse than the physical pain they experience—they suffer the pain of rejection, of knowing nobody wants to come near them or even look at them. They know they have no value in the eyes of most people, that most people see them as unlovable. For me, leprosy symbolizes the true poverty of the human condition. We are all poor. We are all completely dependent upon God. But our money, power, and social status can blind us to the reality of how poor we are and how much we need God's love and mercy.

In April 2014, while working on a film set in Honduras for the Medical Missionaries of Mary, I saw a B &W film made in 1946 featuring the sisters' work with lepers in Nigeria. I included a few minutes of that film in the film I was making. When a sister who had worked with lepers in Africa read my film script, she objected to my calling those with leprosy lepers. In an e-mail to me, the sister dismantled some of the myths and misconceptions about leprosy. The disease is caused by bacteria. It's easily diagnosed, and treatment that prevents the disfigurement associated with the disease is widely available worldwide. The bacteria that causes the disease is similar to the bacteria that causes tuberculosis, and the treatment and drugs used for tuberculosis are similar to those used in the treatment of leprosy. Hansen's disease is actually not very contagious. I had no real reason to have been so afraid of the person with active leprosy that I encountered in Brazil. My fear was based on my misunderstanding of and misconceptions about Hansen's disease. The sister gently informed me that it is not helpful to refer to people with leprosy as lepers. The word leper, she said, is a pejorative term. They are people with a disease. It is far better to say people with Hansen's disease or a person with leprosy. The Medical Missionaries of Mary are living the self-emptying love of Christ and are still treating people with Hansen's disease.

It was a person with leprosy who helped St. Francis enter into his own inner pain and helped him open his heart more fully to God and more fully to the poor. Jesus showed us how to love—how to love unconditionally and without limits. And according to Christ, how we love the hungry, the lowly, and the lost—and yes, even the leper—is how we love him. Every act of love, compassion, and sacrifice transforms our world in which hatred, cruelty, and avarice reign into a new world in which the kingdom of God blossoms.

A CULTURE OF EMPTINESS

Love is not something God does. Love is what God is. And God consistently showers undivided love on each of us. When St. Francis of Assisi began to understand that his life was a gift of love, he desired nothing else than that his life become a loving gift to God and others. This shift in consciousness didn't happen all at once for St. Francis, nor does it happen all at once for any of us. The journey from the assumption of absolute autonomy and the false egocentric notion that we are self-sufficient to a posture of total surrender to God and the recognition of our genuine interconnectedness with all life takes time and requires daily conversion. Day by day, step by step, prayer by prayer, we inch our way along the Way back to God, back to the fullness of life and love. But we easily get distracted, sidetracked by false desires and empty illusions. This is why the discipline of prayer was important to St. Francis and he didn't want to leave it to chance. He carefully carved out time alone, time apart from the roar of the crowd, time for God alone.

Within himself, St. Francis created a culture of emptiness, an empty space for God to fill. To become empty, we need to do nothing; we need to press the pause bottom on our society's addictive need to be productive, to always be doing something. I think we need to create a culture of emptiness more than Francis did, as modern life is so filled with busyness, so cluttered with unfiltered information tirelessly generated by the media and the Internet, so overstimulated by a dizzying array of electronic gadgets, so pressured by the allure of nonstop advertising, and so driven by productiveness that we're almost incapable of stillness and can't tolerate silence. It was in stillness and silence that Francis forged his inner cloister of emptiness and flamed his desire for God.

Francis' form of monasticism had no walls, for the world was his cloister; but he was diligent in periodically retreating to places of solitude where he could be renewed and discover a clear sense of direction for his forays into the wider world of human commerce. God spoke to Francis in the depths of his soul. And in the silence of his innermost being, Francis responded. In time, God, who has no voice, spoke to Francis in everything. Francis became a word of God, echoing all he heard in the inmost center of his being during his prolonged periods of contemplation. Francis' experience of God went beyond faith, dogma, and symbols. His experience of God gave birth to a spontaneous awe at the sacredness of life. The invisible Source of Life touched Francis; as a result, Francis knew beyond all knowing that God was real and that God was always reaching out to us.

St. Francis of Assisi is like an impressionistic painting:

different people see different things in him. Various aspects of his life inspire different kinds of responses in people's lives when they walk with Francis. For some, Francis' understanding of a God-centered peace is his shining virtue. Peace and nonviolence were so integral to Francis' being that it colored all that he did and said. Many people admire Francis' ability to see the goodness within people of other faiths and his willingness to engage in authentic interfaith dialogue. For others, Francis' connectedness to all creation is truly inspiring and makes him the patron saint of ecology. Others are drawn to Francis because of his thirst for silence and solitude. For some, Francis' ability to combine contemplation and action is his greatest accomplishment; and others love his ability to remain faithful to the institutional Church even while disagreeing with it. Some people are drawn to his simplicity and his willingness to take God's word literally and do what it says. Others greatly admire his fiery passion to be like Christ and to live for Christ alone.

For me, all these aspects of St. Francis have changed me in subtle ways. But while my encounter with Francis changed my perspective on peace and nonviolence, solitude and silence, creation and prayer, it was his love of the poor and poverty itself that impacted me the most. Francis led me to the poor, to the deepest and most profound levels of poverty imaginable. It was there that I understood what radical dependency on God truly means. For me, the entire Franciscan spirituality rests on the foundation of poverty. But voluntary poverty is a source of confusion for many of those who strive to follow in the footsteps of St. Francis. Even when Franciscans speak of the poverty of St. Francis, they often speak of it as an isolated concept that leads to a certain amount of vagueness or confusion, and even to idealizing poverty. Are we called to live in abject poverty? No. This is not what Francis wants, nor is it the ideal way to follow Francis.

Francis' concept of poverty was interconnected with his concept of God as the *Summum Bonum*, or the Supreme Good, and that Jesus Christ was the *Summum Bonum* of God given to humanity. Because of his great trust in the supreme goodness of God, Francis could give up everything and depend completely on God to supply every one of his needs from God's overflowing goodness. Francis knew that even in his "poverty" he would be very rich because God out of goodness would supply every one of his needs. Francis was not interested in appropriating the things of God for himself. Francis was focused on abnegation, letting go of everything for God, who gives it back a hundred times more in return.

Franciscan poverty should not be equated with the experience of living in desperation. This is not what Francis or God wants from us. Francis wants us to let everything go and joyfully trust that God will supply every one of our needs. When Francis faced the end of his own resources, he was able to see the vastness of God's unlimited resources. Francis understood that a person's spiritual life will not prosper without an intense awareness of one's own poverty and emptiness. All growth begins in a womb of darkness. Unity with God, Francis discovered, is obtained in only one way: total surrender. This is Franciscan poverty. I believe the lesson is best learned by being one with the poor and helping to liberate them from the prison of unjust, immoral poverty that robs them of their human dignity, a dignity that flows from being sons and daughters of a loving and merciful God.

For St. Francis, voluntary poverty was a way for him to always be dependent upon God for everything. When Francis experienced the self-emptying love of God, it awakened his desire to love God and God alone. He longed for nothing else but God. And most important, Francis put his full trust in the grace of God, the overflowing goodness of God. Every moment was pregnant with the grace to see the boundless love of God in everyone, and to return that love by loving others and all of creation.

In Francis' eyes, everything that is good, every kind gesture, every act of mercy, every gentle touch, every gift of charity, every embrace of forgiveness, every moment of peace flowed from God. Moreover, all loneliness, every disappointment, the very wounds of rejection, the bitter sadness of loss, and the times of suffering open us to the transcendent and allow us to experience the hidden closeness of God. Francis always praised what was good in everyone he met. When he revealed to people their inner goodness, they in turn became better people.

Francis knew two things: without God, he was nothing; with God, he lacked nothing.

THIS IS MY BODY

The story of Francis and the leper is not an easy story to hear or understand. When Francis embraced the leper, he was embracing God. As Francis grew in faith, he saw God in every living creature and in all of creation, which made it impossible for the saint to ignore any suffering he encountered.

Individualism is really an illusion. We are all part of the great whole. Most of us, including me, are isolated from the poor and from others. Down through the centuries, countless people, including numerous saints, believed that we can't find God alone, that we need each other to find our way. The lives of many modern people are marked by isolation. Many people don't even know their next-door neighbors. We tend to deny our interdependence. Awareness of our interdependence is the true basis of compassion. As our isolation deepens, our compassion weakens. The homeless and undocumented migrants, along with those afflicted with AIDS, are today's lepers.

Jesus said, "I was hungry and you fed me." The mercy we share with broken people is the mercy Jesus returns to us. It is not likely that you will encounter a leper, but the next time you see a homeless person—filthy, covered with sores, begging for food—stop and listen, and you may hear these haunting words: "This is my body."

RADICAL OBEDIENCE

Mercy is the holiness of God made manifest; it is God's love in action. Mercy and God are inseparable, one and the same. Mercy is an act of creation, springing forth from unconditional love. God is the energy and passion that drives me to help the poor. But I do so very little in comparison to the people I've filmed, amazing people such as Dr. Tony Lazzara in Peru and Fr. Tom Hagan in Haiti.

When I look at the lives of the truly holy people I've filmed, I see how radical obedience to Christ is not simply a matter of avoiding sin, though that is important. It also requires us to be identified with the poor. Jesus entered humanity in a state of weakness and powerlessness. Jesus gave himself to the weak, the despised, and the forsaken. In turn he became despised and rejected. Christ's life was marked by sorrow and pain. He did not hang out with the poor for a few hours a week and then return to a comfortable home to relax with a glass of wine. He became one with the poor, fully sharing in their misery. He did not become a leader of the poor; he became a servant of the poor. When the poor wanted to crown him king, he fled. Jesus loved and served the lost and the lowly, and he loved being in their company in order to serve them more fully. He did so because it was the will of God.

I'm not implying that the will of God is for everyone to devote themselves fully to the poor. I'm just trying to understand the very narrow path these servants of the poor are walking, and how that path seems to lead to a quicker and deeper encounter with God. I do, however, think their physical journey with the poor has symbolic lessons for the rest of us. We need to encounter our own true poverty, acknowledge our own weaknesses and powerlessness, and be more open to those moments when we can extend mercy in the daily events of our lives.

The radical message for which Christ died is dramatically opposed to our culture of selfish individualism and unchecked consumerism. Should not our Christian faith compel us, by means of our transformed hearts, to live differently from the rest of our culture, whose values are rooted in the material realm and are far from the teachings of Christ?

ORDINARY MOMENTS

The spiritual life does not lift us above the human condition—its misery, problems, confrontations, pain, and difficulties. Spiritual life plunges us deeply into our humanity. It would be wonderful to spend our entire day absorbed in prayer, but that is unrealistic; we must enter into the marketplace and walk the alleys of commerce. We must help each other out of the ditches into which we fall. We encounter God in the streets of life. Everything human is divine. Strive to live the present moment as it truly is: a gift from God.

Every living thing should cause us to praise the Creator of all living things. Every event of our lives is open to God; prayer reveals how. The whole world, including every aspect of humanity, is sacred and a gateway to God. Wherever you are, whatever you are doing, God is there. Strive to feel God's presence and warmth in the ordinary moments of the day. The commonplace is also a divine place. The sacred is not here or there but everywhere. The challenge is to become aware of it. God is rarely where I think God should be. God is on a crowded bus in Port-au-Prince. God is in the quiet whispers of the trees and in the noisy rattlings of a New York City subway train. Everything speaks of God. Thank God.

St. Francis of Assisi found God not in pomp and glory, but in infirmity and foolishness. He found God in what we throw away. Francis found the God of endless light hiding in the shadows on the margin of society. God is on a street corner, at the intersection of everyday life. If we are attentive, we can feel the divine presence in a gentle breeze as God passes by on the street, often in a distressing disguise, hoping for an encounter. In the ordinary moments of the day, the extraordinary loving presence of God is reaching out to us.

TAKE UP YOUR CROSS

Marginalized from the rest of the society of Assisi, these were trying and confusing times for Francis. Julian of Speyer, in his *Life of St. Francis* (which he began to write six years after the saint's death), tells us: "In his soul there was an alternation of joy for the spiritual sweetness he tasted, and a burning desire to realize his plan." Francis spent a great deal of time in fervent prayer, and eventually God graced him with another moment of illumination. St. Bonaventure, in his *Major Life*, describes what happened:

One day as he prayed in one of his usual haunts, he became completely absorbed in God in the excess of his fervor. Then Jesus Christ appeared to him, hanging on his cross. His soul melted at the sight and the memory of Christ's passion was impressed on the depths of his heart so vividly that whenever he thought of it, he could scarcely restrain his sighs and tears, as he afterwards confessed towards the end of his life. He realized immediately that the words of the Gospel were addressed to him: "If you have a mind to come my way, renounce yourself and take up your cross and follow me." [TRANSLATED BY EWERT COUSINS / NEW YORK: PAULIST PRESS, 1978]

At that moment, Christ stepped out of the pages of history and the gospel became vividly real to Francis. He saw, felt, and knew God's love, and it was in the form of Jesus hanging on a cross. In that moment, Francis bore the stigmata on his soul, long before those wounds would appear on his body. St. Bonaventure said that the experience gave birth to "an attitude of profound compassion."

I think St. Francis came to see clearly that the fundamental principle of the gospel requires that the followers of Christ see that the weakest and least presentable people are indispensable to the Church, and that the followers of Christ must be in communion with the poor and must be willing to love our enemies. This has also been the core message of Pope Francis. Each of us is wounded in some way; each of us is an enemy. We need each other, and we need God.

So much of life today is deeply disturbing, especially our attitudes toward poverty and peace. I can't understand the irony of how we seek peace by going to war. Our impulse toward war uncovers our erroneous belief that some people are not important, that some lives, even the lives of some children (the children of our enemies), are expendable. I can't understand how we are undisturbed by the reality that more than 10,000 children die every day from preventable diseases, most stemming from hunger. The economic downturn that is dramatically damaging the lives of the poor reveals the utter lack of moral and ethical constraints on capitalism and consumerism; and the unbridled greed of commodity hucksters is nothing short of idolatry. We've become so numbed by the scope of poverty, as well as by our own self-interest, that we don't even feel the pain of the other; we don't realize that their misery is also our misery.

Our attitude toward the poor is linked to our attitude toward God. Sadly, our response to God's saving love for us is reflected in our failure to love the poor and to serve and care for them without question and as our neighbors. The love of God and the love of neighbor cannot be separated; they are so mutually intertwined as to be one and the same thing. Jesus is not looking for us to give the poor our spare change; he is asking us to give our very lives. The radical message of Jesus clearly indicates that consuming more than we need is actually stealing from those in need, which is certainly a message our consumer-crazed society does not want to hear.

Jesus never treated people as beggars. Instead, he entered into solidarity with the vulnerable, as he did with the man born blind. Jesus shows us that charity is not just about giving, but requires that the giver and receiver become engaged in a human partnership of human dignity, part of a continuing process of creation, a striving toward a completeness that ensures bringing everyone together in caring about mutual dignity and respect for all, regardless of race or religion.

Francis was changed, emotionally and psychologically.

He was a new man in Christ. Still, Francis did not yet have a clear idea of what God wanted him to do. He divided his life between selfless service to lepers and long, lonely hours of prayer in abandoned churches. But he wouldn't have to wait long before once again a voice heard in an empty church would show him the way.

THE LITTLE FIELD CHAPEL

There was another small church that Francis loved to visit. The church was named for St. Damian, a saint revered by both Eastern and Western churches for his charity. The church was not as old as St. Mary of the Angels, but it too was owned by the Camaldolese Benedictines of Mount Subasio. Both churches were perfect for Francis' solitary prayer; both were simple and poor. San Damiano is located just a mile downhill from the walled city of Assisi, an easy walk for Francis. The little field chapel, half in ruins following years of neglect, was empty. Francis, who was now in his mid-twenties, longed to know God's will for his life.

Kneeling in front of a large, painted Byzantine cross above the main altar, Francis prayed for guidance. Light was flooding in through the collapsed roof, creating pools of light and shadows that surrounded Francis as he devoutly and humbly knelt in prayer. We don't know how long he knelt before the crucifix, but I imagine it could have been for hours. Perhaps he grew weary or melancholic, wondering if God would answer his plea. Finally, in the calm stillness of the abandoned church something happened: in the quiet of his heart, Francis heard Christ say, "Francis, go, repair my house which, as you see, is falling completely to ruin."

Francis took the words he heard as a direct order to restore it, and he set about the task of rebuilding the church, brick by brick. Upon leaving the church, Francis spotted an elderly priest sitting in the sun. He approached the priest and gave him money, instructing the priest to use the money to buy oil for the lamp before the crucifix, so that it would be constantly burning, adding that when the oil ran out he would furnish additional money to replenish the oil.

THE CROSS OF SAN DAMIANO

The cross is crucial in Francis' conversion and spirituality. While kneeling at the foot of the large cross that hung in the small chapel of San Damiano, Francis' life was transformed.

Francis was educated by what he saw: creation, beggars, lepers, and Christ's followers. And he looked hard and long at the cross of San Damiano. The cross told a story, a visual story with a profound theological message that acted as a portal through which Francis could enter into the mystery of God.

To the untrained Western eye, icons appear at first glance to be rather odd and strange; the figures and their expressions seem exaggerated and out of proportion. The first few times I looked at the cross of San Damiano, I barely saw little more than the figure of Christ on a cross. I was totally unaware of the symbols employed by the iconographer, a twelfth-century monk, and didn't know how to "read" the picture he had painted. The icon is a visual text that artfully retells the story of Christ's passion as it is presented in the Gospel of John. The story the cross tells highlights humanity's continual struggle between good and evil, and the gospel message that death no longer has power over us thanks to the resurrection of Jesus.

The San Damiano incident, which occurred midway through the year 1206, demonstrated Francis' humanity, showing that he was a saint who made mistakes. Francis misunderstood the message he heard. He took the words literally and began to repair the church. Eventually, he came to understand that God had much more in mind than the restoration of that one church.

The followers of St. Francis believe that the "church" God was talking about was not a building but the institution, and that God wanted Francis to restore the Church universal, which was on the verge of collapse. Even the papacy had been corrupted. I once heard a Zen Buddhist who had a great love for St. Francis say he thought the "church" God had in mind was neither a building nor an institution, but Francis himself. Perhaps God gave Francis a series of progressively more difficult tasks that allowed the saint to build up his spiritual strength by first restoring a building, then an institution, and finally the job requiring the most strength, restoring himself.

God had broken through the silence at San Damiano. And Francis would respond with every fiber of his being; his own private, self-made world came to an end and a new world appeared within him and around him—a world where the impossible became an everyday experience. Francis responded immediately to Christ's request that he rebuild the church. There was no debate, no planning; there was only action, instantaneous and spontaneous.

STONE BY STONE

First, the leper, then the vision of Christ hanging on the cross, and finally the crucifix of San Damiano: These were the three critical events in the life of Francis. God was knocking on the door of his soul; as he knelt in front of the crucifix, Francis was at last willing to throw the door fully open. And the Spirit of God changed him. Before the vision and that divinely charged moment before the crucifix, Francis had been troubled and confused by what was happening inside himself. He was tormented by conflicting thoughts. Peace was nowhere to be found, nor could he find delight in the things that once pleased him, especially nature. Emptiness was part of the process of change, and Francis was still trying to flee the hand of God. God gently extended a hand to Francis. But Francis couldn't give what he didn't have. In this regard, the Zen master was correct: Despite his own weakness, Francis began to rebuild himself. Stone by stone, his own inner fortress was pulled down and rebuilt in the image of Christ. A heart hardened by vanity and a lust for money, fame, and glory was slowly being transformed. As he wandered about Assisi, dazed and distracted, it was clear to all that he was no longer the jubilant troubadour. In the midst of his weakness, at low tide emotionally and spiritually, he was graced with a vision, and shortly afterward, came to San Damiano, and knelt down before the poor, naked, crucified Christ. In the rubble of the church, Francis didn't have one stone fixed upon another in his own life. Yet the more he surrendered to God, the more God visited him with consolations. God gave him a mission, a plan for his life.

Francis' interior experience helped him chip away at his self-centered core and opened him up to the reality of God, which in turn sparked a call to action through genuine service to others. Francis' mission was clear: help people find reconciliation with themselves, others, and God, stone by stone, rebuilding individual lives, communities, and the world. Touched by God, filled by God, Francis now burned with a desire to help others believe in their own goodness. He invites us to rebuild our lives in the image of God, whispering in our ears, ever so gently, "God is simply waiting for your response."

THE ACTUAL SUN AND MOON OVER ASSISI

St. Francis believed in the power of signs. He saw them everywhere. Everything spoke to him of God. I certainly didn't share his ability to recognize a sign from God. Until a sign spoke to me.

I went on pilgrimage to Assisi in 1997. Near the end of cena (supper) on Wednesday July 9, word spread through the dining room at Casa Papa Giovanni that there would be a free concert featuring the Boys' Choir of Westminster Under School that evening at 9:00 p.m. at the Basilica di San Francesco. Two nights earlier, I had attended a beautiful concert at the Chiesa di Santa Maria Maggiore, and so my first inclination was to pass on this second concert. Then I heard one of the team members mention that concerts in the Basilica of St. Francis were special treats because they are the only times all the lights in the upper church are turned on, fully illuminating, with great effect, the church and Giotto's frescoes. I instantly changed my mind; shortly after dinner I began a slow walk to the basilica.

As I walked, my mind drifted to thoughts of the crucifix of San Damiano. Just before dinner we had watched a half-hour-long slide presentation on the crucifix in preparation for the next morning's liturgy, which would be celebrated in the small chapel in the Basilica of Santa Chiara, where the crucifix now hangs. After the liturgy we would be going to the tiny church of San Damiano, where Francis heard a voice tell him to repair the church.

I wished I could hear a voice and get some clear direction from God. The direction I was wishing for as I walked pertained to my first book on Francis. For a few days prior to that night, my mind began entertaining doubts about being able to complete *The Sun & Moon Over Assisi*. The more I learned during this pilgrimage about the depths of Franciscan spirituality—as well as the Christian faith—the more inadequate I felt to the task of presenting another look at the life of Francis. The more I learned, the more I realized how much I didn't know, and consequently how much more work still needed to be done to complete it.

Why me? Why should I be writing a book on St. Francis? I'm surrounded by people who know him better and love him more. That very afternoon I spent a few hours in the library of the Conventual convento where I was staying. So many books. Well-written books. What could I possibly add? "Not much," was my feeling as I walked to the basilica. All I had was my burning passion, my unbridled enthusiasm. Was that enough? I wasn't sure. Should I stop now, abandon the project? I didn't know. If I do abandon it, would I have wasted the last two years? So many questions. So few answers. Was Francis plagued by questions? I wanted to hear a voice. But I didn't think I would.

I was just a few minutes from the basilica when something happened. Something unexpected. Something breathtaking. God spoke to me. Not in words or an audible fashion, but in a symbol—a symbol I could clearly understand. Near the end of the long, narrow street leading to the basilica, the road curves and reveals a wide-open vista. Before me was the grassy knoll in front of the basilica. The basilica was framed by a wide panoramic view of the valley below. To the right of the basilica, the sun was just minutes away from setting. The entire scene was bathed in a golden glow. Then, off to the left of the massive building, high in the sky, I saw the moon. Right there, right at that very moment, was

The Sun and Moon Over Assisi

My heart leapt and then danced in joy. In a place I wouldn't have been had I not overheard something that caught my ear, I saw something that seemed meant for me. A coincidence? I no longer believe in coincidences. Coincidences didn't bring me to Assisi. A few minutes later, a Franciscan sister who is on the pilgrimage came around the corner. I excitedly ran up to her. "Look," I said, just seconds before the sun would slip behind the distant mountain, "the sun and moon...over Assisi!" She smiled. Broadly. She knew the title of my book. I told her about my doubts, and how the sight of sun and moon had just excited me and filled me with confidence. I said, "Is it a sign from God? Or is that silly?"

"No, it's not silly," she said. "God is speaking to you."

As I sat in my room a few hours later, I realized God didn't speak to me the way God spoke to Francis. God spoke to me the way I could best hear the voice. God speaks in unexpected ways, in unexpected moments. Each moment of our lives is pregnant with possibilities for the connection with the divine. Each moment holds the potential to dramatically alter every subsequent moment. St. Catherine of Genoa said it best: "We must not wish for anything other than what happens from moment to moment." A few days later, I came across this quotation from St. Irenaeus: "With God nothing is empty of meaning, nothing without symbolism."

Even a sunset.

GOD DOESN'T TALK IN SOUNDBITES

Rebuild my church," a voice told St. Francis of Assisi. And he did. With stones and spirit. And his very life. We're too modern, too sophisticated, too secular, too educated, too rational to hear God's voice the way Francis did.

By the busload people pour into Assisi every day. Six

million people visit every year. For many the place is simply a museum, a well-preserved thirteenth-century town crammed with fresco-covered churches. But many others come in hopes of hearing God's voice. We come in search of what Francis found: the peace, the sweetness, the stimulation of knowing God's voice. We dash from church to church. We descend to the Porziuncola enshrined within Santa Maria degli Angeli, or we ascend to the Carceri hermitage perched atop a ravine on Mount Subasio. We pray. We light a candle. We buy a statue or a Tau cross. And we move on. The bus is leaving. Can we make it down the hill to San Damiano and back in an hour? No. Got to go. We gave the place a day, maybe two, but we had to get going, had to visit Venice or Siena or Florence—Tuesday, Giotto; Wednesday, Michelangelo—had to visit Rome and Raphael.

But God doesn't talk in soundbites or in sync with the train schedule. God isn't worried about catching the 10:11 train to Foligno, with connections to Rome and Venice. God speaks to the still, not to the restless or the harried. God doesn't use a cell phone to catch us on the run. Do you want to catch God? Stop everything you're doing—and wait. Most of us are too busy and too rational to stop everything and wait. But that, I think, is what God wants, even demands. God is a God who comes, but only to those who wait. Francis knew how to wait. We're too busy to wait for God.

The psalmist was wise when composing the challenge: "Be still and know that I am God." Stillness, silence, and waiting are the portals through which we must walk in order to discover the deeper reality of God. To "be still" means to become peaceful and concentrated. Stillness creates space for deep looking and deep listening, which allows us to gain a glimpse at the reality of God, which leads us to greater understanding and compassion. Stillness allows us to become mindful of each moment and to realize that every moment is pregnant with the possibility of giving birth to God's transforming Spirit. To become truly still, you must penetrate your own silence and enter into the solitude of your heart. In that gentle stillness, the mystics tell us, the voice of God becomes audible. St. Francis heard that voice very clearly.

Deep, spiritually active silence allows us to hear the unity of life. Silence stills the intellect and opens the portal of the heart. Holy silence takes our humble prayers to new and exalted heights of contemplation. Be still and hear the voice of God. It is in stillness that we find our emptiness, the emptiness that can only be filled by welcoming God into our hearts. Seeing my own emptiness and impermanence prompted me to fall to my knees and pray.

HEARING VOICES

I remember reading a well-known theologian, now long-deceased, who suggested that we should always be hearing, with our actual ears, "the gurgling wellspring of our origins in God." The tough thing about Francis' story for modern people to accept is the fact that he "heard" voices. We put people who hear voices in psychiatric institutions and medicate them. We need to resist being turned off by the word "voices" or the idea that Francis "heard" something. The "voice" was inaudible, and was more like a flash of insight, a sense of knowing. The "voice" was so clear, so real, so authentic, so truthful, that Francis had no trouble following it because the "voice" was devoid of conflict, chaos, emotion, or judgment. It was a pure thought, which he followed as he let the insight guide him.

Like St. Benedict, Francis listened with the ears of his

heart. This contemplative listening grew out of his experiential consciousness of God in the mundane events of his life. Through his intimacy with God, Francis slowly developed a spiritual mindfulness that allowed him to see the light of God in everything. Down through the centuries, mystics of all faiths have used poetic language—"seeing God," "hearing God," "tasting God," "being embraced by God"—to describe their unexplainable experience. The great Jewish scholar Rabbi Abraham Joshua Heschel offers lucid insight into how prophets "hear" voices:

> The leading exponents of Jewish thought exhort us not to imagine that God speaks, or that a sound is produced by Him through organs of speech....In being "told that God addressed the prophets and spoke to them," our minds are merely to receive a notion that there is a divine knowledge to which the prophets attain....We must not suppose that in speaking God employed voice or sound.

What Francis heard at the foot of the cross of San Damiano arose from the depth of his being and flowed out of his tasted intimacy with God. It was an intensely personal phenomenon that subsisted entirely in the realm of faith. It cannot be explained; it can only be experienced. And it can only be experienced if you take the time to listen. It was Francis' faith that did the hearing, not his ears, just as it was their faith that allowed Abraham to see an angel and Moses to see the burning bush.

NAKED IN THE SQUARE

The experience of San Damiano eventually led Francis to a painful break with his family and the world of business. He realized the restoration of the church would require a lot of money. While his father was away on business, Francis took (or as Chesterton puts it with brutal frankness: "He stole...") cloth from his father's store and traveled via horse to Spoleto. He sold the cloth—and the horse too—in order to raise money to restore the tiny church. He returned to the church with the money and tried to give it to the old priest. But the priest would not accept it. He suggested that Francis spend some time in prayer, and he offered to let Francis stay with him, either in his house or in a cave near the church. Francis left the money in the church and retreated to the cave, where he embarked on a period of prayer and fasting. Meanwhile, Francis' father returned and was outraged when he discovered that Francis had taken the horse and the cloth. He immediately began looking for his son, determined to drag his son home and knock some sense into him.

Pietro Bernardone's search eventually led him to the church. Francis, learning of his father's anger and imminent arrival, fled in fear. The old priest returned the money Francis had left behind. Once he recovered the money, Pietro gave up his search for his son and returned home. Francis, now in hiding, continued his fasting and prayer for nearly a month. During this time, Christ was no longer in the throne of his heart: fear was. Francis agonized over his father's recrimination, the scorn of his neighbors, and the mocking disdain of his friends. He must have been in the grip of fear and must have wondered if he was making a huge mistake.

Thomas of Celano, in his *First Life*, says, "He prayed always with a torrent of tears that the Lord would deliver him from the hands of those who were persecuting his soul, and that he would fulfill his pious wishes in loving kindness; in fasting and in weeping he begged for the clemency of the Savior, and, distrusting his own efforts, he cast his whole being upon the Lord."

This was a time of real anguish, and Francis clung to the hope that God would hear his prayer and help him cast off his fears. In this "darkness," Thomas of Celano tells us, one day [perhaps in April, 1207] "a certain exquisite joy," beyond anything Francis had ever experienced before, penetrated the void, and the "fire" from this joy prompted Francis to abandon his hiding place and return to Assisi, knowing full well that he was about to "expose himself openly to the curses of his persecutors."

His emaciated body was covered with dirt. His eyes had dark rings under them, and his hair was disheveled. Children were tormenting Francis as they followed him down the street, calling him names, shouting insults, and throwing stones and garbage at him. "You're mad; you're demented," they shouted. St. Bonaventure notes: "But the Lord's servant passed through it as if he were deaf to it all, unbroken and unchanged by any of these insults." Hearing the commotion, Francis' father ran to the street to see what was happening. When Pietro Bernardone spotted Francis walking down the street, he was horrified by his son's appearance. Filled with sorrow, shame, and anger, Pietro became so enraged at the sight that he seized his son, dragged him home, and locked him in the store's dark basement.

Francis remained a prisoner in his father's basement for weeks. His father only provided bread and water, in hope of somehow breaking his son's spirit and curing him of his crazy ideas. According to *The Legend of the Three Companions*, Pietro "used threats and blows to bend his son's will, to drag him back from the path he had chosen." While Pietro's treatment of his son was harsh and cruel, it reflected the fact that he desperately wanted the "old" Francis back, wanted his son to be "normal," to enjoy life and follow in his footsteps and help him run the business. Francis stood firm.

The situation filled Pica with anguish. She could see her son's unwavering determination and realized nothing was going to change his mind. Eventually, when Pietro was away, Pica, filled with tender compassion, released her imprisoned son. Upon his return, Pietro was so angry he denounced his son as a thief and set legal proceedings in motion to disinherit him.

Francis repudiated his father in a public square in front of the bishop's residence, giving back to him all he owned, including the clothing he was wearing. Standing naked in the square, Francis declared he would call no one "Father" except God. Francis was now free—free to follow the Lord. Some saw it as a bold act of faith; others as a foolish act. Either way, Francis was from that day on going to follow the gospel. He had forsaken everything, picked up his cross, and walked in the footsteps of Jesus. As it was for Jesus, Francis' ascent along the road that lay ahead of him ended with the Cross.

A number of people from Assisi, including Bishop Guido, who covered the naked Francis with his cloak, surrounded Francis in the square as he made his bold and daring break with his father and his past. It is hard for me to imagine anyone publicly performing such a radical act. I know I couldn't. But what if I thought—fully believed—God was asking me to do something equally as radical? Could I do it? Would I do it?

I can't imagine doing something so bold when all the eyes around me were looking at me as if I were mad, the way the crowd must have looked at Francis that fateful day in the square. Francis, however, was unconcerned about what his friends and family thought; his only concern was pleasing God and doing the will of God. The grace of prayer is given to the pure of heart, those who seek only the Lord with all their heart and soul. But at the same time, authentic prayer will put you in conflict with all who reject the demanding message of Jesus.

STRIPPED OF EVERYTHING

Today we place great emphasis on clothing. We make fashion statements, and all too readily judge others solely on the basis of what they are wearing. Conversely, we also glorify nudity, which has become commonplace in movies and television. Magazines and the Internet use nudity to attract subscribers. For Francis, clothing and nakedness were symbolic and a means of expression. He dressed as a troubadour, in the finest of silk, in his party days. He dressed as a knight to enter battle. He wore beggar's rags in the early days of his search for God. Eventually, he created and wore a habit that perfectly reflected his devotion to poverty and simplicity.

Francis wanted to truly imitate Christ. Christ died naked on the cross. We don't show the slain Lamb of God naked on the cross because we simply could not take such a graphic image. We need to cover Christ up. We need to cover ourselves up, and not just with clothing. By removing all his clothes in public, Francis stripped himself of his fear and pretense. He stripped himself of his parents and their influence, prestige, and security. He stripped himself of his friends and neighbors. He stripped himself of his past and his future family wealth. Francis stood naked with only a thin wall of flesh between him and God. Naked, he had nothing and had nothing to lose. Naked, he had no plans, no prospects for the future. Naked, both literally and symbolically, Francis was the freest man in the world. Naked, Francis had to rely upon God for everything. Naked, his faith was lived on a minute-to-minute basis. Naked, Francis only wanted to be clothed in the glory of God.

The symbolism of his bold and spectacular gesture prompts me to ask myself a very tough question: what in my life needs to be stripped away? Am I willing to stand naked before God, stripped of everything that stands between myself and the divine?

A BEGGING BOWL

Life during these first solitary years wasn't easy for Francis. Change is always hard, and Francis was remaking himself; the process of making the gradual transition from a life of easy, prodigal self-indulgence to one of heroic self-abnegation in imitation of Christ was painful. The emerging saint took every opportunity to conquer himself so God could rule.

Early one evening, Francis went up to Assisi to beg for oil, which he needed for the lamp he always kept burning before the crucifix at San Damiano. When he saw a house with lamps burning, he walked up to it, but before knocking on the door, he noticed through the window a gathering of his old friends inside the house. They were having a party. Francis must have recalled the days when he was the life of such parties. Suddenly he was too ashamed to knock on the door. Not wanting to cause embarrassment for them or himself, he turned and walked away from the house. Within a few steps, Francis knew his own weakness was causing him to be a coward. He returned to the house. His old friends let him in. They must have been stunned by his appearance. His worn, patched clothing looked strikingly out of place. As they looked on in astonished silence, Francis proclaimed he was a coward too ashamed to enter the house. His confession must have baffled them. He then asked them for some of their oil for the love of God.

Francis went to extreme ends to conquer himself. For instance, the old priest at San Damiano, who came to love Francis, grew increasingly distressed over how exhausted Francis was at the end of a long day's work restoring the church. The priest was so worried about Francis' frail health that he began preparing hearty meals for him. But Francis saw this kind gesture as a temptation that could easily divert him from his commitment to true poverty. Francis realized that even a simple meal in the humble surrounding of the poor priest's home could be as addictive and comforting as all the luxuries he had once enjoyed in his father's house, and so he refused the food and opted instead to beg for his meals. Each day, Francis would take a bowl to Assisi and go door to door begging for scraps of food. When the bowl was filled, he would find a quiet spot to sit and eat the leftover morsels of food he had gathered. When the contents of the begging bowl looked like a nauseating and disgusting mess, Francis managed to see his poor meal as a sacrament of divine providence, which he ate with joy.

I think St. Francis was extreme in his fastidious avoidance of any comfort and security, and even a nice meal lovingly prepared by a kindly old priest. Yet I understand the motivation behind his extremism. I'm trying to emulate the poverty of spirit that Francis so fully embraced, yet I really don't want to be more than a few miles away from Starbucks and my daily double tall latte.

Francis' willingness to follow God anywhere is what made him so simple, pliant, and totally responsive to even the slightest prompting of the Spirit. It is perfectly understandable that the worldly people of Assisi could not tolerate his incessant wanderings. They could only sneer at the future saint because they acted out of their own self-interest, and any other kind of behavior was incomprehensible.

My faith in God is so easily shaken that it is hard for me to understand how Francis overcame the loneliness of his new life and the numerous setbacks he encountered along the gospel road. He was just one man. Yet he undertook the Herculean task of fighting the physical decay of crumbling churches and suffering lepers. He didn't weigh the hugeness of his task, a task far beyond the reach of one frail man. He didn't see the obstacles. He only listened to his heart. Stone by stone, he restored the churches. Bowl by bowl, he fed the lepers. He did what he could and left the rest to God.

I would have caved in under the enormity of the problem. The decaying churches and the agonizing suffering would have filled me with sadness and doubt. Yet St. Francis faced the hardships and heartbreaks with hope and joy. In contrast, the joys I've experienced in life have all been lined with sadness. For me, joy has been fleeting; sadness, enduring. And I know I'm not alone in that regard. All around me, I see people fighting to suppress their inner sadness by searching for joy in a wide array of ways: sex, power, fame, fortune, drugs. We crowd into gigantic malls and gobble up all the goodies on display. We consume more than we need because we think we need more than we have. Credit cards in hand, we chase after the hottest fashions, the fastest cars, the quickest computers, or the latest electronic gadgets in order to find happiness and dull the sadness. But the sadness remains. Francis chose a different path.

PART III

The Founding

A STATE OF PENANCE

In the beginning of his journey to God, Francis lived as a hermit for nearly two years, calling himself a penitent and living according to the gospel as he understood it. It was a time of prayer and fasting and living in a "state of penance." For Francis, penance was the most effective way of entering into the unceasing renewal required to achieve the gospel imperative of *metanoia*, a complete change of mind and heart through renouncing all self-love, all self-will, and all self-seeking. Francis practiced acts of vigorous mortification as a means of breaking down any resistance within himself toward fully living the life of Christ in his own life.

It was also a time of restoring small, dilapidated chapels

in the countryside near Assisi. Without any money and possessing nothing but the warmth of his personality and the
fire of his faith, Francis went from town to town begging,
often asking only for stones to use in rebuilding the Church
of San Damiano. He carried the stones on his own shoul-
ders. He quickly learned the skills of a stonemason. He also
cared for lepers, going door to door with a bowl begging for
food for them to eat. He even briefly worked as a servant
in a Benedictine abbey near Gubbio. In short, Francis was
a beggar and a homeless, itinerant worker. Worse, he was
cursed by his father when they crossed paths. In *Tales of
St. Francis,* Murray Bodo paints a picture of the harshness
of life for a beggar: "Begging...is not sublime; it is demean-
ing and small, and actually quite ugly. And the only reason
Francis insisted on it was that it enabled him...to feel the
Incarnation the way God felt it, for God had to come among
us as a beggar, his hands open, asking us humbly to receive
Him." In time, the people of Assisi resented his begging,
even mocking him.

The gospel life certainly wasn't an easy life. God, it seems,
asks hard things of those who love him. Yet all the accounts
of this time of Francis' life indicate he endured all these hardships with great joy in his heart and often a song on his lips.
Out of the darkness of detachment and utter deprivation,
Francis slowly emerged to sparkle with sunshine and mercy.

By letting go of his old life, Francis discovered a new life.
The less there was for him, the more there was for others. By
banishing his illusions, he was able to see what was truly real.
The spiritual life has more to do with subtraction than addition. As Francis journeyed to God, he had to gradually let
go of his fears, doubts, and prejudices, along with his need
to be right or his natural human instinct to blame others.

This is the same journey we all must make. It is not an easy road…and few take it.

A LIFE OF PENANCE

In thinking about Francis and his penchant for penance, my mind drifts back to my two visits to Isola Maggiore in Lago Trasimeno, the island where Francis fasted forty days during one Lent. The natural beauty of the island made it hard to think about the starkness of Lent and the idea of penance. Yet Francis summarized his life before his dramatic and transcendent encounter with a leper in four words: "I was in sin." And with a kiss of a leper he embarked upon a "life of penance."

We don't like the word "penance." For us, it's an ugly word, bearing connotations of guilt and shame. Yet the foundation of St. Francis of Assisi's spiritual life is built on harsh penance, which bordered on the extreme edges of asceticism. The people of Assisi were dumbfounded by the nearly inhuman aspects of the austerity of his life. St. Bonaventure tells us that the saint "curbed the stimulus of the senses with a discipline so rigorous that at great pains did he accept what was necessary for his sustenance."

Lent was not merely a season for Francis, but a way of life.

If conversion and faith require this kind of change—the "metanoia" of the New Testament—then we're not interested in it. But for Francis, his understanding of penance, manifested in the extravagances of austerity, was not tied to punishment. For him, penitential mortification was a means for growth, creating a "new man." Francis wanted to put his abounding passions to death so that their creative power could be put to the service of a higher goal, namely, holiness. Francis wanted only to serve God in a full and radical way, and personal privations and penance was the path he chose to follow.

As Francis began to attract followers, he did not demand that his brothers emulate his relentless drive to subjugate his own earthly passions. On the contrary, St. Bonaventure notes, "he rejected [for others] excessive severity [in penance] that was not, at the heart, clothed in mercy, nor sprinkled with the salt of discretion." Francis was only hard on himself, which made it easy for him to be soft with everyone else...especially the poor and the poorest of the poor, the lepers.

For St. Francis, profound penances were the gateway to his profound humanity. His gentleness was derived from the strength and discipline he acquired while silencing everything within him that was not in harmony with the love of God.

Slowly, I'm learning to say "no" to the things in my life that are blocking me from a fuller relationship with God. The spirit behind St. Francis' desire for a life of penance has taught me that small acts of mortification in my personal life can be effective teachers. In the lives of many saints, the road to holiness was paved with authentic penance.

NO PAIN, NO GAIN

Poverty was not Francis' goal; it was an ascetical path to holiness. The aim of his asceticism is the attainment of poverty of spirit. Poverty of spirit is the manger of gentle receptivity, which allows the divine to be born within us. To be wholly present to God, with all of our heart, mind, and soul, we must be poor in spirit. This is the entire message of St. Francis.

Poverty of spirit, as Francis clearly understood, is far more than material poverty. While material poverty may help to facilitate poverty of spirit, it is nonetheless important to realize that a person without possessions can still be possessed by a craving for things. It is the craving that makes us restless, distracting our hearts and minds from being present to God alone. Poverty of spirit frees us from being divided by false idols and uncurbed passions.

Without self-denial and sacrifice, my prayer life will wither on the vine. Poverty of spirit is a means of maintaining a continual attitude of dying to self without succumbing to self-hatred or causing a lack of self-esteem. We need to die to self because it is the only way to be fully alive to God. A cluttered heart is a deaf heart.

When it comes to our careers or business endeavors or succeeding in art or athletics, we all know the importance of discipline. No pain, no gain. Yet when it comes to our inner life, or life of the spirit, it seems we easily succumb to the temptation of slipping into indiscipline. But our lack of spiritual discipline, our avoiding any form of asceticism, leaves us vulnerable to be influenced by the empty allurements and false realities of our culture. To arrive at a point of true selflessness, a point of wanting nothing for yourself, living fully for God and others, requires the same kind of focused discipline that we exercise in our external endeavors. When our wills are dulled by impure and selfish desires, our spirits in turn become deaf to the silent voice of God that is always gently whispering the truth, gently calling us into the abandonment of our ego so we can enter fully into the essence of the divine.

Asceticism plays a part in the spiritual life just as discomfort plays a part in the natural life. We do what we need to do in order to fight cold and heat; so also, we need to fight sin and weakness. But compulsive asceticism is of no use. At the very least, asceticism can be an effective self-management tool. When asceticism and mysticism wed, the saints tell us, they give birth to a luminous creation—as long as both are hidden with Christ in God.

OUR LADY OF THE ANGELS

After finishing the restoration of San Damiano, Francis began the work of restoring a small, abandoned chapel hidden in the woods in the valley below Assisi. The church was named Santa Maria degli Angeli (St. Mary of the Angels). Located a little more than a mile below the walls of Assisi, the tiny church, built on the ruins of a Roman villa, is often referred to as the cradle of Franciscanism. Built in ancient times, the church had been dedicated to the Blessed Virgin; it had long ago been deserted and was in terrible shape when Francis, moved by his fervent devotion to Mary, decided to restore it. Francis had a deep love for this humble church. Bonaventure said that Francis felt that angels often visited it.

In Francis' time, the area surrounding where the basilica now stands was heavily wooded. A simple footpath through the forest led to a small plot of cleared land where the ancient chapel stood. It was built in 352 by hermits returning from the Holy Land. Until well into the tenth century, pilgrims traveling to and from the Holy Land often stopped in the small, rustic chapel, which was originally named St. Mary of Josaphat, because enshrined within the chapel was a fragment of the Blessed Virgin's tomb, given to the builders of the church by St. Cyril. In time, the chapel became known as St. Mary of the Angels, because angelic songs were supposedly heard there, and even occasional angelic apparitions had been reported. The change in the name might also be more realistically traced back to a very old painting on the wall behind the altar that depicts the Assumption of the Blessed Virgin into heaven. In the painting, Mary is surrounded by a bevy of floating angels. Hence, the peasants, most of whom were illiterate, probably began referring to the church as St. Mary of the Angels.

Eventually, the church became known simply as the *Porziuncula*, a word that means "little portion of earth." That designation was originated by the Benedictines who lived on Mt. Subasio. In 576, the chapel was given to them. By 1075, it had fallen into such a state of ruin that the Benedictines abandoned the property even though they still retained the rights to it. More than a century later, Francis, of course, would see the beauty in the ruins and restore the church.

When the restoration was completed, Francis continued to live in a nearby camp known as Rivo Torto. On occasion a monk would come down to celebrate Mass in the rebuilt church. Francis had prepared a home for the Eucharist and the word of God, and his reverence for churches where the word could be proclaimed and the Eucharist celebrated gave birth in his heart to a prayer he would teach his followers, a prayer still said by the friars today:

> We adore you, most holy Lord Jesus Christ,
> here and in all your churches throughout the world;
> And we bless you because by your most holy cross
>   you have redeemed the world.

According to the *Legend of Perugia,* the church was "the poorest church of the whole region around Assisi" before Francis restored it. It is hard to overlook the symbolism at play here. The institutional Church at the time was rich and powerful. The Church was a dominating, secular feudal power that owned half the land in Europe. Even monks were rich in land and material goods. Rather than enter the "system," Francis moved to the periphery, where he found the environment ripe for creatively responding to the call of conversion. On the margins of society, far from the center of power, Francis chose the path of foolishness, following the crucified Christ in absolute poverty and simplicity. Prophets are always planted on the periphery. Even the Son of God was born on the margin of Jewish society.

THE BASILICA DI SANTA MARIA DEGLI ANGELI

The French-Jewish intellectual Simone Weil had a mystical experience in Assisi. She wrote: "In 1937 I had two marvelous days in Assisi. There, alone in the twelfth-century Romanesque chapel of Santa Maria degli Angeli, an incomparable marvel of purity where St. Francis used [to] often pray, something stronger than I was compelled me for the first time in my life to go down on my knees."

The enormous Basilica di S. Maria degli Angeli, which clearly can be seen from Assisi, dominates the valley's landscape. On my first visit to the church in 1995, the day was bright and beautiful. The deep blue sky was clear, with only a few puffy cottontail clouds snuggling together at the top of Mount Subasio. The sun was bathing the basilica, causing it to shimmer in the distance. The bus from Assisi slowly wound its way down the hillside, lazily traversing the three-mile distance to the church.

What draws people to the Basilica of St. Mary of the Angels is not its impressive size or architecture, but what is housed inside the church. The grandiose church functions as a womb for the two humblest and most sacred shrines connected to the life and death of St. Francis: the little field chapel known as the Porziuncula [often referred to as the Portiuncola], the first permanent home for Francis and his first followers, and the Chapel of the Transitus, where Francis died.

When Francis was dying, he asked to be taken to his favorite spot on earth: the Porziuncula. He was placed in a small infirmary, little more than a cell, near the small church, where he died on the evening of October 3, 1226. The infirmary was converted into the Chapel of the Transitus (Cappella del Transito), so named because it was from there that Francis made the transition from this life to eternal life. Today, both the Porziuncula and the Chapel of the Transitus stand just a few feet apart under the great dome of the basilica.

Construction of the huge new church began in 1569. The exterior of the majestic church is powerfully beautiful, a balanced blend of columns and arches crowned by a gold statue of Mary. The golden Mary wistfully looks down on the piazza, which is usually filled with tourists taking pictures or eating picnic lunches, vendors selling statues and postcards, and local kids kicking a soccer ball. When I entered the basilica, my attention was immediately drawn to the Porziuncula. I felt as if I had stepped into a magnificent tabernacle housing the humblest of guests, in much the same way as ornate, draped, cabinet-like shrines on altars house consecrated pieces of bread mysteriously containing the essence of Christ. The small, simple, stone chapel, once surrounded by a dense, green forest, contains the essence of St. Francis.

Inside this chapel Francis prayed, cried, sang, heard the voice of God, and nurtured his disciples. When I passed through the arched entrance of the chapel Francis loved, I sensed I was entering into the heart of the Franciscan spirit: *simplicity, serenity, sincerity, silence, and song.* I smiled, thinking of Brother Francis humbly walking into the chapel with a broom in his hand and quietly sweeping God's house. A swell of emotion swept over me as I knelt down and prayed for the grace, with Francis as my guide, to follow Christ more closely.

O Lord, my mind and heart are centered on so many things other than you. Mostly good things, but not you. Help me this day to desire you first and foremost, and not to be distracted by all the things that pull me this way and that way, fragmenting my being. Teach me this day, O Lord, how to forget my fears and anxieties, and put all my trust and hope in you alone.

THE EYE OF A NEEDLE

When Francis embraced the gospel, he embraced a life of letting go. The gospel is countercultural in countless ways. Take the story in Mark's gospel of the rich man who has observed all the laws of his Jewish faith who asks Jesus what more he must do to gain entrance into eternal life. Jesus tells him to sell all he has, give away the proceeds to the poor, and follow him. The countenance of the rich man's face turns sullen. He turns and walks away, dejected. Jesus turns to his disciples and tells them that it would be easier for a camel to pass through the eye of a needle than for a rich person to enter the kingdom of God.

On the face of it, the story says a rich person will find it impossible to get into heaven. But actually the story has less to do with money than with surrender. I'm certainly not rich, at least by American standards; but compared to the two-thirds of the world's population locked in the punishing prison of poverty, I'm indeed a rich man. Even though I feel as if I'm giving my life in service of the poor, is Christ asking me to literally give everything I own away? I do not think so.

In the Jewish culture at the time of Jesus, being rich was a sign of God's blessing; conversely, being poor indicated God was not pleased with you. The rich felt secure in their knowledge that God favored them. Jesus turned that idea upside down, saying that our external possessions are not a sign of our internal harmony with God. God's capital, according to Jesus, was love, not money. We will be judged not by what we have, but by what we give away in love.

The rich man in the story walked away sad because "he had many possessions." He was unable to let go of the things he valued, the things that made him feel safe and secure. Jesus is saying that security is detrimental in the spiritual life because it thwarts full surrender to God. As I've walked with the poor, I've come to see how so much of what I once thought was important or valuable has turned out to be rather worthless. In our culture, even those of us who are hardly considered rich have so many resources at our disposal that we feel no need for God. Our culture tells us to be strong and independent. The ever-countercultural Jesus says God is found in weakness, that we are all connected, all one in the loving and merciful eyes of God. Perhaps Jesus was asking the rich man to become poor in order for him to experience the deepest need and longing of his heart: unity with the Creator, the source of all life. Whether we admit it or not, we need God. None of us is truly rich, because we lack the fullness of God. I think Jesus was telling the rich man that self-reliance was detrimental to the spiritual life and that spiritual growth requires surrender and total dependence on God. I may not have much money, but I fear I am just as self-reliant as the rich man in the gospel.

Christ is asking us to give away all that is blocking us from the deepest longing of our hearts—unity with God. That could be money, or it could be any of a litany of things that we hold on to for dear life—things like excessive worry, the need to control, the urge for unrestrained carnal pleasure, addiction to drugs or alcohol (or any addictive behavior), the need to consume more and more, the unrelenting desire to succeed at all costs, the need to be constantly entertained, or the need to be always on the move, always striving for something we don't have. The list is endless. So much of modern life distracts us from God. Every day we face an onslaught of images and messages hurled at us from the media, Hollywood, and the world of business in the form of nonstop commercials. Life has become a whirling dervish of frenetic activity. We live life in fast-forward. There is no time for stillness and silence, no time for reflection. No time for God. We are too rich, too busy, too preoccupied with satisfying our own desires. Jesus is saying: stop. Stop everything that leads you away from God.

The more we are focused on the material world, the less we will be focused on the spiritual realm. Jesus was telling the rich man to give away all he was clinging to, and to cling to God alone. Jesus is asking us to become radically dependent upon him alone. I'm slowly learning that I can accomplish nothing on my own; but with Christ, nothing is impossible. But I easily forget that truth. Following Christ is truly hard because it is truly countercultural. I once met a humble Franciscan friar who had dedicated his entire life to serving the poor. He told me the only things he owned were his sins. Sin, at its root, is nothing more than a failure to love. This ultimately is what Christ is asking us to give away: anything that hinders love. Thich Nhat Hanh, a Vietnamese

Buddhist monk and Zen master, once said: "If you have compassion, you cannot be rich...You can be rich only when you can bear the sight of suffering." He understood what Christ was saying to the rich man in Mark's gospel. God is calling us to deeper and deeper levels of love, mercy, and compassion, and we need to give away anything that thwarts our response to that call. And so our faces turn sad and we walk away dejected because we have so much.

For me, capitalism is becoming a dirty word. I'm an artist, and the world of economics and global markets and corporate culture is far beyond me. I suppose the idea of capitalist-style competition has some merit, as long as corporate leaders and independent business people at least make an attempt at remembering that the purest goal of all economic endeavors is the well-being of the entire human community, especially the weakest and poorest members. The capitalist system needs to be constantly on guard against the dangers of greed and structural injustice, while at the same time fostering a sincere concern for distributive justice and the common good. It is sinful that so many people around the world do not have access to clean and safe water and enough food to at least prevent death by starvation.

According to Catholic social teaching, our concern for the poor should go far beyond mere moral concern. More than forty years ago, Pope Paul VI said economic decisions should focus on the poor because in God's eyes they occupy a privileged place. In other words, our first concern should be the poor. Of course, profits are our first concern, and the poor are relegated to an afterthought, if at all. Wealth rarely trickles down to where the poor are: living on the mean streets of our big cities and hidden in massive slums around the world. When Pope Francis expressed his reservations about capitalism, a popular radio talk show host called the pope a communist.

My head spins just thinking about all these issues. These are complex times. We lead complex lives. We live in a hectic, fast-paced society that is filled with moral dilemmas, financial worries, ecological disasters, criminal violence, racial bigotry, corporate greed, decaying inner cities, global political unrest and economic instability, and deadly wars fueled by religious differences that pit neighbor against neighbor. We are stressed and anxious as we breathlessly chase after more and more possessions. Our passion to possess blinds us to the reality that much of the world is enduring poverty and starvation on a scale unmatched in human history. Millions of malnourished and abandoned people are living on the edge of extinction. What can I do? I think St. Francis of Assisi would recommend that I take a close look at the virtue of simplicity. By way of simplicity, Francis was able to enter into the deep silence of his heart.

Simplicity is hard. Attaining it will not eliminate the complexity of modern life and all its intricate personal and global problems. I think simplicity allowed Francis to live in harmony with the ordered complexity of his day. As his heart grew in simplicity, he was better able to understand the Lord and the world around him. Pope Saint John XXIII said, "The older I grow, the more clearly I perceive the dignity and winning beauty of simplicity in thought, conduct, and speech: a desire to simplify all that is complicated and to treat everything with the greatest naturalness and clarity."

Francois Fenelon, in his book *Christian Perfection*, wrote: "It is a wise self-love, which wants to get out of the intoxication of outside things." Before I can free myself from the lure of material things, I must become more sensitive to the things of the spirit, which will diminish my chances of being dazzled by the superficial, such as the latest sports car from BMW or the latest computer from Apple. More important will be the latest revelation from God on how I can love my neighbor while at the same time deflecting my own self-centered greed. Through simplicity, we learn that self-denial paradoxically leads to true self-fulfillment. Simplicity allows us to hold the interests of others above our self-interest. Real simplicity is true freedom. The constant drumbeat of materialism is no longer deafening. We desire less and are happy with less.

Simplicity is the best method of stripping away excess baggage and nonessential adornments that weigh us down. As these distractions disappear, the reality of God becomes clearer. Simplicity is a much more profound concept than voluntary poverty, which is much smaller in scope, because simplicity not only reduces your material possessions, it also diminishes your desire for them. Simplicity immunizes you from the plague of consumerism.

Our future depends on more and more people learning to live more simply. Mahatma Gandhi once said that the world has enough resources to meet everyone's need, but not enough to match everyone's greed. While Americans, who make up five percent of the world's population, gobble nearly thirty percent of the globe's resources, large segments of the world's population live without hope, tottering on the brink of cruel deaths by starvation. Simplicity is not an option; it is a vital necessity. Reckless, out-of-control consumption needs to be curtailed before it destroys us. Unlimited growth, which fosters a throw-away culture, is a dangerous illusion. Voluntary denial is liberating. As Christians we must become advocates for the poor and the forgotten.

We must become poor ourselves, living simply so others can simply live.

Jean Vanier, the remarkable founder of L'Arche, said: "Simplicity is no more and no less than being ourselves, knowing that we are loved." Francis knew, to the core of his being, that he was loved by God. Francis' inner life was so serene, his thirst for the truth so palpable, and his freedom from attachments to material possessions so great that he became a magnet for people wanting something deeper and more meaningful from life. From the simplicity of disentangled living, Francis learned how to enter the fullness of integrated life. He possessed nothing while enjoying everything.

St. Augustine said: "All plenty which is not my God is poverty to me." What an amazing thought. Is it possible to get to the place where we can truly understand, not on a theoretical level but in practical reality, what St. Augustine felt? St. Francis did.

THE COMMUNION OF SAINTS

As a child growing up in New York City in the 1950s, stories about the lives of the saints always fascinated me. Down through the centuries, the great saints were always larger than life, heroic figures whose dedication to and love of God knew no boundaries. The gospel was truly alive in them; their hearts, minds, and actions reverberated with the spirit of Christ. But my childhood enthusiasm for these spiritual heroes didn't survive my passage through puberty. Gradually, I came to see saints as quaint, pious remnants of the past, whose deep faith and dynamic lives had been reduced to lifeless statues of wood or plaster. For me as a teenager, their stories, filled with drama and miracles, began to recede into the realm of fairy tales; the saints eventually took their place next to Santa Claus and the Easter Bunny—irrelevant and fanciful myths from my innocent childhood that had lost all meaning in the confusing world of adolescence. By the time I reached my fortieth birthday, I was an atheist.

Today, I clearly can see that the decline in my fascination with the lives of the saints came in direct proportion to the decline and eventual death of my faith. And conversely, after the rather dramatic resurrection and renewal of my long-dormant faith in March 1995, my interest in saints has not only been fully restored but also deepened and intensified. In order to love the saints, one needs to believe in an infinitely supreme being of immeasurable love, goodness, and wisdom, with whom the core of our being is united by the act of creation.

As I began afresh reading the lives of the saints, I quickly realized saints were not always saints. That is, they weren't born saints with halos firmly affixed over their heads; they became saints, overcoming doubts and intense struggles with temptations and their own human weaknesses by accepting the healing grace God offers to everyone. Sainthood emerges from the depths of human frailty. The saints were one of us. They got mad, they were testy and impatient, they made mistakes, and they had firsthand knowledge of sin. Many, many saints, at one point in their lives, denied the existence of God. Most saints fought heroic battles as they transformed their natural urges towards selfishness and meanness into a desire for communion and a life of self-giving sharing. Saints represent the best we can be. While the saints were not perfect humans, they became, through hard work, truly authentic people, people who have demonstrated that the gospel can be lived if you are willing to pay the price.

As I struggle to live more and more the way Jesus taught

us to live, the saints serve as irrefutable evidence that it really is possible to live the gospel ideal. The lives of the saints challenge us to hear—really hear—the message of Jesus and allow it to transform us. The saints show us how to take our lives in our hands and offer them to God, without knowing what will be asked of us in return. In the age of cynicism in which we live, the saints teach us how to trust. The saints show us what we might be, what we should be. Look into the heart of a saint and you will see the heart of God. Enter into the communion of saints; allow the saints to become your friends, to hold your hands as you journey toward God.

THIS IS IT!

Francis attended Mass one day in the restored church of Our Lady of the Angels, and as he heard the gospel being read he felt his heart burn with passion. He could not have known he was on the verge of making the transition from a hermit and restorer of churches to an apostle and evangelist. It was the feast of St. Matthew the Apostle. As Francis listened to the priest reading from the Gospel of Matthew, he believed God was talking directly to him, and so the words of the gospel became marching orders for Francis:

> [At the time Jesus said to his disciples...] And as you go, proclaim the kingdom of heaven is close at hand. Cure the sick, raise the dead, cleanse the lepers, cast out devils. You received without charge, give without charge. Provide yourselves with no gold or silver, not even with a few coppers for your purses, with no haversack for the journey or spare tunic or footwear or a staff, for the workman deserves his keep.

Those powerful, challenging words spoken by Christ reverberated through Francis' mind and heart. This is what he
had longed for with all his heart. His pulse must have been
racing. He had to respond to the gospel invitation. Every
word of the gospel reading made a profound impact on his
mind. It can be seen in his Rule, his Testament, and in all
his writings. Christ had given Francis the formula of unre-
served abnegation. He heard it with his own ears and his
soul danced in delight: *This is it!*

The words from the gospel reading are often far less powerful to our modern ears. The words long ago were tamed
and stripped bare of their transforming potential. We are
able to rationalize them away. We debate whether or not
they were the actual words of Jesus. We contend that even
if Jesus actually uttered the words, he certainly addressed
them to his time and place and surely could not have meant
them for all times and all places. Heck, it's hot in Palestine,
so you really don't need to take much on a journey, and
they didn't have suitcases with wheels. We assert, with good
reason, that it would be foolish to guide your entire life by a
single passage from the gospel.

In order to make sure he understood the words correctly,
after Mass, Francis rushed up to the priest and breathlessly
asked him the meaning of the text. I can almost hear Francis
pleading: "How can we deny those words? Are they not a
command from God?" What a solemn moment! Francis'
whole future hung on an impromptu consultation with a
humble priest in a shabby, little country chapel. But the
meaning of the text was clear, even though no one, not even
the priests, seemed to adhere to it, and so its true meaning
could not be explained away. The old priest went over the
text with him point by point, and Francis, ecstatic with joy

and filled with the Holy Spirit, said, "This is what I want, this is what I long to do with all my heart!"

Francis now knew what he had to do. He had to act on the words. He had to go out into the world, proclaiming that the kingdom of heaven was near. Selecting the coarsest material he could find, he made himself a habit shaped in the form of a cross. He fastened the simple habit about his waist with a rope. And off he went. Dressed like a peasant, he walked barefoot through the countryside and towns, bringing the peace of Christ to all who wished to receive it. He preached the word of God in public squares, always beginning his sermon by offering a blessing to those assembled: "The Lord give you peace." Filled with conviction, he spoke with great passion. His enthusiasm and assurance electrified his simple, plain words, giving them power to move his listeners.

The gospel said to take nothing for the journey, not even a pair of sandals. And so Francis took nothing, trusting God for all he needed. Unlike Francis, we wouldn't literally follow such harsh—and even foolish and senseless—directives. We know better. We would take ample supplies and have contingency plans drawn up. Still, the gospel does challenge us to travel lightly. After all, Jesus always stressed that our identity and security are not to be found in material possessions or clever strategies, but in God alone.

Francis took nothing for his journey, and still he had all he needed. God alone is not yet enough for me. I still need more than that. I still want more than that. And so I never seem to have enough.

CRAZY OR INSPIRED?

The gospel has the power to make all things new. Yet sadly in our culture, for the most part, it does not. This failure does not reside in the gospel, but in us. We have failed to make a link between mysticism and action. Such a connection is vital for us to deepen our awareness of the immanence of God. We experience the God we "see." Some people "see" a judgmental God, others a merciful God; still others see a distant and detached God, while some see an immanent and involved God.

God sees a reflection of God's own image in all people. And so we too need to see and experience this same phenomenon of seeing God in each other. When we see as God sees, we have no choice but to actively resist evil and alleviate suffering. Such a vision compels us to stand up against injustice, whether it is found within our governments or within our churches. The gospel is not making all things new because we do not always live the gospel, have not fully embraced the beatitudes and truly followed down the narrow path of peace and love where Jesus all but walks alone.

From the time Francis heard Matthew's gospel, he was certain of his calling. *Certainty*—I wish I could feel it regarding my "calling" to make films on poverty. At times, I think it is exactly what I should be doing. At other times, I think it is the craziest thing I could possibly be doing.

Was Francis' impulsive and literal reaction to the gospel story he heard mumbled in Latin crazy or inspired? Did a literal response to words uttered so long ago in a vastly different cultural and religious setting make any sense in medieval Italy? Does it make any sense in the United States today? Knowing how to interpret the gospel is a very difficult task for most people today. Should it be? What would Francis of Assisi say to us? Would his response have any relevance in our time and culture? How we answer those questions determines how we interpret the gospel and how God speaks to us.

Francis doesn't want us to do what he did; he isn't interested in people becoming copies of him. He said, "I have done what was mine to do; may Christ teach you what you are to do."

Francis knew each person is an individual, a unique creation loved by God as an individual. Francis would have agreed with the Japanese poet Matsuo Basho (1644-1694) when he wrote (in his famous work *The Narrow Road to the Deep North*): "Do not seek to follow in the footsteps of the men of old; seek what they sought." Francis would tell us to listen, listen intently with a pure and humble heart, and we will know what we are to do.

In making my poverty films and writing books like this, I'm doing what is mine to do. And the doubts I feel at times come from some dark corner within me where my false self is clinging to the hope it can still get its own way, that it can knock God off the throne of my life. But I know that nothing finite can ever satisfy the infinite longings of my heart. Julian of Norwich said it best: "In the Only I have all."

SIMPLE WORDS

By 1209, Francis' austere way of life began to attract others. Impressed by Francis' kindness, sincerity, and holy demeanor, men from all walks of life asked to join him in his new way of life. The first to follow him was Bernard of Quintavalle, a wealthy and respected citizen of Assisi; he was followed by Peter Catani, a lawyer; and then came Giles, an illiterate layman with a great gift of prayer who was known for his heroic virtue. They set out on preaching tours to the Marches of Ancona, a hilly country northeast of their native Umbria, to the Valley of Rieti, to the south, and to Florence in Tuscany, to the north.

When Francis began his preaching mission to the people of Italy, it was a bold move, because at the time it was the custom for only bishops to preach. Sadly, many bishops were more interested in amassing wealth than tending to the flock. The common people had little instruction in spiritual matters, and as a consequence many sank deeper into an abyss of spiritual ignorance and superstition. Sin was more prevalent than prayer. These were truly dark days for the Church. Francis was as a joyful light, a poor man serving the poor and delivering a message of peace and love. With outstretched arms he welcomed everyone. He spoke from the depths of his heart, and his simple words penetrated the souls of his listeners. This seemingly illiterate man, the very antithesis of the pedantic clergy, had the power to hold and sway an audience, and he gave all the credit to God.

WHERE LOVE IS

Francis shows us that the spiritual life is a twofold journey: an inward movement to the depths of our being and the source of love, and an outward movement to the broken world and the margins of society, where love is manifested in acts of kindness. But when we are enslaved by obsessive desires, we are not free to pray. When our interest in power, money, and material things is greater than our longing for God, we are still far from authentic prayer. The deeper we journey into prayer, the less interested we are in thoughts rooted in worldly desires and sensory perceptions. At its essence, prayer isn't about asking for divine favors. The primary purpose of prayer is to assist us in continual abandonment to God. Prayer stimulates a mindfulness of God, which in turn stimulates acts of love and mercy.

Our prayer, Francis would suggest, should be dressed in

reverence and humility, unsoiled by a mind still cluttered, impassioned, and impure. It is helpful to calm the restlessness of your mind by an awareness of your breathing and by acts of compassion. The altar of our spirit should be unadorned and free of false and unhealthy desires. We should strive to imitate God, who stoops down in mercy to touch us. So we too must stoop down in mercy to touch others.

BUON GIORNO, BUONA GENTE

The Valley of Rieti was practically a second home to Francis. Only his beloved Valley of Spoleto (below Assisi) occupied a higher place in his heart. The Valley of Rieti, located northeast of Rome and far to the south of Assisi, was the site of Francis' first efforts at preaching, but in time it came to represent the contemplative dimension of the Franciscan charism.

Francis loved the mountains that ring the valley. The valley floor, which once was a lake until it was drained by the Romans, is covered with wheat fields, olive trees, vineyards, and an exuberant assortment of flowers. The ancient city of Rieti sits on a low hill at the southern end of the valley; the city is still partially surrounded by medieval walls. Near the end of his life, Francis traveled to Rieti seeking a cure for his eye disease, and during his stay he was consoled during a night of prayer by the sweetness of heavenly flute music. Four important Franciscan sanctuaries are located in the valley: Greccio, Fonte Columbo, La Foresta, and Poggio Bustone. They each resonate with the simplicity and humility of Francis' spirit. Nature and silence take precedence over art and architecture.

Poggio Bustone is located about ten miles from the city of Rieti and is the northernmost Franciscan sanctuary in the valley; it sits in a high, rugged, and remote area that provided Francis with ample solitude. The Convento di San Giacomo is believed to have been founded by St. Francis in 1217. Down a flight of stairs from the Convento is a small hermitage where Francis planted a cross to remind him of his redemption. There is a steep path leading from the Convento up to the crest of the hill. Along the path, there are six little chapels. At the end of the path there is a small hermitage cut out of rock.

Francis first came to Poggio Bustone in 1209. As he entered the little village, he greeted the inhabitants with the cheerful words: *"Buon Giorno, buona gente"*—"Good morning, good people." The greeting reflected the saint's ability to see good in everyone. Poggio Bustone was a place of pardon for Francis. One day, Francis found a place for solitary prayer and stayed there for a long time. He was concerned about the future of his little band of friars and was praying for some sense of direction. While praying, his mind became preoccupied with the sins of his past. He began to repeat over and over again the words, "O Lord, have mercy on me, a sinner." Eventually the repetition of his plea gave way to a great joy. The depths of his heart were washed in a soothing sweetness, his spirit danced in the certainty that his sins had been forgiven, and his soul was filled with an abundance of fresh grace. God showed his humble servant that his little band of men would increase into a great multitude who would announce the good news of salvation to the world.

Francis' compunction over his sins was not a simple matter of feeling sorrow about wrong actions. It was a sincere attempt to separate himself from those things within him that were harmful to his relationship with God. He no longer wanted any behavior from his past to have any power over his present, which was consumed by a love of God. God heard his cry and graced Francis with an unshakable peace and joy.

A STATE OF ALERT STILLNESS

Life demands that we be useful. Many people feel the need to at least have the appearance of being hard at work, even during their personal free time. It is as if we fear what lies beyond our usefulness. Our society is focused on chasing the transient quest of business and pleasure, and it views monks and hermits with suspicion because a life devoted to seeking God is incomprehensible to a materialistic culture. But without inner stillness, it is virtually impossible to know yourself; and without knowing yourself, you really can't know the world or God.

Our drive for usefulness, for action, seems to far outweigh our desire to be still. We want to just plunge immediately into deep contemplation, but it doesn't happen. It takes a lot of time to still the restless movement within us. We are doers, performers who always have an itch to be acting. It is hard for us to simply sit before God and listen. How can we speak about God or share God's love when we haven't fully experienced it ourselves? Francis knew he had to spend time listening to God before he could speak to others about God.

In deep solitude, Francis transformed his loneliness into an interior empty space where he was able to hear the silent voice of God speaking about the necessity of love. Solitude became a place of engagement with God, a place of true peace. Solitude allowed his soul to look upon the pieces and see the unity. In the solitude of Poggio Bustone, Francis did not so much pray as he became a prayer. It was here that he experienced the spectacular greatness of God, which he shared with the world.

For most of my life, I was moving away from God, carried along on the tide I created. All along I had been fighting a divine wind that had been trying to turn me in the opposite direction. My initial movement away from God was propelled by the influence of sin and was powered by my ego and illusions. The habits acquired while traveling in the wrong direction are hard to reverse. The superficial, fictional me I saw in the mirror was far from the reality of God. The guy in the mirror was incapable of transcendent experiences. Only my openness to God's call put me on the path to becoming more receptive to the mystical dimension hidden within me. I still have a long way to go. Francis showed me that I needed to find a quiet place, and sit. Being still, mentally and physically, was—and is—the most difficult thing in the world.

Prayerful silence is more than a lack of words; it is a state of alert stillness and attentive waiting. The point is not to rest, but to concentrate and focus the heart and mind on God. Beneath the appearance of passivity is an active state of attentiveness. Silence is an expression of love and strength. Within the silence of our hearts lies a mystery beyond our hearts. In deep silence, we are fully awake, fully open, and one with God. To enter the silence of meditation is to enter our own poverty as we renounce our concepts and intellect and sit alert, waiting to hear from God, even if we must wait a lifetime.

Prayer helps us transcend our preoccupation with the self, and it teaches us how to embrace the other. Grace prompts us to pray, and praying opens us up to even more grace. Our journey to God begins in earnest when we still our senses, desires, and mind. In stillness, real movement begins. Stillness stills unruly passions. Contemplation quiets our restless, relentless quest for sensual pleasure. The cornerstone of the spiritual life consists of stillness, prayer, love, and self-control. In stillness we feel the movement of God's Spirit transforming our hearts.

TWEETING AND TEXTING

While God is beyond words and shrouded in silence, God nonetheless is in a perpetual conversation with each of us, even if most of us are rarely listening; our failure to recognize and appreciate this divine conversation has caused us to turn a deaf ear to the other, to anyone who does not believe as we do, which in turn stifles communion and compassion. We are drowning in words and shrouded in noise. Silence was once a natural part of life. Max Picard, the famous Swiss philosopher, accurately observed: "Nothing has changed the nature of man so much as the loss of silence." And he wrote that long before such noise-making devices as television were invented. Today, it is normal for earphones to be almost permanently jammed into ears, earphones connected to myriad devices that are channels for endless chatter. We watch life through little screens that distract us from the real life in front of us. We film our lives with our cell phones and then e-mail selected scenes from our self-centered lives to everybody we know. No one looks up anymore; we are all looking down at our i-Whatevers and typing something that someone else needs to know. Writing has become "texting." We tweet away the day and keep God at bay.

Society is becoming increasingly fragmented and polarized, which poses a great danger. Many people are questioning the very meaning of their lives. Many are eagerly seeking God because their lives seem empty even though their homes are stuffed with every gadget and convenience imaginable. But their search finds little trace of God or peace, because they do not realize that God cannot be found in noise and restlessness. As the saints and mystics of all faiths down through the centuries have learned, God is a friend and lover of silence. For us, silence has become a foreign language. Simplicity is a friend of silence and is the key to unraveling the complexities of modern life.

We need to find someplace, some quiet corner, where we can press the pause button on our minds, forget the concerns that plague our lives, and slip into a silent space where we can hear the wellspring of life. On the road to God, words eventually dissolve into silence. To become more and more silent—to enter deeply into creative silence—takes courage. The wordless is foreign to us. Yet God transcends language and intellect. In silence, we are able to meet our deepest self. When we have found our authentic self, we are free to give ourselves away, to give ourselves back to God. St. Maximos the Confessor, a great saint of the Eastern Church, said: "Love and self-control free the soul from passions; spiritual reading and contemplation deliver the intellect from ignorance; and the state of prayer brings it into the presence of God Himself."

Through prayer, we become aware that God is present. Through prayer, we become at home with the living presence with whom we can share everything. And in the presence of God, we become aware of our complete dependence on the Creator. Prayer fosters within us a spirit of humility and the realization that we cannot truly live without God.

The best way to approach God is to proceed in humility, simplicity, and poverty, to enter the silence of God's presence, and then patiently sit in prayer and wait until God elects to speak. The primary focus of prayer is to lead the mind to stillness. Prayer helps us become more aware of God's presence. Prayer acknowledges our dependency on God. The goal of prayer is communion with God—and each other. In solitude, St. Francis became deeply aware of the world's needs. The life of St. Francis suggests we should approach God with open hands, a searching mind, and a loving heart.

NO FATTED CALF FOR THE GOOD

During my first visit to Assisi, I began to be drawn to Francis' radical interpretation of the gospel. In the last few years, I've come to better appreciate just how radical the gospel *itself* is. The truly radical nature of the gospel is clearly evident in the parable of the prodigal son. In this story, Christ says, in essence, that the just person who has never sinned will be less well received in heaven than the person who has sinned and has repented. So it seems that straying from the straight and narrow path has it rewards, as long as you return to the path. There was no fatted calf or feast for the son who did not kill or steal or commit adultery, and who instead obeyed all the commandments. This is hard for us to understand, because it goes against our nature. We want to reward the good and punish the bad. The prodigal son's brother was enraged and filled with bitter indignation at his father's joyful reaction to the return of the brother who had brought shame to the family. The father's response: *your brother who was dead is now alive; he who was lost is now found.* That response recurs again and again in the gospel, like a leitmotif with endless variations: *for the one who exalts oneself shall be abased*; and *the one who humbles oneself shall be exalted*; and *the first shall be last, and the last, first.*

Jesus didn't spend his time with the good and the just. He consorted with outcasts, with publicans and sinners. He ate with prostitutes and with vagabonds he found along the highways and hedges. Why? Perhaps because they, like the prodigal son, were capable, in the extremity of their evil or pain, of a sudden awakening that enabled them to convert their utter deprivation into a new reality and true clarity. Moments of great suffering and failure often lead people to scale the heights of their souls—perhaps because they have nowhere else to go. Crying out for God in the darkness isn't something an honest person, who believes he or she stands well with himself or herself, society, and God, is likely to do. The prodigal son risked all and lost all, and yet in the moment of loss he came nearer to God than ever before. It's not the way most of us would have organized things. But that's what makes the gospel message so radical. And truly hard to follow.

NO STRINGS ATTACHED

When you look more deeply at the gospel parable of the prodigal son, you see how the story illustrates God's unconditional acceptance and forgiveness. God is a God of endless second chances. No human being can escape making mistakes. If we are wise, we learn from them. I've been a very slow learner. The deeper message of the parable of the prodigal son is that God allows us to make our own way through life, even when the path we choose is a dead end. God gives us the freedom to make mistakes, to make bad choices. But God is always there, always ready to warmly embrace us when we turn around and head in the right direction. God gives us the freedom to be co-creators of the gift of life God gave us. Whether we choose to walk with God or without God, God's love remains constant. No matter what we do in life, no matter how bad our screwups, God is there to help us pick ourselves up and start over. The journey through life is a twisting path, filled with ups and downs, possibilities and potholes, consolations and desolations. The journey is hard. We must climb mountains of problems and traverse deserts of doubt. But God is there walking with us, pointing the way; and so there is no need to fear or falter.

Life, the gospel proclaims over and over again, prevails over death. The story of Jesus does not end on the cross but in the resurrection. God is not finished with me or with you. God is always laboring to bring about a new creation in each of us, especially when others seem intent on judging and destroying us. Jesus wants us to know joy and fulfillment, even in the midst of our suffering. Jesus calls each of us out of the tomb of our mistakes. Like he did with Lazarus, Jesus wants to unbind us so we can be fully alive.

On my desk is a small picture card featuring a detailed look at the father and son from Rembrandt's famous painting *The Return of the Prodigal Son*. For me, the picture represents the ideal of the all-merciful, all-forgiving father from the gospel story. But there is more to the painting than meets the eye. The father in the patriarchal social context of the biblical story would never run to embrace a son who dishonored him. Such a gesture would have been an act far too undignified for the venerable head of a family to perform, especially since the son had not yet even sought forgiveness. Moreover, the son had thrown away any privileges he may have had; he lost all his money and was on the brink of ruin. In those times, the son would have been considered a complete disgrace to all, and not worthy of the father's trust or affection. Yet the father forgave his son without asking him for any reparation or proof of the sincerity of his repentance.

For those who heard Jesus tell this parable, it was truly an astounding story, because he was telling them that God's forgiveness was an easy thing to obtain. You simply had to walk into God's loving arms. God gives love away. There are no strings attached, no conditions to be met. It is ours for the asking. The father's embrace of the son healed the son of the disastrous effects of his wrongful behavior. When you experience that level of generosity, totally unmerited, you become more acutely aware of your failures, and you make a sincere effort not to repeat them. That is the transforming secret of confession.

The story of the prodigal son tells us that we don't have to feel guilty over the reality of our human frailty and weakness. God is not standing behind some bush waiting to jump out and sternly judge us. No. God, Jesus says, is running down the road toward us, eager to wrap his arms around us and kiss us until we are healed. The enormity of God's love, which is so vast it is beyond measure or comprehension, creates an awareness of the depth of my insufficiency. But that awareness does not trigger feelings of unworthiness or emptiness. Rather, it creates a sense of poverty that allows me to trust fully in God and abandon myself fully into God's bountiful love.

The painting and the parable also remind me of my need to forgive others without hesitation and without question. That is hard to do, which only illustrates more clearly the radical nature of the parable and God's love.

Jesus says, "Be merciful, just as your Father is merciful" (Luke 6:36).

Much of life hurts. Forgiveness helps life hurt less. Sadly, our hurts often become who we are, forming our very identity. Forgiveness helps us forget our ego, our pain, and our feelings. Forgiveness is possible when your heart overflows with compassion. Forgiveness is freedom, radical freedom, divine freedom. Outside of forgiveness, God is unknown and unknowable. Forgiveness is the sweetest word there is.

A KNAPSACK AND WALKING STICK

St. Francis of Assisi said, "When the brothers go through the world, let them take nothing for the journey, neither knapsack nor purse, nor bread, nor money, nor walking stick." It is good to realize we're on a journey, a journey to God. What are we taking with us? Me? I'm lugging a lot of stuff—far more than can fit in a knapsack. Mostly, I'm carrying my sins. They wear me down and slow me down.

Slowly as I travel, I'm learning to see that my sins do not erase from my soul the fundamental dignity that God stamped on it at my conception. God does not want to see my demise. God's mercy continuously desires to give me new life. I don't have to change before God will love me. As Richard Rohr points out, "God loves us so that we can change." Sin alienates me from God. But God does not reject me because of my sin. God simply wants me to refrain from sinning, because my sins prevent me from experiencing the love God wants to shower upon me.

For so long, I thought my sins were beyond redemption. They had me bound so tightly, it was impossible to free myself from their choking control. But I didn't understand the power of grace. I underestimated the unlimited power of God. Dimly, I'm beginning to see that God can overcome my personal weakness. All I have to do is let him. But before God can work, I must wake up and admit I need God's help. Genuine, sincere contrition is always fully embraced by God's tender, loving mercy.

THE ONLY QUESTION

One time when Francis was praying in the house of Bernard of Quintavalle, it was reported that he repeatedly said, "My God, my God, what art thou? And what am I?" Of course, the question was also asked by St. Augustine, but it nonetheless represents Francis' frame of mind: this was the only question he thought worth asking. And it is the question every mystic asks as he or she begins their journey to God; and sometimes the answer is discovered by the end of their quest.

St. Francis saw God in the tensions and conflicting forces within himself. He accepted his own complexity, and created something new and fresh for himself. He responded to the Christ he saw in everyone by living a life for others. But he also paid attention to his need for solitude by finding (or making) a time and place for withdrawal so he could enter fully into contemplative prayer. He was able to do this because he centered his life on Christ, listening to and experiencing both the suffering Messiah and the risen Lord in his daily life. Christ himself went into the marketplace, preaching and curing the sick, and he also went into the desert, praying and seeking the will of the Father. Francis found unity for his life by imitating the life of Christ.

SEEKING PAPAL APPROVAL

By the spring of 1209, Francis had twelve followers, and he felt it was necessary to write a rule of life for himself and them. Using simple words, Francis based the rule on the solid foundation of gospel principles, adding, according to St. Bonaventure, "a few other things that seemed necessary for their way of life in common." Francis harbored a hope that the rule he composed would be endorsed by the pope, in part because some people thought Francis and his followers were heretics or just another radical fringe group. And so he and a few of his friars set out for Rome seeking approval for their form of life (*Forma Vitae*) from Pope Innocent III. But approval of his gospel way of life would not be easy to obtain. During that time, many different sects that the Church considered heretical were sprouting up under the leadership of laymen, some of whom even espoused the same kind of evangelical poverty as did Francis. Francis could easily have been viewed as the leader of yet another politically tinted splinter group, such as the Albigenses, the Humiliati, the Waldensians, and the Cathars.

It is almost impossible to imagine the initial meeting between the pope and the pauper, the former an icon of power and the latter an icon of humility. Francis, dressed in rags and dirty from the ordeal of the long, grueling walk from Assisi, was a simple penitent whose coarse hands gave clear evidence that his primary "ministry" was little more than rebuilding crumbling churches. And this insignificant little man was about to stand before a towering figure, Pope Innocent III, whose papacy, which began in 1198, brought the Church's temporal power and influence to its zenith. Innocent was a famous and learned man whose books on the Mass were among the bestsellers of medieval times. Moreover, he was a skilled statesman, a consummate politician, and a fiery orator. He was thirty-six years old when he was elected pope and went on to be one of the most powerful pontiffs in the history of the Church. Innocent loved order and beauty; he was the first pope to use the title Vicar of Christ. While he lived simply and chastised wealthy clergy for their excesses, his sponsorship of the Crusades darkened his chapter in papal history. He is remembered more for his political ruthlessness than for his pastoral activities, which were considerable, including encouraging the Humiliati, a poverty-based reform movement, to return to the Church.

The following description of what happened when Francis arrived in Rome was added to St. Bonaventure's *Major Life* by Jerome of Ascoli, minister general of the Order from 1274-1279, who later became Pope Nicholas IV. According to Professor Ewert Cousins, whose translation I'll use, Jerome heard the story of how Francis and the pope met from Cardinal Riccardo degli Annibaldi, who was a relative of Pope Innocent III.

> When he arrived in Rome, he was led into the presence of the Supreme Pontiff. The Vicar of Christ was in the Lateran Palace, walking in a place called the Hall of Mirrors, occupied in deep meditation. Knowing nothing of Christ's servant, he sent him away indignantly. Francis left humbly, and the next night God showed the Supreme Pontiff the following vision. He saw a palm tree sprout between his feet and grow gradually until it became a beautiful tree. As he wondered what this vision might mean, the divine light impressed upon the mind of the Vicar of Christ that this palm tree symbolized the poor man whom he had sent away the previous day. The next morning he commanded his servants to search the city for the poor man.

They found Francis in a nearby hostel and immediately brought him to the pope. Francis humbly explained his gospel way of life and how he wanted his followers to live and act. St. Bonaventure writes that the pope detected Francis' "remarkable purity and simplicity of heart," his "firmness of purpose," and his "fiery ardor of will," and he was inclined to approve the rule. However, the pope hesitated because a number of cardinals who were present felt the radical way Francis wanted to live was too innovative and far too difficult to follow.

But Francis found a worthy advocate in John of St. Paul, a cardinal who was impressed by Francis' unselfishness and love of the poor. Addressing the pope and his fellow cardinals, he said, "If we refuse the request of this poor man as novel or difficult, when all he asks is to be allowed to lead the gospel life, we must be on our guard lest we commit an offense against Christ's gospel. For if anyone says that there is something novel or irrational or impossible to observe in this man's desire to live according to the perfection of the gospel, he is guilty of blasphemy against Christ, the author of the gospel."

Struck by the force of the cardinal's reasoning, the pope asked Francis to seek God's will on the matter in prayer, and after doing so, if he was still certain that this is the path God was leading him down, then he should return to him and he would eagerly give Francis' new community his blessing. After a period of prayer, Francis returned to the Lateran filled with conviction. He boldly told the pope a parable based on the Scriptures, concluding that if Jesus had promised us eternal life, surely he would not deny us the things we need here on earth. After listening to Francis, the pope fully believed that Christ had spoken through the poor man from Assisi. The pope then recounted a vision that he recently had in which an insignificant poor man was holding up the Lateran Basilica, which was on the verge of collapse. Francis, according to the pope, was the fulfillment of that prophetic vision. He said, "This is truly a pious and holy man by whom the Church of God shall be restored." The pope then gave

Francis his verbal consent and ordered the brothers to live strictly according to the gospel.

THE BREAD OF TEARS

Having secured the pope's blessing, which gave them juridical status, Francis and his followers returned to Assisi. Depending totally on God's providence for their food, the brothers vowed never to turn their back on holy poverty. St. Bonaventure tells us, "They spent their time praying incessantly, devoting themselves to mental prayer rather than vocal prayer because they did not yet have liturgical books from which to chant the canonical hours." Francis often taught them lessons from the Scriptures. They set up camp at Rivo Torto, located just a few miles from St. Mary of the Angels Church, where they lived in a large mud and stone hut for nearly two years. This wasn't some happy-go-lucky campout. Poverty for Francis and the friars was not merely a matter of living simply. No, poverty, for them, was true poverty: they were dirt-poor, living without sufficiency in a constant state of need. A story from Lawrence Cunningham's *Brother Francis: An Anthology of Writings by and About St. Francis of Assisi* illustrates holy poverty as practiced by Francis.

> An old and poor woman who had two sons as friars once came to Saint Mary of the Angels to beg alms from Saint Francis. The saint went immediately to Brother Peter of Catania (who was the minister general at the time) and asked if there was anything to give the woman, adding that a mother of one friar was a mother of all friars. Brother Peter answered, "The only thing in the house is a copy of the New Testament, which we use to read the

lessons during the night office." Saint Francis said to him, "Give her the Bible; it will be more pleasing to God that she should have it than we should read from it." Thus, she got the first New Testament that the brotherhood owned.

During those early days of the brotherhood, they worked hard and barely subsisted, "drawing nourishment," St. Bonaventure writes, "more from the bread of tears than the delights of bodily food."

Francis' love of poverty flowed from his belief in God as the creator, and that all creatures belong to God and owe their existence to God's sovereignly free love. Because he felt everything belonged to God, Francis renounced all forms of ownership. He wanted only to stand naked before God. Because he saw himself as a brother to all, he was able to reject having any possessions. Francis knew that money and possessions were not bad in and of themselves, but that they could easily become a hindrance to enriching one's spiritual life. In her book *The Essentials of Mysticism*, Evelyn Underhill writes: "Mystics know that possessions dissipate the energy which they need for other and more real things; that they must give up ownership, the verb 'to have,' if they are to attain the freedom which they seek, and the fullness of the verb 'to be.'"

Francis believed in the liberty of poverty rather than in the power of money.

Before my first trip to Italy in March 1995, I thought the meaning of my life resided solely within me, and after years of searching I found none. I simply existed, trying to squeeze moments of sweetness out of the bitterness of life. But during that trip I discovered the meaning of my life could only be found in responding to God's love for me. Knowing and loving God has helped me know and love myself, and others, too.

BROTHER BMW

The cornerstone of Franciscan spirituality is poverty. Francis took Lady Poverty for his bride. Of course, for us moderns, poverty is a strange choice for a mate. The goal of our lives is to escape or avoid poverty. We chase after Brother BMW. When we look at the millions of indescribably poor people around the world, people living in unthinkable squalor in far off places such as Africa or in the shadows of our own cities, we cannot even remotely begin to picture poverty as an ideal.

For Francis, a life of poverty didn't just mean living a simple, uncluttered life. Francis knew poverty, at its core, was a condition of being perpetually deprived, of being in a state of constant need. The virtue of poverty is that it leads one to recognize that God alone can provide us with what we truly need. Francis believed that to travel down the road to God required him to rid himself of all possessions. Buddha understood the same thing. He was born a prince—Prince Gautama—and was raised in a luxurious palace. When he was around age thirty, he left his father, his wife, his son, the palace, and his fortune and set out to solve the problem of human suffering. He knew that the road to enlightenment was paved with detachment, and that he had to break free from all desire and karma.

Down through the ages, mystics of all faiths have claimed that God speaks in the quiet of our hearts and that we can hear the voice only when we silence the noise of our selfish desires. Francis turned his back on all the things of the world that might turn his heart away from God. With the help of Lady Poverty, Francis gladly gave up all his desires except one—to do the will of God. Joy, he discovered, was in giving, not in having.

Even though I'm drawn to Francis' ideal of poverty and have no consuming desire for riches, nonetheless the last thing I want to be is poor. I don't want to have to beg for food or not be able to buy a book or the latest recording of Gregorian chant by the Benedictine Monks of Santo Domingo de Silos. I can't help but think perhaps Francis took the idea too far and that his impetuous literalness that demanded that he own nothing but one ragged, old, brown robe was a mistake. Mahatma Gandhi didn't think it was a mistake. Gandhi said that Francis' renunciation of every conceivable human consolation was so complete and profound that he "made himself zero." In effect, Francis created a void in his life, a void that could only be filled by God. Francis' understanding of poverty didn't leave room for him or his early followers even to live in the security of a sturdy building or to have the assurance of daily food. Francis wanted his friars to live from moment to moment, trusting completely in God, and giving "no thought for the morrow"—just as the gospel said. Without denigrating the rich, he nonetheless called money dung and became angry when a friar even touched a coin. This is hard to understand or appreciate.

WE DON'T HAVE ANY POTATOES

In fall 1996, I spent a few weeks at a soup kitchen in the Kensington section of Philadelphia that was operated by Franciscan friars. The area, known as "The Badlands," is one of the worst slums in America. I wanted to learn more about St. Francis' love of the poor; unexpectedly, I ended up making a film about the place. St. Francis Inn has a team of dedicated Franciscan friars, nuns, and lay volunteer ministers who serve the poor and homeless. Besides the soup kitchen, which feeds up to 500 people a day, the team also runs a men's shelter that accommodates ten men a night, a women's center that offers counseling during the day to prostitutes and drug addicts, and a thrift shop that provides clothing for the poor. What I saw shocked me, saddened me, and, eventually, inspired me as I slowly gained insight into the spiritual wisdom of poverty.

I went to Kensington expecting to find a soup kitchen. What I found was a community of remarkable yet very human people offering not just a hot meal to the poor and homeless but also love to all those who were hungry and hurting. The staff gave their all to those who had nothing. As I observed them, I saw people who saw Jesus in people most of us do not even see. They looked at the broken, dirty, and disheveled people who live on the margins of society and saw a spark of divine beauty and goodness. The drug addicts, the prostitutes, the mentally ill, as well as the poverty-plagued elderly and families who live each day without hope or enough to eat, come to St. Francis Inn and are treated with dignity and respect.

One young Franciscan volunteer minister told me that when she goes home and hears people talking in a condescending manner about drug addicts and prostitutes, she gets angry because they are talking about "my friends." That was the amazing and unexpected part; the staff doesn't just feed the guests—they enter into a relationship with them. They listen to them. They laugh with them. They cry with them. They hug them. They encourage them. They pray for them. In short, they give themselves—completely and without reservation—to the guests. And what is even more unexpected, the staff claims it is the guests who give to them, enriching their lives in innumerable little ways each day.

Before spending time in Kensington, the plight of the homeless always troubled me, but the problem was beyond not only my comprehension but also my ability to do anything about it. It's hard to care about the homeless when you don't know anyone who is homeless. My time in Kensington helped me put a face on the homeless: the face of Sheila from Tent City, whom I came to care about very much. Tent City is not a campground. Located on an empty, corner lot, it consists of a collection of small, ramshackle dwellings made of cardboard, scraps of discarded wood, and large pieces of plastic. A dirty mattress, standing on its side, formed a wall of one of the dwellings. Perhaps a dozen people live in the four or five huts. I tagged along with one of the friars who was delivering some leftover food that had to be eaten before it spoiled.

It was a damp, cold night. As we loaded the van, the light drizzle began to intensify. I began to shiver as we drove, which made me wonder how the homeless endure the winter nights. As we pulled up to the lot, we could see a group of people gathered around a fire. Some were standing, warming their hands over the bright flames; others, bundled under blankets wrapped around their heavy coats, were seated on the old junk furniture that encircled the large barrel in which scraps of wood were being burned. The friar introduced me to his friends, who were thrilled by the surprise late-night food delivery. "Hey, we got some good stuff here. It came from a gourmet Japanese restaurant. It was left over from their Sunday brunch. It won't last long. Gotta eat it quickly."

No need to worry. Starving people do not need to be told to eat quickly. Sheila asked me to sit on the tattered couch with her. I did, though it felt awkward sitting on a couch that sat in the middle of a vacant lot. The friar sat down on a wooden crate. As they ate, we talked about all kinds of things. Perfectly normal conversation. I couldn't help but feel as if we were in their living room, except it was raining in this living room, and the occasional loud truck that passed made it difficult to hear each other. The main topic of discussion was the coming winter. The temperature at night will regularly get well below freezing. Some of the people were going to try to find an abandoned building in which to squat. They needed to get their hands on a kerosene heater, which would be instrumental to their hopes of surviving the winter.

I don't know why, but I was drawn to Sheila. Perhaps it was her broad, infectious smile and hearty laugh. If this littered lot were my living room, could I manage to smile or laugh? But beyond her smile, Sheila's eyes told a different story. In them, I could see deep sadness. The sadness of someone who couldn't break the addiction to drugs. The sadness of a mother who had her daughter taken away by the state because she was not able to care for the child. The sadness of a woman who confronts relentless suffering and violence on a daily basis. The sadness of a woman whose home was a cardboard hut in a lot off a busy street. In the distance, through the drizzle and over the roofs of the boarded-up buildings, I could see the skyline of Philadelphia, the City of Brotherly Love. Sheila and her friends experience very little brotherly love. Rejection is their lot; hopelessness, their brother.

I ran into Sheila a number of times. She often came to

the Inn to eat. Whenever I drove past Tent City with one of the staff, I asked to stop for a few minutes to visit Sheila. I asked if I could photograph her. She let me. She was a large woman. Her face was round, and her smile made her cheeks look puffy. Her skin was weathered by constant exposure to the harsh winter. Her teeth were crooked. Her thrift shop clothes fit her poorly. Yet she was beautiful, beautiful in her openness.

One morning, during my second visit, I saw her waiting by the side door of the Inn. The poor are always waiting; they are powerless to do anything else but wait. When I approached, I could see she had been crying. There were no smiles that morning. She was clearly troubled by something, so I asked her what the problem was. I wasn't ready for what I heard. Sheila and a couple of other people from Tent City had moved into an empty building to escape the bitter cold nights. It was a "crack house." One of the women living there had a young baby, whom Sheila had grown very fond of. She missed her own daughter very much, and so Sheila showered her motherly affection on the infant. The baby's mother was a "crack" addict. Sheila made it her business to look after the child when the mother was stoned. Sheila heard the baby crying in the middle of the night, but she didn't get up to see what the problem was. She said, "I was cold and tired. I thought about getting up, but I couldn't. I fell asleep."

When Sheila came downstairs that morning, she made a horrific discovery. The mother and child had been sleeping on the couch. During the night, the mother had rolled over on top of the child. The child must have cried. But to no avail. Under the weight of her drugged mother, the child suffocated. Sheila and the mother screamed as they shook the baby. Someone ran to a pay phone a few blocks away and called for an ambulance. The paramedics said the infant had lapsed into a coma. They rushed the child to the hospital, where she was reported to be in critical condition. Sheila blamed herself for not responding to the cries in the dead of the night. I tried to comfort her. But there was little I could do. I expressed the hope that the hospital could help the baby and everything would end up OK. Sheila needed some change to take a train to a clinic, where she had an appointment. She had been troubled by pains in her stomach for over a month. I gave her the money. As she walked toward the train station, I thought about just how tough her life was. If living in a "crack house" in order to escape some of winter's bite wasn't tough enough, now she had the added burden of guilt over a child's tragic accident, not to mention her own chronic stomach pains.

Later that night, Sheila was in the courtyard of the Inn, waiting her turn to come in and get a hot meal. They were serving turkey soup that night. I noticed a woman come up to Sheila and say something to her. Sheila began crying. A couple of homeless women surrounded her and tried to comfort her. I went over to see what the problem was. One of the women whispered in my ear, "The little baby from the crack house died." I backed off in order to give Sheila and her friends space. After a few minutes, Sheila left the courtyard and began to walk alone under the Kensington Avenue elevated train. I ran after her. As I approached her, a train roared by overhead. I just looked at her. Her eyes were filled with tears. She said, "The baby died." I could hardly hear her. I said, "I know. I'm sorry." The train passed. Stillness suddenly filled the dark night, as we stood alone looking at each other. I gave her a hug. As I did, I said something that was so unplanned it caught me by surprise as the words punctuated the cold stillness of the night: "I love you." She hugged me even tighter and said, "I know. Thank you." There was a brief pause as we both looked at each other. "I'll be OK," she said. We parted. I stood watching her as she walked alone under the elevated tracks as another train loudly rumbled past. It was a moment I shall never forget. I felt a real, vital connection to a large, homeless woman who was a drug addict. Before spending time at the Inn, I would have considered such a person to have been repulsive, someone I could never embrace. By embracing the lepers, whom he found repulsive, St. Francis of Assisi was able to discover their beauty. That same miracle of discovery happens every day in Kensington.

The staff at St. Francis Inn thought I was doing them a favor, offering my time and expertise to make a film about their ministry. No way. It was the community of St. Francis Inn who did me a favor, by showing me how willingly embracing Lady Poverty can lead one to know and love the poor and the outcast and all who suffer. By becoming poor themselves, the staff depends completely on God for everything. They are fed each day at the altar, where they receive the strength in turn to feed the poor. The spiritual poverty espoused by Francis recognized that there was nothing wrong with material things, but he did not want the friars to appropriate anything for themselves. Not owning anything meant they had nothing to defend. Francis did not want to even cling to his own ego. During a homily, Fr. Charles Finnegan, OFM, quoted the martyred archbishop of San Salvador, Oscar Romero: "Without poverty of spirit there can be no abundance of God."

During my stay at St. Francis Inn, I learned two important lessons. First, I needed to empty myself in order to be filled by God. Second, charity is the antidote to the poison of self-absorption. St. Francis of Assisi would feel very much at home on this island of hope in the midst of a sea of despair. He would be glad to see his followers depending on God for everything and living simply so others might simply live. St. Francis would have smiled had he been in the kitchen the day a volunteer asked Br. Xavier de la Huerta, OFM, "What are you making, Brother?"

"Potato soup," Brother Xavier answered without hesitation. The volunteer looked around the kitchen for a few seconds and then asked, "Where are the potatoes?"

"We don't have any potatoes," responded Brother Xavier. A perplexed look crossed the volunteer's face. He asked another question: "How can you make potato soup then?"

Brother Xavier's answer reflected his faith: "The Lord knows what we need, and he will provide."

I can imagine the volunteer rolling his eyes and thinking, "What a nice pious thought, but there are 400 people standing in the cold waiting for something to eat." Amazingly, a few minutes later there was a knock on the side door. The volunteer opened the door, and standing before him was a man who said he had been to a farmers' market, adding, "When I saw the potatoes I had this sudden thought that I should pick up a couple of 50-pound bags for the Inn. I hope you can use them."

Embracing Lady Poverty means learning to admit that we don't have any potatoes. It also means letting go of self and entrusting ourselves to God. The essence of Lady Poverty is fulfillment and inner freedom. Lady Poverty is not rich because she has given up much, but because she has found much. God's love and grace are all the riches she needs.

LOVE NEEDS THE NEED OF ANOTHER

Everyone experiences heartbreak; everyone is in need of tenderness and compassion. At some point in our lives, we all have to face the difficult journey of coming to terms with feelings of rejection, humiliation, and fear. These very real and very painful feelings, in time and in prayer, become an authentic path from despair to hope. Tragedies and disasters become places of courage and perseverance, places where we learn to plumb the depths of our inner life, our true essence, and where we are able, by God's grace, to move from rejection and terror to healing and hope. Love grows from that deep-rooted pain within the universe where God is present and ever-willing to embrace us and bless us.

The mystery of God is buried in solidarity with those who suffer. In the midst of suffering, divine compassion is revealed as a loyal companion that transforms pain into praise, discomfort into consolation. The road to authentic healing begins with forgiveness. Forgiveness emerges from pain and leads to love. Love requires self-surrender, which allows us to enter more deeply into the mystery of God. Love needs the need of another. In our need we find God's love, which heals and renews us. Christ is the answer to our deepest need.

A HOTEL FOR DONKEYS

"One goes more quickly to heaven from a hut than from a palace." ❋ **ST. FRANCIS OF ASSISI**

Francis and his followers stayed at Rivo Torto for nearly two years. Rivo Torto takes its name from the winding, serpentine brook that crosses the plain, a brook in which Francis most surely washed his feet. This humble settlement of humble men is the birthplace of Franciscanism. But Francis and his entourage didn't get a chance to plant their roots in Rivo Torto, because they were practically chased from the site by an ill-tempered peasant who insisted on boarding his donkey in the main hut. One evening, shortly after dusk, the man approached the hut and, thinking it was vacant, decided he and his donkey would take shelter there for the night. When he entered the hut he was surprised and angered to find the friars silently praying. He caused a great deal of commotion, pushing the donkey into the hut, tripping over the friars, and interrupting their prayer time.

Francis humorously claimed he wasn't running a hotel for donkeys; in response, the man began to shout, cursing the brothers. Even though Francis abhorred profanity, he remained calm, trying his best to see what God was trying to tell him through the foul mouth of the mule driver. Francis told his brothers that God was giving them the opportunity to liberate themselves from the temptation of claiming ownership of the hut, reminding them that where there is ownership, there is security, and where there is security, there is no room for his beloved poverty. Rejoicing, Francis told his brothers they must vacate the hut immediately. Without another word, they abandoned their dwelling and headed for Saint Mary of the Angels, where they set up camp not far from the Porziuncula.

Shortly afterwards, Francis went to the abbot of Mt. Subasio and asked his permission to occupy the chapel and the surrounding "little portion of earth." The abbot, impressed by the holiness and growing numbers of men entering the new order, gave the little chapel, the poorest church his order owned, to Francis, without any restrictions or payment. Francis was delighted, especially because the church was so poor and had such a humble name— Porziuncula— yet he could not accept ownership of the church. Each year he insisted on sending a basket of small fish to the monks of Mt. Subasio as rent in return for the privilege of being allowed to stay there.

During this time, the brotherhood continued to grow. Among the new followers was a priest named Sylvester, who was known for his avarice. At Rivo Torto, five men who played an important part in the life of Francis joined the Order: Giles, Leo, Rufino, Masseo, and Juniper. The friars preached throughout the towns and villages of Umbria and Tuscany. They served lepers and ministered to the needs of the poor. As he traveled to Perugia, Cortona, Arezzo, and Pisa, Francis' way of life and his preaching attracted even more followers. These were the golden days for Francis. But soon, not only would the number of his followers dramatically increase, but also the number of his problems. Many of the problems stemmed from the way some of his followers interpreted their vow of poverty.

LADY POVERTY

Francis had so fully embraced poverty, he poetically called her Lady Poverty and took her for his bride. This was his symbolic way of expressing the spiritual principle of liberty, which freed him from the unnecessary pleasures of the world and, more important, freed him from the tyranny of his false self. With Lady Poverty at his side, he could cling to God and God alone.

Poverty fueled all of Francis' thinking and teaching. In what is known as the apostolic command, Christ said, "Take nothing for the journey." For Francis, that is the end of the story, and it required his strict adherence.

Perhaps Francis loved poverty because the Lord had made himself poor by entering into the world, and because Jesus, the Son of the all-powerful God, was not ashamed to be so poor as to be born in a stable. Moreover, Christ was poor, suffering, naked, and hung on a cross. Jesus not only dedicated himself to a preference for the poor but also shared their social condition. For Francis, Christ made poverty a royal virtue, and so he clung to it with an inviolable fidelity. Poverty was a means of liberation and freedom. The end and aim was love. Love was the unifying force of his life and personality. Poverty removed all obstacles blocking the full glow of love. Love of poverty was really love of Love.

Francis did not become one with the poor because he liked poverty. Hardly. He did it because he loved God. Poverty was the road he traveled to get to God. In poverty he saw his wealth and he felt the immense wealth of God. A hundred years after Francis' death, the papacy, employing reasonable biblical exegesis, condemned the Franciscan doctrine of poverty. In the view of the papacy, Francis was holding poverty to a higher standard than Christ did.

The problem is simple: Francis isn't practical—and neither is the gospel.

All wars, whether between individuals or nations, begin with one word: mine. For St. Francis, his practice of poverty was not about not having things. "Things" are part of life; some "things" are even essential to life. Francis did not want to "own" or "dominate" things. He was brother to all and nothing was subordinate to him. He lived in relationship with everything. Poverty was, for him, a complete letting go of everything but God. The Brazilian theologian Leonardo Boff explains Francis' insightful reasoning: "Possession creates obstacles to communication between persons and with nature, for by possession we are saying, 'This is mine,' and 'That is yours,' and so we are divided." In poverty, Francis was completely dependent upon God for everything. In poverty, Francis practiced a deep asceticism that aided him in his ability to renounce the instinct to possess and to satisfy every desire. He made the journey from being a self-centered playboy to a humble man who simply tried to be present to all while being free from everything. His was a life of total abnegation and utter availability. With Lady Poverty as his bride, he lived in peace and harmony with all things. He owned nothing, yet he was one with everything, a brother to all. The "letting go" that St. Francis (and all spiritual masters) advocates also includes letting go of unhealthy attitudes.

When I tell the story of St. Francis and his love of Lady Poverty during my presentations at churches, I can sense some people squirming when I speak about Francis' contempt for money, consumerism, and materialism. The saint lived in a time when conspicuous consumption began to fill the hearts of the middle class. Francis considered the idea that material possessions could create happiness to be absurd. When it comes to personal economics, most Christians today do not make countercultural choices that would set them apart from the rest of society's hyper-acquisitive lifestyles. Francis believed the Church's languishing spirituality could be directly attributed to her vast wealth and rise to great political power, and that the Church of his day needed to be reminded of—and strongly exhorted to follow—the example of absolute and voluntary poverty, along with the resulting detachment of worldliness, as exemplified by Christ and his apostles.

RADICAL TRANSFORMATION

So much of our trouble comes from thinking we are the focal point of reality, that the world revolves around us, and that we can pass judgment on everything that touches us. Because of this egocentric thinking, everything in the world becomes an object that exists for our personal benefit. We even turn God into an object, another tool in our arsenal of weapons of destruction and survival. But I am not just another individual object in a world of objects. I am, as the mystics of all faiths came to see, a "no-thing." Not "nothing" but "no-thing." That means I'm more than my body, and reality is more than my consciousness. When I become aware of my true reality, that is, my "no-thing*ness,*" I suddenly have room for "some-thing" else—namely, God. This kind of transformation of reality changes everything. We see goodness and unity. We see as God sees. We are no longer chained to our unruly emotions, no longer prisoners of our exalted feelings, opinions, and judgments. We have room for the other. The great twelfth-century Sufi philosopher and mystic Ibn 'Arabi said, "The hero is he who smashes idols, and the idol of every man is his ego." I think Francis would agree.

St. Francis believed in the absolute reality of God. Moreover, he believed that while God transcended the material world in which we live, God manifests divine presence in this world and in doing so has sanctified the world and made it real because it has been charged with the reality of God. The modern person, even those who claim to believe in God, is far too "non-religious" (or secularized) to believe the way Francis did. We either deny or find it hard to accept transcendence.

For most of my life, I harbored strong doubts that human existence had any meaning whatsoever. I saw none. I saw nothing but random chaos. I regarded anything sacred as a threat to freedom and an insult to the intellect. I equated transcendence with magic, something only the gullible or needy could fall for. St. Francis was far beyond my understanding. I thought his was an ancient and medieval faith that has all but disappeared. But, by the grace of God, Poverty's little brother showed me a richer way.

SMALL TALK

Early biographers of St. Francis, such as St. Bonaventure and Thomas de Celano, wrote of the saint's tremendous reverence for the name of Jesus. Just hearing it filled him with joy, as if he had "suddenly tasted something marvelous or caught the strain of a beautiful harmony." The early friars who lived with Francis told how he continuously talked about Jesus in the most loving manner imaginable. The love of Jesus seemed to always be oozing out of Francis. He seemed totally occupied by Jesus, even to the point of forgetting to eat if the meal conversation turned to Jesus.

Thoughts of Jesus never distracted me from eating. Even though the picture of Francis presented by his early biographers was intended to show Francis as a saint, I doubt they were exaggerating very much when they says Francis' daily conversation was filled with "continuous" talk of Jesus. What is our conversation filled with? Certainly not Jesus. If we mention Jesus in our conversation just once during the course of the day, that's a lot. We prefer small talk. It's easier, less troublesome.

Francis knew what the word "God" meant. It was a reality that burned in his heart. St. Bonaventure wrote: "Jesus Christ crucified reposed continually on the breast of Francis like a bouquet of myrrh, and the fire of love with which he burned made him desire to be entirely transformed in Jesus."

The fire of love needs to be lit in our hearts.

When we look at the reality of the world around us, we see death and destruction, revenge and retaliation. A culture of death seems to dominate our spirit of life. We have lost our prophetic voice and we no longer defend the undocumented, the lonely, and the alienated—those who are hurting and have no voice. Poverty exists because we as the human family have forgotten God and turned our backs on God's children. The only way poverty will be reduced is with love and goodness. We need to see God in each other. We need to turn away from hatred and more fully embrace love. We need to make compassion the foundation of our lives and actions. Tolstoy said that our great duty as humans was to sow the seed of compassion in each other's heart. It is only compassion that will change and save the world.

Christ's work of reconciliation and healing beckons us to build bridges to unity, bridges to a distant shore where common ground is found and peace prevails. Our very woundedness is waiting to be transformed into compassion. Our emotional and physical pain helps us understand and respond to the suffering of another. Compassion is as elegant as any cathedral.

A CHILD TALKING

How is it that I rarely forget to wear my tau cross around my neck, but frequently I forget that I carry within me the Holy of Holies, the living presence of God? If the indwelling presence of the Creator truly permeated and influenced my life, how utterly changed I would be.

Humans are very complex beings. I think we all too frequently bring that complexity into our relationship with God. St. Francis came to understand that God, on the contrary, is the mirror of simplicity, and consequently the simpler we are, the closer we come to God. In Matthew's gospel, Christ tells us "to be as simple as doves." Instead, for most of my adult life, I frittered away my time philosophizing about God instead of talking with God. Francis sought God in the simplicity of his heart. And he spoke to God in a simple, unaffected way, as a child talking with his father. That is the essence of true and real prayer.

Perhaps the banality of our daily conversation, which is rarely imbued with talk of God, is due to the collective dryness of our daily prayer life. For most of us, prayer is left to chance and squeezed into a few brief, hurried moments. I recall reading in *The Pilgrim Continues His Way*, the sequel to the spiritual classic *The Way of a Pilgrim*, a striking passage in which a priest helps the pilgrim prepare for confession. During the conversation the priest claims any honest examination of conscience would reveal that we neither love God nor our neighbor, that our religious convictions are shallow, that we are full of pride and sensual self-love, and that our prayer life is marked by dryness and boredom. As I read the passage I found myself nodding in agreement with the priest.

I say I love God, yet I wonder if I could prove it in a court of law. St. Francis de Sales reminds us: "The will loves only by willing to love." I take that to mean that I must act "as if" I truly loved God, despite the compelling evidence to the contrary. Hypocrisy? No. It is merely an honest assessment of the spiritual reality that I must live by faith, not feeling or knowing. God doesn't measure the quality of our love. We can't, no matter how perfect and selfless our love might be, earn God's love. It is pure gift. Grace is everything. No matter how poorly I may love God, I am always guaranteed full access to God and assured of a divine embrace. My imperfect love can only be perfected by prayer.

Vatican II instructed us that "action is subordinated to contemplation." Moreover, Scripture tells us we should pray ceaselessly. But it doesn't tell us how we can possibly do such a thing. It sounds totally unreasonable. Francis knew the importance of prayer, and his life reflected the richness of his prayer, the fruit of which did not allow him to distinguish between the righteous man and the sinner, loving them both equally and judging neither.

I've got a long way to go. Francis, I'm sure, would advise us not to become overly troubled by the dryness of our prayer. Instead, he would gently suggest we await with patience the fruit of persevering in prayer, and he would encourage us to set up an altar to God in our hearts where we can pray wherever we are, no matter what we are doing. He would whisper to us: Fly to God on the wings of prayer. Pray always, no matter how poorly, and do not be disturbed by anything. Rest in God. Free yourself from the servitude of your passions; disengage yourself from those amusements of the mind and attachments of the heart that distract you from God, who is your only delight. In humility, make the effort to pray, for this much is within your power, and grace will surely purify your prayer. And remember what James wrote in his letter: "Pray for one another and this will cure you."

POVERTY AND SIMPLICITY

For Francis, poverty created a spirit of detachment that liberated him from everything in order for him to love everything without possessing anything. It is so easy to depict St. Francis as some kind of carefree minstrel who loved simplicity, as if it were a poetic virtue to be cherished. Francis wasn't naturally inclined toward simplicity. The simplicity that underscores his life was merely a by-product of his love of poverty. Francis loved the radical insecurity of poverty because for him it was the ultimate act of faith in the providence of God.

In practical terms, his embrace of radical poverty meant he had no clue where his next meal would come from or how long it would be before he ate again. I have witnessed firsthand this kind of severe poverty in massive slums around the world. Of course, the residents of those slums do not choose to live in such extreme poverty. Nonetheless, poverty's impact is the same: fear. The fear grows out of the realization that one's world is fragile, insecure, and often malignant. The poor and homeless I've met feared getting sick because they don't have the money for proper medical treatment. Francis' trust and faith in God was so strong, he had no such fear. And it was his vow of poverty that fueled the growth of his faith.

To imitate Christ, which was his sole goal in life, meant living a life of extreme self-denial. But self-denial as practiced by Francis never gave way to some twisted form of self-loathing. While denying himself everything, he fully loved everything, joyfully entering into a healthy relationship with all of creation. Following the self-emptying example of Christ and trusting fully in the providence of God enabled Francis to see the entire world as a free gift of God and a manifestation of God's presence and love.

FOLLOWING THE WRONG ROAD

Progress along the spiritual road seems painfully slow. As I listen to friends who are serious about their spiritual lives, I hear a common concern: "Why, after so many years of prayer and varying degrees of asceticism, years of trying to lead a more spiritual life, must we struggle with the same weaknesses, the same faults?" I'm frustrated with the slowness in which I'm able to eradicate sin from my life. Is this just the way it is, or are we missing something, doing something wrong? Or worse, are we following the wrong road altogether?

As I looked more closely at the ascetical life of St. Francis, one thing became clear: the purity of his motivation. Often for us moderns, spirituality has become just another tool to help us become better people. That is to say, our spirituality is egocentric: *what is it doing for me?* Not so for St. Francis. His goal was not self-perfection; his goal was God alone. Asceticism for St. Francis was inspired and animated by a simple principle, found in the sixth chapter of the book of Deuteronomy: "Thou shall love the Lord thy God with thy whole heart, with thy whole soul, and with thy whole strength." To deviate from this reality is to return to a self-centered perfection that misses the essence and profound purpose of Christianity.

St. Francis took seriously the words of Christ; and in John's gospel, Jesus said, "Without me, you can do nothing." Taking those words to heart changed Francis' entire outlook: God alone must be the source and expression of all his actions. As we grow in awareness that of ourselves we can do nothing but that in Christ we can do all things, we will no longer be discouraged by our own faults, nor will we be proud of the virtuous acts we perform through the promptings of God's grace. Once St. Francis arrived at the realization that he was nothing and that God was all, his own weaknesses and failings were no longer obstacles, but instead were transformed into a means through which his faith was strengthened by the exercise of heroic acts of self-sacrifice, echoing the words of Paul in his second letter to the Corinthians: "Gladly will I glory in my infirmities that the power of God may dwell in me."

The more you pray, the more you will become poor, plain, and empty. And ready for God. Prayer consists of becoming aware. We experience God's love in proportion to our experience of our own weakness. Day in and day out, God the divine Sower liberally plants seeds in the soil of our lives. Prayer tills the soil, making it receptive to the flowering power of the seed. But far too often the soil is hardened by sin, worries, and an unhealthy preoccupation with money, power, and success; and so the seed is trampled on or blown away. God's love goes unnoticed.

To make visible the hidden love of God, to feel more intensely the inexpressible marvel of God, Francis knew he needed to spend time in prayer and time with the poor. Because each of us is a child of God, each of us possesses the eminent dignity of a child of God. Divine mercy is incarnated in human weakness.

INTO THE WOODS

St. Francis became who he was in solitude. He spent about half his adult life alone in seclusion. In his journals, Gandhi made a reference to his personal practice of reserving one day a week for total silence: "A periodic decree of silence is not a torture but a blessing." Modern life leaves little space for silence.

From the very beginning of his new life in Christ, Francis

wanted to know, with clarity, what he should do. He was drawn both to solitary prayer and to a combination of doing good works and proclaiming the good news. But before Francis could actually "do" anything, he had to "become" something, because "being" must come before "doing." Thomas Merton, in his book *Contemplation in a World of Action*, expressed this principle well: "He who attempts to act and do for others or for the world without deepening his own self-understanding, freedom, integrity and capacity to love, will not have anything to give others. He will communicate to them nothing but the contagion of his own obsessions, his aggressivity, his egocentered ambitions, his delusions about ends and means, his doctrinaire prejudices and ideas."

Near the top of Mount Subasio, built into the cliffs at the back of a ravine and surrounded by a thick forest, quietly sits a hermitage known as the Carceri, an isolated spot high above Assisi where Francis went for solitude. The friars lived in individual caves, which they called cells. The word *carceri* means prison. However, when the word is applied to the mountaintop dwelling used by Francis, it is not used in the sense of a jail, but rather in harmony with the religious concept of seclusion. For Francis, *carceri* meant solitary, a private hermitage where he could be alone with God. The Carceri is located about two and a half miles from Assisi. The steep road leading to the Eremo delle Carceri begins at the Porta del Cappuccini (The Capuchin Gate).

At first, the incline is gentle and the road gradually ascends through lovely olive groves. But quickly the slope becomes steeper, and the olive trees give way to the thick vegetation of small bushes, yellow broom flowers, and small bay oak trees. As the road twists and winds its way to the summit, it graciously offers arresting views of the valley below. Off in the distance you can see Santa Maria degli Angeli and the towns of Bastia and Cannara. Some locations along the road offer beautiful views of Assisi and the ancient fortress, the Rocca Maggiore. These vistas are paid for with the sweat and strain of the climb. With each step along the steep road leading to the Carceri, you can feel the air becoming lighter and cooler. Birds playfully dance in the currents of wind and updrafts. As you near the end of the hour walk, you realize the hermitage sits atop a deep gorge just below the summit and is hidden by a dense forest of tall oak trees. This is isolation. In the silence of the mountain Francis found the space to be receptive to the speechless language of God and to respond with all of his heart. I made the following entry in my journal after the first time I made the climb in 1995.

The arduous hike up to the Carceri is rewarded with a spectacular view of the Valley of Spoleto and the hills upon which Assisi sits. As I climbed higher and higher, my appreciation for the beauty spread out before me rose steadily. A thought expressed by the nineteenth-century Jesuit poet Gerard Manley Hopkins suddenly became electrified with meaning: "The world is charged with the grandeur of God."

During the exhausting climb up to the Carceri, I felt God's presence in the beauty of the natural wonders before me— and it had nothing to do with the design argument for God's existence expressed by some philosophers. The feeling was too poetic to be philosophical. However, as my spirit danced before the grandeur, my mind recalled something penned by Marcel Proust, which voiced a totally different reaction to the same beauty: "It has been said that the highest praise of God consists in the denial of Him by the atheist, who finds creation so perfect that he [or she] can dispense with a creator."

Bathed in the brightness of the day, questions about how all this came into being seemed irrelevant. In the beginning...*who knows?* Who knows from where it has come and how it happened? It is the riddle of all riddles. Questions about what God did before creation or how God created the world without using any raw materials or why if God was perfect and complete within the divine being did the need and will to create arise in God—all these questions have no convincing answers.

Hindus offer a dazzling variety of answers to the riddle, all of which include a wide assortment of gods and mythologies, but ultimately they are more content with doubt than dogma. Buddhists offer no answers to the riddle. Jews, Christians, and Muslims offer what many perceive to be rigid answers provided by one book authored by their one God. Many thoughtful people, such as the followers of Confucius, are indifferent to the riddle of creation and don't trouble themselves with thinking about it. The scientifically minded among us can't agree on one theory that explains it all.

As I looked over the vast valley pulsating with life, I pledged to rejoice in creation instead of trying to explain it. Francis was so inspired by the beauty of creation that he too created something beautiful out of nothing: himself!

THE SILENT VOICE OF GOD

The Carceri was a place of stillness and solitude. God can't be found in noise and restlessness. Our real pilgrimage is into the depths of silence, which leads to a true light. The quest for God is a journey, a pilgrimage to the depths of the soul. The quest requires a listening heart, an ear quickened to the silent voice of God, and a vigilant spirit actively waiting and watching. Each day needs to be a pilgrimage into my own heart. To be a pilgrim is to live on life's threshold, walking on the edge of reality, striving for what lies beyond the reality we see with our flawed human eyes.

Jesus often sought the emptiness of the desert to experience a fuller union with God. God never shouts to be heard over our noise. Only silence gives God a chance to speak. To effectively listen to God—or even to another human being—one needs to be silent and attentive. If we are truly listening to God or another, truly paying attention, there will be no hint of self-reflective consciousness; there will only be silent receptivity. To listen is to be silent. We need to empty our hearts, to sit in stillness. Silence allows us to live within; it helps us to concentrate on the serious, profound inner mysteries of life. Noise takes us out of ourselves and distracts and scatters our thoughts.

THE RULE OF HERMITAGES

Amid the oldest manuscript collection of the limited writings of St. Francis, there is a very short, simple document composed of only four paragraphs that sets down a Rule for Hermitages. Francis wrote the rule sometime between 1217 and 1221. Francis was keenly aware of the need for the brothers to occasionally interrupt their preaching and their work among the poor and to withdraw into solitude for a period of time. In the peace of a cave or austere hut, they could strengthen their souls for the apostolic work that had been entrusted to them. A hermitage was little more than a collection of huts in an isolated area, usually high atop a mountain. The hermitages were places of spiritual respite, where the focus was on prayer and renewal.

Occasionally, a brother desired to spend longer periods

of time in isolation. Francis wrote a rule governing life in a hermitage, which cleverly allowed some brothers to live entirely in silence as children—being served and protected by other friars acting as loving mothers. Francis said a hermitage should consist of three or four brothers. Two brothers should act as mothers, following the example of Martha, caring for and serving the other one or two brothers who are living a life of Mary. The brothers who are mothers must not permit anyone to disturb their sons or allow anyone to talk with them. The sons should spend their time alone in their enclosed space. Both the mothers and the sons should pray the Office. After a time, the friars would switch roles. It was as simple as Martha, Mary, and Jesus.

That was it: not long on rules or regulations, but shimmering with grace and simplicity. Francis had a wonderful knack for applying gospel stories to the life he lived. The rule reflects the maternal instinct within Francis, whose tenderness was always at the service of all in his care. The short rule uses the word "mother" six times, as he instructs the brothers to be mothers to each other. Essentially, a hermitage is a place of silence. The silence of the hermitage taught the brothers how to speak in the noisy streets of the city.

Eremitical solitude is an essential part of Francis' spirituality. He did not consider solitary adoration as an optional extra. Francis founded at least twenty mountain hermitages. They were primitive, poor, and simple. St. Bonaventure was washing dishes in a hermitage when he received the news he had been made a cardinal. While Francis and his followers were deeply involved in evangelization, they recognized the importance of maintaining a certain distance and perspective from society. The hermitage experience kept them from becoming too deeply submerged in active cares, and also safeguarded them from becoming physically and spiritually drained by the demands of their exhausting work of caring for the poor and preaching the good news. Prayer does not flourish without help, and the hermitage helped revitalize prayer by providing it with time and space.

We all need time in a hermitage.

PART IV

The Mission

PREACHING TO THE SULTAN IN EGYPT

After receiving papal approval, Francis' years of more active ministry were truly remarkable, the stuff of an epic film. As someone who once earned his living producing television dramas, I cannot help but be struck by the sweeping, colossal drama of the saint's heroic life. His two failed attempts at reaching the Holy Land pack enough dramatic potential to make a compelling film. He survived harrowing storms at sea and endured a strenuous walk across Europe and over the Pyrenees. Along the way there was illness and heroism. He preached to a sultan and told sparrows to shut up so people could hear his sermon.

Of course, people tend to remember the sweet stuff: preaching to birds and taming a wolf. But Francis' life as the head of a rapidly growing Order was far from sweet. These were years of suffering and deep anguish. Detailing the full story of the next dozen years of the saint's life would gobble up far too many pages to be included here. I simply want to offer an outline of one significant episode—Francis' attempt to reach out to Muslims—which will illustrate the explosion of energy that propelled Francis to new horizons of outreach and spirituality.

Francis made three attempts to meet peacefully with Muslim leaders. He hoped to counteract the violence of the Crusades by bringing them a message of peace. The first attempt, in 1212, was thwarted by a terrifying and violent storm that forced the ship to return to Italy. The following year his second attempt ended when Francis became seriously ill in Spain, after an arduous walk across Italy and France.

In June 1219, during the Fifth Crusade, Francis embarked on a long trip to Egypt, knowing full well that some of his friars in Tunis and Morocco had been beheaded by Muslims. It seems plausible that Francis wanted to set foot on the soil of Islam and offer his own life as a holocaust for his Muslim brothers. So many friars volunteered to go with him to Egypt that they all could not fit on the ship. Not wanting to show favoritism, Francis left the selection of friars in the hands of God by calling on a small boy to pick eleven friars out of all those assembled at the port. Randomly, the little boy touched one friar after another, saying "This one." The twelve men boarded the ship and set sail from Ancona. Francis was about to undertake an unimaginable mission: he would attempt to reverse the Crusades by embracing the enemy instead of killing them. As they sailed, Francis reminded the brothers that Jesus said they were to love their enemies and that in the eyes of God the sultan was their brother because everyone was a child of the God of peace.

It was a long and grueling trip. After a brief stop at Cyprus, the ship reached the seaport city of Damietta in the Nile Delta of northern Egypt near the end of July. Damietta, a city of 80,000, was well fortified, defended by a triple ring of walls with many high towers. The city was under siege by the Crusaders, who only a few days earlier had won an important victory. But on the last day of July, the attack on Damietta was beaten back by the Muslims, and in the process the Christian army suffered considerable losses. The orgy of slaughter on the battle lines and the wanton debauchery of the Christian military camp horrified and depressed Francis. He felt a profound sorrow and deep conflict within himself over the excessive cruelty of the crusaders. From a distance, Francis the idealist believed the Crusades were a sacred venture; up close, Francis the humanist viewed the Crusades as a sacrilegious act.

Francis saw how the Crusades violated the ideals of the gospel: namely, not to return evil for evil but instead to promote a spirit of reconciliation. Those ideals had been honored by the early Church. God's people, according to the early Church, had to be a people of forgiveness. Violence was never advocated. By the thirteenth century, war and violence had become a way of life. Crusaders ruthlessly slaughtered Muslims, Jews, pagans, and even Christians whom the pope declared to be enemies of the faith. The Crusades were considered to be a holy war, and killing Saracens was thought to be a religious act. Worse, the mass slaughter was blessed by the Church as fulfilling God's purposes on earth—*Deus vult* (God wills it) was the battle cry of the crusaders. Killing was justified and sanctioned, and the victims were looked at as less than human. St. Bernard wrote, "To kill a Muslim is not homicide." The popes called for the Crusades to eliminate rather than to convert the Saracens. Moreover, the Crusades exploited the penitential system to raise funds to extermi-nate unbelievers. Christianity had taken on a warlike spirit.

The lived reality of the gospel in Francis' life made it im-possible for him to accept what he saw as the fundamental goal of the Crusades: purging the land of Arab Muslims by killing them. He was appalled by the fact that many of the crusaders participated in the carnival of violence simply to gain wealth and land for themselves. Even if the Muslims were in error, Francis did not understand how followers of Christ could violently eliminate the error rather then gently try to correct it. Francis was out of step with his Church and the rest of society. In Egypt, he realized that violence and killing should never be advocated or sanctioned by the Church; moreover, the followers of Christ needed to put down their iron sword and pick up the sword of the Spirit. All killing and all wars are unjust and immoral.

The crusaders planned on storming Damietta again in late August. Francis believed God was telling him the forces of the cross would suffer a great defeat. Risking ridicule, Francis warned the crusaders, even taking his plea directly to the Christian commander, Cardinal Pelagius, but his warn-ing fell on deaf ears. On August twenty-ninth, the crusad-ers launched an offensive that was handily turned back. Six thousand crusaders were killed or captured.

It was time for Francis to act, to do what he came to do: preach to the Sultan Malek el Kamil. It was a foolhardy mission, especially in light of the fact that the sultan had offered a gold ducat for every Christian head presented to him. Accompanied only by Brother Illuminato, Francis fearlessly marched toward the enemy line, where he was immediately seized by soldiers armed with curved swords known as scimitars. Francis repeatedly shouted the sultan's name. The soldiers believed he must have been an emissary sent to seek a peace treaty and therefore elected not to lop the saint's head off right there on the spot; instead, they beat and bound Francis before escorting him to the sultan's palace.

Exactly what transpired during the meeting is not clear. Hard facts are clearly outnumbered by tall tales. We do know that the sultan, who was a nephew of Saladin, was a cultured and courteous man; he had a skeptical mind but was open to debating the merits of the gospel and the Koran as an intellectual exercise. Perhaps the sultan consented to see Francis merely to amuse himself. Assuming his visit was connected with the Crusades and was sponsored by some diplomatic authority, the sultan asked Francis for a letter of accreditation. Francis said he was sent by God, not man, to announce the "good news" and that his visit had nothing to do with the Crusades. Francis then told the sultan about Christ the Savior and the Trinity. His fervor and boldness impressed the sultan. It seems safe to conclude he was charmed and intrigued by Francis, for Francis did leave the palace with his head still attached.

One story that seems to have garnered historical acceptance claims that the sultan tried to trick Francis by spreading before him a carpet with crisscrosses woven into the design. The sultan said if Francis walked on the crosses he would accuse the Christian of insulting his own God; and if Francis refused to walk on the carpet he would accuse Francis of insulting him. Francis' response to the challenge displayed the same degree of ingenuity as the challenge itself. Francis said the crosses on which he walked belonged to the thieves between whom Christ had been crucified and so he was not ashamed to tread on them.

Francis, in an effort to prove the superiority of his faith, proposed a trial by fire in which he offered to throw himself into a fire on condition that a Mohammedan priest do so also. Francis told the sultan that he should believe in the faith of whoever emerged from the fire unharmed. The sultan, being a wise man and noticing that his priests did not like Francis' proposal, declined the offer. Francis then said he would still throw himself into the fire, if the sultan would only pledge to accept Christ if he was not consumed by the flames. The sultan was touched that a man who did not even know him would be willing to throw himself into a fire for the sake of the sultan's own soul and salvation. He offered Francis gifts of gold and silver. Of course, Francis, concerned only with souls, refused. The sultan was even further impressed with the saint and marveled at his contempt for worldly goods.

The sultan asked the religious leaders of the palace what he should do with Francis. Behead him, was their response, because he had preached against the law of Mohammed. The sultan told Francis that he would not behead him because he couldn't put to death someone who was willing to give his life for another's salvation. The sultan ordered that Francis be set free and further decreed that he and his companion be permitted to travel without restriction through the Holy Land.

Giotto, the famous Renaissance artist, graced a wall in the upper Basilica of St. Francis in Assisi with a painting that depicts the saint and the sultan and the "trial by fire," yet the historicity of that story has never been fully proven. It should be noted that St. Bonaventure in his *Major Life of*

Francis does not even mention the episode. However, a horn given to Francis by the sultan, which the saint eventually accepted at the sultan's insistence, is kept on display in the Sacro Convento di San Francesco in Assisi. According to a passage in the *Little Flowers*, the sultan secretly converted to Christianity, a claim that has no historical foundation but is simply a legendary embellishment that has been believed by some people for centuries.

In Francis' day, most Christians viewed the prophet Mohammed as a devil, and his followers as heretics. However, Francis told the sultan that Muslims were people of faith among whom God was present through grace. He was impressed by their prayerfulness, answering to the call of the Muezzin five times a day. He said he accepted the sultan as a brother. He proposed that his friars be nothing more than a simple, peaceful presence among the Muslims, a gentle witness to the depth of Christian life, and not to engage them in useless polemics or try to refute their religious convictions. Francis said he preached only when he knew that doing so would please the Lord. However, when he preached he did so in a manner that allowed reverence and respect for the Muslims. Francis said he came to the Muslims not with power and a sword but in humility and with a spirit of nonviolence and peace and heart for true dialogue among people of differing faiths. This was a far cry from the goals of the Crusades, which wanted only to root out the infidels, crushing them into submission. Francis' approach to dealing with Muslims was radically new, and not all the brothers could accept it. Francis had a willingness to learn from those who believed differently than he did.

Francis clearly demonstrated that he was a liberating visionary, showing us a way to encounter and even embrace "the other." He has much to say today to those who are in-terested in inter-religious dialogue—after all, he invented it. I believe that Francis, as a little brother, desired first to befriend (not convert) the sultan, and that is the real reason why the saint left the palace with his head still attached.

Francis failed in his attempts to get the crusaders to scale the heights of the true Christian ideal; he wasn't even able to lift them out of their debauchery. He also failed in his preaching of the gospel of Christ to the sultan. Surely these setbacks must have saddened the saint.

The sultan allowed him to travel to the Holy Land. There is no record of what happened there, but we can only imag-ine what it was like for Francis to visit the sacred sites of the life of Christ. Oh, how it must have nourished his soul!

Often in my life, I have known the pain of sadness and failure. Not knowing what to do with the pain, I simply carried it with me for far longer than I needed. When life knocked Francis down, when he failed to accomplish what he thought God wanted him to do, he knew how to reach out to God for a helping hand, a hand that never failed to lift him back up. Francis knew how to look to the crib and the cross for all that he needed, and he experienced both mysteries every day at the altar.

A TRUE BROTHERHOOD

The sacrilegious brutality of the Crusades shocked and sick-ened Francis. He could not fathom mocking and torturing prisoners of war. For him, judgment was God's job, and Christians should have no part in it; moreover, because God was all-merciful, Christians had responsibility to be kind to everyone and condemn no one. Francis had undertaken a crusade for peace.

Years ago, long after I had lost my faith, I read about the Crusades in detail for the first time. I was horrified by the brutality employed by the Church and disgusted by the political corruption that had infected the Church. My reading helped reinforce my belief that God did not exist. Now, rather than focus on the abuses of the past, I prefer to follow Vatican II's wise counsel that is found in "Declaration on the Relationship of the Church with Non-Christian Religions":

> Upon the Moslems too, the Church looks with esteem... although in the course of the centuries many quarrels and hostilities have arisen between Christians and Moslems, this most sacred Synod urges all to forget the past and strive sincerely for mutual understanding.

St. Francis' spirituality grew out of the tumultuous times in which he lived; it was an age of tremendous social change and horrific violence. Francis was a man of his times. His conversion didn't happen in a flash or vacuum after reading the gospel. He had the same passion and aspirations that sparked the revolution brewing in the depths of society. The gospel, however, slowly showed Francis the limitations of the hopes of his times. In Jesus, Francis saw a different and better path to transformation in individual hearts and in society. In Jesus, Francis saw that wholeness was possible. For Francis, the gospel became life and light as it rubbed up against the aspirations within himself and within his society. In his thought-provoking book *Francis of Assisi: Return to the Gospel*, Eloi Leclerc, OFM, writes:

> Francis discovered an aspect of God very different from that current among the adherents of ecclesiastical prin-

cipalities and holy wars. For him, God ceased to be the external, dominating, and Transcendent One, the Lord in a more-or-less feudal dress. To him, God appeared as mysteriously present in our history, bereft of all trappings of power, bound instead to what was weakest and most despised in man's world. Francis rediscovered God's humbleness, God's humanity. Not merely as an object of devotion, but as a new principle on which to reconstruct society. He understood that if one acknowledges the God of the Gospel, then one can no longer be satisfied with just any form of social organization. This acknowledgment is bound to bring about a transformation in human relationships; it involves seeking and bringing into being true brotherhood, a brotherhood that excludes nobody. The God of the Gospel lets himself be seen through other men, where there are no more lords and no more subjects, where no one is kept out. The dawn of true brotherhood is the light in which God is truly found.

In the midst of a dark night of barbaric cruelty, the meeting between Francis and the sultan had the potential to be the dawn of a true brotherhood that excluded no one and could have produced a transformation in human relationships. But the forces of ecclesiastical kingdoms, holy wars, pride, and intolerance darkened the new morning light and the ideal of a true community of all people, excluding no one. But a seed had been planted, a seed of interfaith dialogue and respect that is, eight centuries later, beginning to sprout in our day, but is still a long, long way from being fully realized. The blueprint that Francis discovered in his time in the gospel and which the sultan found in the Koran is there for us to discover. Our survival depends upon it. We need to talk to each other, listen to each other, learn from each other, and grow in love and compassion together.

DIFFERENT TONGUES

As a child, I was taught that I was created in the image of God. Anne Lamott turned that idea upside down in order to humorously illustrate the difficulty surrounding interfaith dialogue. She said: "You can safely assume you've created God in your own image when it turns out that God hates all the same people you do."

As a Catholic, Franciscan Christian, my understanding of the world has a distinctly Christocentric character. For me, personal communion with Christ is at the center and heart of all reality. I believe Christ is the Wisdom of God, the "unknown and unseen" Sophia, in whom the cosmos is created and sustained. That belief should not, however, hinder me (but it often does) from affirming the other *as other,* from saying yes to the other, from saying yes to everyone. But this is not easy; and this is why authentic dialogue is difficult. It is not easy to hold onto the core of your beliefs without denigrating conflicting beliefs held by people of different faiths. But we must.

Interfaith dialogue requires that people of differing faiths avoid dogmatic assertions when speaking with each other. Theological arrogance and rigidity stifles any authentic exchange. Nor will dialogue succeed if our aim is advancing our own theological perspective. True dialogue requires an honest mutual exploration of our respective theologies and felt experiences of God; it is a journey toward understanding, not convincing.

The world's faiths speak in uniquely different tongues of a transcendent reality most consider common to them all.

The path of peace is dialogue. Dialogue transforms a stranger into a friend. Perhaps people of differing faiths can each grow closer to God by drawing closer to each other. A few years ago, I spent ten days traveling through Turkey with a friend of mine who is a Sufi Muslim living in Istanbul. We prayed together in many mosques and churches. I saw myself within my friend, and he saw himself within me—and we were both better for that experience. As we shared our experiences of divine light, we became brothers. While our religious differences may be beyond resolution, we saw our hidden unity. We all need to find the common thread, to reveal the hidden wholeness, to see the inscape of the soul. We must do more than preach tolerance at a comfortable distance without listening, without relationship, without growth. We must open ourselves to one another. We must risk learning something new and essential on the path to God, and thus risk altering the presumptions that have shaped our respective faiths. Perhaps our faiths need to be more lyrical and less dogmatic. Friends can unite in the struggle against poverty and evil.

Our modus operandi should be: *more poetry and less prose*. Prose flattens the world, sees it as unchangeable, accepts unthinkingly the status quo, perpetuates the royal consciousness, and causes numbness and conformity. Poetry bursts forth with new life, upsets comfortable conformity, imagines new realities, resists the predominate consciousness, and sees the world from an alternative perspective to the mind-numbing prose.

I harbor no illusions about the manifold differences across seemingly impenetrable religious and cultural boundaries or the difficulty of dialogue across deep and often painful historical and conceptual divides. Nevertheless, authentic dialogue is not only possible but gives access to a deep communication that is not merely communication, but communion that is beyond words and dogmatic assertions.

Pope John XXIII's prophetic, universal, and all-inclusive vision for the Second Vatican Council in 1962 helped ignite a worldwide ecumenical dialogue. One of the council documents clearly states:

> The Catholic Church rejects nothing that is true and holy in these religions. She regards with sincere reverence those ways of conduct and of life, those precepts and teachings which, though differing in many aspects from the ones she holds and sets forth, nonetheless reflect a ray of Truth which enlightens all people....The Church, therefore, exhorts her children, that through dialogue and collaboration with the followers of other religions, carried out with prudence and love and in witness to the Christian faith and life, they recognize, preserve and promote good things, spiritual and moral, as well as socio-cultural values found among these people ["Declaration on the Relations of the Church to Non-Christian Religions," in Documents of the Second Vatican Council, proclaimed by Pope Paul VI, October 28, 1965, no. 2].

MADE BY LOVE

We do not know peace because we do not know love. We do not know love because we do not know God. God is love. We were made by love and for love. But we have turned our backs on love, and have become unloving. The world has been disfigured by our failure to love. The world will only be transformed when all people learn how to love each other.

Our human love is limited, unable to reach beyond ourselves, our family, our friends. Our love is feeble, unable to withstand the storms of life. Our love is egocentric, unable to put others first. Love requires humility, mercy, kindness, trust, patience, perseverance, and sacrifice. Sadly, these noble traits are underappreciated and in short supply in our troubled world. Only divine love allows us to embrace all, even our enemies. Peace can only flow from self-emptying love. Peace creates unity and works for the common good. Faith in God should unite us and lead us to a peace rooted in mercy and compassion. But our flawed faith divides us and pits one faith against another. It says my religion is better than yours; my religion is the only true religion. And so we pray, and kill,and ignore the poor, the weak, and the suffering. And cause God to weep.

God is neither Christian, nor Jewish, nor Muslim, nor Buddhist, nor Hindu. God is love. Different religions are different ways at trying to understand God. God is beyond all faiths, beyond all understanding. We can grow in knowledge of God every day until the day we die, and God will still be unknown to us. My love for my Christian faith is enhanced by my embracing all religious faiths. Every faith needs to root out hate and cultivate love. Where there is hatred, there is the absence of God. Where there is love, there is God.

PREACHING TO THE BIRDS

Both Thomas of Celano's *First Life* and St. Bonaventure's *Major Life* contain the charming story of St. Francis preaching to the birds. It is one of the best-known stories from the saint's life. Here is Bonaventure's version of the story, as translated by Murray Bodo, OFM:

> Once near Bevagna in the Spoleto valley St. Francis saw
> a large flock of birds of various kinds. There were doves

and crows, and those popularly called daws. Now Francis was always fervent towards creatures and showed them great tenderness, so as soon as he saw these birds, he left his companions and ran eagerly to the birds. And when he got close to them, he greeted them in his usual way. They seemed to be waiting for him; they didn't fly away as he expected them to do. And so, filled with joy, he begged them to listen to the word of God. Among other things, he said this to the birds: "My Brother Birds, you should always praise your Creator and love him. He covered you with feathers and gave you wings to fly with and granted you a kingdom of pure air. He cares for you, too, without any worry on your part, though you neither sow nor reap."

At these words, as Francis and his companions later reported, the birds acknowledged his words in a wonderful fashion. They stretched out their necks and flapped their wings, and gazed at him with beaks open. And St. Francis walked among them in fervor of spirit, brushing their heads and bodies with his tunic, and not one of them moved until he made a sign of the cross over them and gave them permission to fly away. And Francis and his companions went on their way, as well, praising and thanking God whom all creatures venerate and humbly acknowledge.

Thomas of Celano goes on to offer us a bit of commentary:

Francis, who was not simple by nature but through grace, then began to accuse himself of negligence for never having preached to the birds before then, given that they had listened to the word of God so reverently. From that day on, he promptly began to exhort all birds, all animals, all reptiles and even unfeeling creatures to praise and love the Creator, for every day he experienced their obedience when the name of the Savior was invoked.

The Basilica of St. Francis in Assisi houses a famous fresco that graces the rear wall to the right of the main door of the upper church. The fresco beautifully depicts Francis preaching to the birds. Following closely the story from Celano and Bonaventure, the fresco contains birds of varying sizes and species. Birds of different species normally don't mingle together. The story and the fresco are trying to tell us something.

First, we must understand that Francis was not merely a nature lover. That's too simple. Francis loved God; and because God created nature, Francis loved nature. The different kinds of birds symbolize people: people of all races, nationalities, and personalities who together make up a single diverse flock of humanity. And Francis gathered them all together so they could hear him proclaim the good news of the gospel. Francis is telling us that we must not only take care of nature and each other, but we must also share the good news with all creation.

I have no doubt that Francis preached to birds. Whether they listened doesn't matter—but I have a hunch some did. A dodo bird named Gerry did.

MYSTICISM VS. MORALISM

Even the most ordinary moments of the day are charged with mystical possibilities. To see the mystical in the ordinary, we need to pause often during the day and be attentive to what is really happening all around us and inside us. In that unexpected and transforming moment in the empty church in Rome nearly twenty years ago, I felt a deep sense of union. While I have never since had such a profoundly deep experience, I've had fleeting moments of awareness in which I experienced a deeper sense of connectedness with God and all of creation. For so many years, I earnestly tried to be perfect, to be sinless. It seems clear to me that merely striving for perfection will get us nowhere, or at least not get us even close to a place of wholeness with God where our true identity resides.

St. Francis of Assisi was one of the many mystics who reached a place of wholeness that enabled him to see God in all things. This kind of union with all seems impossible to us. So many of us strive to reach God by trying our best to be perfect, and we always fall far short. It is as if we think we can achieve wholeness on our own without any help from God or another. Such a path to God is rooted solely in our ego. Private perfection is not possible and is doomed to failure. Sin always seems to defeat us. And so we end up either giving up on religion or continuing to go to church without ever believing we will be going to heaven. I know from personal experience that it is very possible to go to church on a regular basis and not really believe that God exists.

Those truly mystical moments always enlarge the soul and help us see the possible. The path of perfection is egocentric and rooted in a strident moralism that makes holiness and wholeness impossible to achieve. Mysticism unites; moralism divides. Those who mount the high horse of moralism love separating people into camps of lost and saved. Mystics of all faiths never condemn or exclude anyone.

When I shared this reflection with my friend Fr. James, who is an Orthodox monk and priest, he replied with: "When we place before our eyes this idea of 'perfection,' we think in terms of a goal...entirely missing the key characteristic about our spiritual life, which is that it is a journey, not an arrival, and that it is HOW we TAKE the journey that constitutes our spiritual growth...or not...toward becoming more like God."

ELIMINATION AND RESTORATION

"When I was in sin...." That's the way St. Francis described himself before his conversion, before he "put on the mind of Christ" and began to live his life through Christ in the spirit and slowly started to die to his self. We don't much like the word "sin." I don't, even though I am acutely aware that I am a sinner. Despite my progress in curtailing sin, I still sin a lot. Sin, the way I understand it, is a failure to love. I fail often. I fail when I put myself first.

Conversion involves a "metanoia," a turning away from sin and becoming a "new creation." In that sense, Francis did not restore himself, because restoration implies a return to an original condition. According to Christian theology, we were born in sin. In other words, thanks to original sin, sin has always been a part of our nature. In that light, Francis was not engaged in a process of restoration but one of elimination.

Eliminating sin in my life has proven to be a difficult chore. I can't seem to get out of my own way, and my own way sometimes reverts to a self-seeking persona that is not in harmony with the life of Christ. Francis let go of his own way, let go of everything he knew and loved, and, leaving all behind, jumped into the unknown abyss of God, where he became so united with God that he became a new person, a new creation. The old man had died; Adam no longer lived within him. Adam is still alive and kicking within me. Sin keeps me alienated from the fullness of God.

Thomas Merton saw sin as a symbol of our state of alienation from God and our true selves. Our identity hinges on the realization that we are, at our deepest core, one with God. I am not just me and me alone. I am me and God. In other words, if I view myself as just me, I am divided from God—and from everything. If I see myself as being united with God at the core of my being, then I am whole. On the way to God, our false self—that is, the self that is divided from God—begins to dissolve and eventually disappear, until we are, as Merton put it, "no one." To be "no one" is to be our true self, one who is united with God.

The self that disappears along the way is our false self, the descendant of mythical Adam's disobedience, an egocentric act that caused our spiritual death by destroying our relationship with God. The resurrected Jesus restores that relationship and allows us a way to once again become grounded in God, to become who we were meant to be.

Over and over again in the New Testament we read that we are supposed to actively participate in the life of Christ: to die with Christ by dying to sin in order that we may rise with Christ. The journey of conversion begins with a death to self so we can "put on the mind of Christ" and live our lives in unison with Christ through the power of the Holy Spirit. Living a "life in Christ" is something that does not just happen; it's not like putting on a new coat. It is a process, a long and arduous struggle. Why? Because we stand in our own way. Our false self resists and rebels every step of the way, fighting for its own way, the way of sin, the way of self-seeking pleasures. To live a life in Christ means we must die to this false self. For Christ to flourish, our false self must vanish. Ditching a lifetime's worth of false understandings is not an easy task as we desperately want to hold onto what we think is the truth about ourselves and the world around us. We don't want to really believe that sin slowly destroys our intrinsic relationship with God, even though God never stops loving us. We think sin is simply a matter of morality, when it is really a manifestation of our false self. Sadly, the false self wants to listen to the serpent's song of lies and illusions instead of God's song of true harmony. We may say otherwise, but we seem to like stumbling around in the dark rather than being bathed in the light of God.

The first time I read about the concept of a false self and a true self, my intellect understood the theological principles underpinning it, but the idea didn't resonate in my heart. But gradually I began to see the inner struggle that was going on inside of me really was a matter of my old self, my false self, resisting my efforts to live a life in Christ. Prayer was not easy. Often it was dry, arid. It was difficult to see God in the daily, mundane events of my life; God still seemed distant, beyond my reach. Years of unbelief and skepticism caused me to often question the merit of trying to live a more God-centered life, trying to live a life in Christ.

Sometimes during Mass, my mind would wander and entertain the thought that my attendance is a waste of time, that the Mass is nothing more than an antiquated, lifeless ritual or that the concept of transubstantiation is nothing more than theological mumbo jumbo and that the consecrated host is merely a symbol and not the body of Christ, so there is really no need to eat a symbol. The false self has a very active mind, continually questioning, doubting, and constantly trying to restore itself to the throne of my life, trying to force God to abdicate. I was also troubled by my frequent inability to resist the temptation to sin, which in some cases had become rather habitual. Yes, I had professed Christ with my lips and in my heart, yet my false self shouted back, "No! You alone are all you need. Jesus is a fairy-tale messiah and God does not care. Wake up. Live for yourself. You are your own ultimate fulfillment."

In the nearly twenty years since my rebirth in Christ, I have slipped and betrayed him often. But grace and mercy help me to get back up and try again to live a life in Christ. Day by day, little by little, the false self dies. I have no idea how long it will take for the rebellious Adam who lives within me to vanish.

In his excellent book *Merton's Palace of Nowhere: A Search for God Through Awareness of the True Self,* James Finley writes: "Adam is not seen as some historical figure who committed a particular act that brought about a kind of ontological birth defect that is handed down from child to child. Rather, Adam is now. Adam is ourselves in disobedience to God. The garden of Eden prior to the fall is just as much in the future as it is in the past. Both heaven and hell live not only beyond us but also within us, and it is through the door of ourselves that we enter both."

The false self makes life hell. I know; I've been there. Dr. Finley correctly points out: "the serpent's lie is a dark and twisted echo of God's creative act in which he made us sharers of his own divine life. Indeed, for us to want to be like God is simply for us to want to be who God created us to be in his own image and likeness. The spiritual life for Merton is a journey in which we discover ourselves in discovering God, and discover God in discovering our true self hidden in God."

St. Francis made that journey. It was a long, hard trip, and he suffered greatly along the way. He discovered what Thomas Merton expressed centuries later: "The secret of my identity is hidden in the love and mercy of God." Merton went on to say: "There is only one problem on which all my

179

existence, my peace and my happiness depend: to discover myself in discovering God. If I find Him I will find myself and if I find my true self I will find Him."

St. Francis, the helper and the hermit, discovered his true self and God through his selfless service to others and in the inner desert of prayer and contemplation. In the process, he removed the shackles of sin and the mask of illusion and was able to have a face-to-face relationship with God. I can't help but think of the way Francis described himself before his dramatic encounter with the leper: "I was in sin." Thomas Merton identifies sin with the illusions of the false self that hinder us from recognizing Christ. He writes:

> Every one of us is shadowed by an illusory person: a false self. This is the man I want myself to be but who cannot exist, because God does not know anything about him. And to be unknown of God is altogether too much privacy. My false self and private self is the one who wants to exist outside the reach of God's will and God's love—outside of reality and outside of life. And such a self cannot help but be an illusion. We are not very good at recognizing illusions, least of all the ones we cherish about ourselves—the ones we are born with and which feed the roots of sin. For most people in the world, there is no greater subjective reality than this false self of theirs, which cannot exist. A life devoted to the cult of this shadow is what is called a life of sin.

During my 1997 pilgrimage, I composed this prayer for myself: "St. Francis, help me to walk out of the shadow of sin and into the glorious sunshine of God's presence. Help me liberate myself from anxiety and fear and inordinate desire.

Help me keep the flame that was rekindled two years ago burning, and don't let the winds of doubt and skepticism blow it out. Help me cherish all you have given me. Help me surrender all that is unloving in my life. Help me be guided by God's holy will, not by my unhealthy desires and whims."

I was frustrated by my failure to fully live a life in Christ. I've come to see that the transition from the false self and a life of sin to the true self living in oneness with God is a very slow and long process. That doesn't mean I'm satisfied with the pace of my progress; it only means I won't become depressed or distressed by my inability to instantly and completely make my false self vanish. He's been around for a long time, and he's a stubborn cuss.

The spiritual life is a journey—a journey of elimination and restoration.

TWO SMALL LOAVES OF BREAD

Whenever St. Francis wanted to be alone with God, he always sought out some mountaintop cave that would become his hermitage, with one notable exception. In the year 1211 (or possibly 1213), Francis spent Lent on an island. The island is the site of a fanciful story recounted by St. Bonaventure in which a rabbit was caught and given to St. Francis. Although it fled from everyone else, the rabbit trusted St. Francis and the saint was able to hold the rabbit in his hands before releasing it. The island, Isola Maggiore, is one of three small islands located in Lago Trasimeno (Lake Trasimene), the largest lake in the Italian Peninsula. In memory of the Lord's forty days' fast, Francis went to the island in order to fast. Lent, of course, is a time of fasting and penance, which were both important elements in Francis' spirituality. Penance, for Francis, was an open channel to complete absorption in

God. Fasting helped him curb his appetite for anything not of God, so God alone could fill his heart and his entire being.

Prior to Lent that year, Francis had been preaching in the hilltop city of Cortona, which is not far from the shores of Lake Trasimene. The *Fioretti* tells us that Francis was staying in the home of a devoted friend, when, during the night, he was inspired to spend Lent on an island in the lake. Before dawn on Ash Wednesday, his friend ferried Francis to the island in his small boat. Francis instructed the man not to reveal his whereabouts in order to secure his privacy. He also asked the man to return for him on Holy Thursday so he could spend Easter Sunday with the friars living at Le Celle, the hillside hermitage located outside of Cortona. According to the boatman, Francis took with him to the island two small loaves of bread.

According to a legend still told by the people living on the island (but which can't be found in the Franciscan sources), there was a storm on the day that Francis crossed the lake in his friend's boat, yet he managed to keep a candle alight for the whole trip. Likewise, on the return trip there was another storm, this one of far greater intensity, and according to the legend, Francis calmed the fury of the lake by merely holding up his hand.

The important part of the story has nothing to do with keeping a candle lit in the wind or calming a storm. The heart and soul of the story is the forty days Francis spent in rigorous fasting. Raphael Brown's translation of *The Little Flowers of St. Francis* states that Francis, after being dropped off by his friend,

> went into a very dense thicket in which thorn bushes and small trees had made a sort of little cabin or hut. And he

began to pray and contemplate heavenly things in that place. And he stayed there all through Lent without eating and without drinking, except for half of one of those little loaves of bread. His devoted friend came for him on Holy Thursday, as they had agreed. And of the two loaves, he found one whole and half of the other. It is believed that St. Francis ate the other half out of reverence for the fast of the Blessed Christ, who fasted forty days and forty nights without taking any material food. And so with that half loaf he drove from himself the poison of pride, while according to Christ's example he fasted for forty days and forty nights.

What drew Francis and his brothers to fasting and penance? Murray Bodo, in his book *The Journey and the Dream,* suggested a reason: it was a way for them to "be united with God on a new level of consciousness and understanding." Fr. Bodo goes on to say:

So the pain of detachment was only a means of union. It was a stilling, of quieting everything that would prevent them from hearing that hushed knock of God within. That is why Francis left his father.

Pietro's world, his values and what he lived for, clamored so loud in Francis' ears, he could not hear the Voices in the heart of his real self. That is why he was willing and able to bear the insults and hooting of the citizens of Assisi; he heard a voice within him that was even louder and more real than all the citizenry of the world. That is why he mortified his body when it clamored so loudly for attention that it threatened to drown out the peace of the "Voice" inside. Everything then that he and the brothers had done and suffered was for union with God, who dwelt inside them. They had sacrificed everything that their love might be consummated...

The focal point of the faith and holiness of St. Francis was his love and imitation of Christ. His spirituality grew out of his unconditional love of Christ, whom he believed was tangibly present in all of creation, as well as in Scripture and the Eucharist. His love of Christ was so deep he wanted nothing else but to imitate Christ down to the smallest detail. Francis' faith was nurtured, fed, sustained, and deepened by the word of God and the Eucharist. Francis burned with love for the Eucharist. In his *First Admonition*, St. Francis wrote:

> He shows himself to us in this sacred bread just as he once appeared to his apostles in real flesh. With their own eyes they saw only his flesh, but they believed that he was God, because they contemplated him in the eyes of the spirit. We, too, with our own eyes, see only bread and wine, but we must see further and firmly believe that this is his most holy Body and Blood, living and true.

St. Francis of Assisi experienced the Eucharist as a sacrament of love in which God became his spiritual food. Through the Eucharist, the saint became more intimately united with Christ and the world. He needed the refreshment of love's presence the way his lungs needed air. Nourished by love, Francis was able to love in turn all of creation. As Christ's Body and Blood became one with Francis' body and blood, Francis was able to become Christ to everyone he met. Through the Eucharist, eternity and time, heaven and earth, both became one.

A LITTLE BREAD

The same Jesus Christ who humbled himself at the Incarnation "when he came down from his heavenly throne" continues to do so every day, as Francis emphasizes in his *First Admonition*, for he "comes to us and lets us see him in abjection, when he descends from the bosom of his Father into the hands of the priest at the altar." Francis saw in the Eucharist a continuation of the self-emptying of Christ, which took place not only at his birth but throughout his earthly life. In fact, Francis cannot contain his wonder when he contemplates Christ's continued presence among us in such humility: God in the form of bread!

Francis beautifully expressed his love for the Eucharist in his *Letter to a General Chapter:*

> Our whole being should be seized with fear, the whole world should tremble and heaven rejoice, when Christ the Son of the living God is present on the altar in the hands of the priest. What a wonderful majesty! What stupendous condescension! O sublime humility! O humble sublimity! That the Lord of the whole universe, God and the Son of God, should humble himself like this and hide under the form of a little bread for our salvation.

In the mystery of humility, poverty, and weakness—in the mystery of the Cross—Francis discovered the fullness of love and the omnipotence of God, who lives with us in our condition.

Jesus is sacramentally present in the Eucharist; he is also present, in a different way, in the poor. St. John Chrysostom saw the connection between the presence of Jesus in the Eucharist and his presence in the poor. In a homily on the

Gospel of Matthew, the great saint of the Eastern Church wrote:

> Would you honor the body of Christ? Do not despise Him in His nakedness, that is, in the unclothed poor; do not honor Him here in church clothed in silk vestments, and then pass Him by unclothed and frozen outside.... What is the use of loading Christ's table with gold cups while He Himself is starving? Feed the hungry, and then if you have any money left over spend it on the altar table. Will you make a cup of gold and withhold a cup of water? What use is it to adorn the altar with cloth of gold hangings and deny Christ a coat for His back...Adorn your house if you will, but do not forget your brother in distress. He is a temple of infinitely greater value.

The once visible Christ who walked on earth, while now present in the Eucharist, has existentially passed to the poor, and to all those whom Jesus referred to when he said, "You did it to me." Raniero Cantalamessa, OFM, Cap, in his powerful, little book *Poverty*, makes this clear when he writes:

> The poor person is Jesus, still roaming the world un- recognized, rather like when he appeared in different guises after the resurrection to Mary as a gardener, to the disciples on the road to Emmaus as a traveler, to the apostles on the lake as an expert fisherman standing on the shore—waiting for *their eyes to be opened* with a cry of recognition: "It is the Lord!" If only that same cry of recognition—"It is the Lord!"—could issue from our lips even once, at the sight of a poor person.

St. Francis, who strove to combine radical detachment with loving care of the downtrodden, learned to see the poor person as a living tabernacle of the poor and despised Christ.

THE CRIES OF THE POOR

We pray for our daily bread. Yet for millions of people around the world, their daily bread consists of violence, famine, and destruction. Did God hear our prayer and not theirs? No. God hears the cries of the poor. We do not hear the cries of God asking us to be divine hands tending to the needs of the poor. God took on human form as a vulnerable baby, the child of homeless refugees, who needed human help in the ongoing work of creation. We are God's messengers delivering food and hope to those living with hunger and death.

Around the world, so much of life is so unjustly ordered that it stands in the way of God's hope for humanity. The reign of God, which is a reign of peace, justice, and mercy, is being blocked by the disorder we have created by our indifference to social justice, the plight of the poor, and our lack of mercy. We have suppressed the liberating energies of the gospel and ignored the witness of Mary who, as stated in *Marialis Cultus* (no. 37), is a "promoter of the justice that liberates the oppressed and the charity that succors the needy, but above all active witness to the love that builds Christ in hearts."

When we hear the cries of the oppressed, the cries of the poor, we hear the voice of God. Where there is weakness, there is God. We need to ask God to shatter our complacency, to strip us of our need for comfort. God wants us to be poor; but not poor in the sense that we don't have enough money to buy food or secure housing. The poverty God wishes for us is not monetary poverty. The poverty God wishes for us is that we live a radical dependence upon God alone, willing to respond, like Mary, in purity and fullness to the divine will. To be poor, in God's eyes, is to have the attitude of a servant of the Most High: "I am the servant of the Lord. Let it be done to me as you say" (Luke 1:38).

TO BECOME BROKEN BREAD

Jesus could have done anything he wanted, but chose to be bread meant to be broken and handed out to the hungry. He chose to be a cup of wine poured out for us. And Jesus asks us to do the same thing—to become bread broken for the nourishment of the poor and the hungry, to be like cups poured out in service to others. A little piece of bread, a handful of rice, a cup of clean water, an old pair of pants or frayed shirt of no value, a small coin, a smile or a hug…this is the price of righteousness in the eyes of God.

Part of the Lord's Prayer is a request for the bread we need to sustain life. Even though we work to obtain the bread we need daily, our daily bread is a gift and a grace. For many people, having bread every day is not something they even have to think about or pray for: their cupboards are full. But for countless millions of people, having bread every day is a rarity: they live with hunger, with barren cupboards.

Bread is about relationship. It comes from the earth and from work and is for everyone. The earth produces the grain, we harvest and produce the bread, the bread is distributed, and we give thanks for it and consume it. Bread is meant to be shared, to give life to all. The earth sustains humanity and is in a life-giving relationship with us. We need to respect and protect "our sister, mother earth," as St. Francis so poetically called her, so she can continue to produce our daily bread, bread meant to sustain the benevolence and beauty of the kingdom of God. Our praying for daily bread brings with it an obligation to share the bread. An essential part of eucharistic communion is the obligation to share the Bread of Life. As St. John Chrysostom would say, the sacrament of "one's neighbor" cannot be separated from the sacrament of "the altar." Too often we participate in the sacrament of the altar and easily forget the sacrament of the neighbor.

Part of the eucharistic mystery is the fact that the consecrated bread already contained the sacred before the words of consecration were uttered. Nurtured by the sun and watered by the rain, the unconsecrated bread is the fruit of the earth and the work of human hands. Bread is the gift of God's benevolence, and like all of life, it is therefore sacred and a manifestation of God's presence and love.

Change comes slowly: hunger will not be wiped out in a heartbeat. But if more and more people's hearts beat with love and mercy for the poor, hunger will slowly disappear. Each of us might consider consuming our daily bread in moderation so we can share more of it with those who have none of it.

BITTERNESS AND SWEETNESS

In his book *The Sacred Exercises of the Love of Jesus*, which was published in 1623, a Franciscan friar named Severin Ruberic wrote: "Throughout the entire life of our Seraphic Father St. Francis we see, on the one hand, nothing but the bitterness of sacrifice and penance, and on the other, the sweetness of God's impulses. He began by ridding himself of his possessions and went on to the utter stripping of himself, seeking nothing but God." Three hundred and sixty-four years later, another Franciscan friar, Murray Bodo, said this in his book *The Way of St. Francis*: "A conversion is a turning around, a change of heart; and mortification is the process of saying good-bye to what is not of God, to what is preventing us from experiencing true peace and joy."

The twin pillars of Francis' life were love and abnegation. He knew the bitterness of sacrifice and the sweetness of God's love and mercy. For Francis, the soul's love of God increased in direct proportion to its detachment from and renunciation of its own selfish interests. Love of God covered all his actions, including his extreme acts of abnegation, which he undertook to weed out the roots of self-love and all its carnal inclinations and all-consuming passions that prevent the soul from uniting itself with God.

But love came first. Francis knew that renunciation, either internal or external, had no meaning or merit apart from and without love. Love took possession of Francis, devouring his heart while burning away everything earthly within him. Francis became so riveted to Christ through holy compassion for all creation that he bore on his body the wounds of his crucified love.

Underlining Francis' fasting and acts of mortification, which sound dreadfully harsh to our modern ears, was his belief that it was not possible for him to be interested in himself and interested in God at the same time. Francis knew that God loved him more than he could love himself. And so he made a decision to no longer be concerned about himself or his own needs, but instead, he strove with every fiber of his being to enjoy the delights of God and trust completely that God would take care of him. Francis totally disregarded his own misery and suffering, trusting God would either dispose of it or help him bear it. He gave his full attention to God's all-embracing goodness, finding in God's grasp true joy.

Francis no longer offered incense to vanity or his own satisfaction. His only aim was to please God alone. Fasting and mortification helped Francis die to himself so he could live more fully for God. By renouncing the delights of the world, Francis was not merely engaging in some form of strenuous self-mortification; it had much more to do with the reality that the transient delights of the world had lost their charm for him because the only thing that mattered was God and God alone.

BLESSED ARE THE POOR IN SPIRIT

Francis understood that it was impossible for a soul that still finds some satisfaction in other creatures or in any created thing to completely enjoy a truly deep level of divine intimacy without first emptying itself of everything other than the divine, pruning away every vestige of self-interest, and it was equally clear that the best way to accomplish this was through the mortification of the senses. To be with God meant to abandon everything else. He also knew that mortification of the senses was in and of itself useless, unless it stemmed from the purest of motivations—that is, unity with God, not self-improvement or to avoid the detrimental effects of sin. Listen to the words of St. Francis:

> There are many servants of Christ who are given to prayer, doing good for the sake of others, fasting, and practicing self-denial so as to abstain from sin. And yet they miss the mark. How quickly are you offended, scandalized and stirred to anger by a single word—all because you count it as a personal injury? How quickly are you offended when something you feel is yours is wrongfully denied you? If you find this true, then it simply means

you are not yet "poor in spirit," counting nothing of your own—neither reputation, nor position, nor possession. When you are truly "poor in spirit," you will despise everything that causes you to be selfish and self-centered. Soon you will become so free in God that you take no notice of offenses, no matter how great or slight, so that someone might actually strike you on one cheek and you would not fail to respond in love.

To enter more fully into the presence of God, to experience the divine from moment to moment in even the most mundane things of life, we need to let go of everything that is not of God. As the heart empties itself of everything but God, it inherits the riches promised by Christ to those who are "poor in spirit." The consuming fire of divine mercy that Francis fully experienced created within him a tremendous purity of life that allowed him to see the Creator in every creature.

NO TELEVISION

On the forty-ninth day of my 1997 trip to Italy for the pilgrimage and teaching at the Pontifical Gregorian University, it suddenly dawned on me that it had been nearly two months since I watched any television. I made this comment in my journal: "It seems almost unthinkable to have gone so long without seeing *NYPD Blue, Homicide: Life on the Streets, ER,* or *The CBS Evening News with Dan Rather.* 49 days without CNN, or *Baseball Tonight* on ESPN. Unthinkable."

Yet—amazingly—I didn't miss it.

I think again of the candid observations of the unnamed man traveling across Russia in the 1850s found in *The Way of a Pilgrim,* and how despite his love of God he finds it difficult to spend time with God in prayer. He laments his sloth and is troubled by how eagerly he occupies most of his time with unimportant trifles and does not spend time alone with God.

I can't begin to imagine how many hours I have wasted in front of the television. Taoism suggests that when the mind is wild, the spirit is distracted. The onslaught of images and ideas from both the frivolous programs that pander to our basest instincts and from the commercials that often use sex and empty promises to stimulate sales combine to create a wild mind—wild in the sense of being over-hyped or stimulated. For many people, if not most, television offers a distraction from the cares and pressures of the day. Even though we sit passively in front of the television, the effect it has on us is far from calming. As a Taoist would say, "When the spirit is distracted, it will attach itself to the ten thousand things." Henri J.M. Nouwen said, "Solitude is the furnace of transformation. Without solitude we remain victims of our society and continue to be entangled in the illusions of the false self."

The distracted mind is running wild with things of the world: fame, fortune, passion, possessive love, alcohol and drugs, sex, riches, and out-of-control emotions. Out of this distraction, craving and desire emerge, and the mind is disturbed. The mind is attracted by what it sees, giving birth to cravings, and subsequently the desire to satisfy those cravings. Slowly, the forces of earth become stronger than the forces of heaven. Yet out of our worldly desire and craving, stress and anxiety emerge, and the peace of heaven is hidden. This may all sound oversimplistic, yet out of this notion arises the understanding the saints had of the importance of detachment.

I'm slowly coming to see that detachment is forged in the furnace of solitude. And silence. We need solitude almost as much as we need air, water, and sleep. Yet society's marketing machine claims we need the latest fragrance of perfume or the fastest new car for survival. Detachment frees us from the control of others and introduces us to the indwelling presence of God.

Solitude, by enabling us to be genuinely alone, frees us from the panicked need for acquisitions, approval, and acclaim. From his time alone, St. Francis learned to be prompted not by the opinions of others but by the divine center within him. Walking hand in hand with solitude is simplicity, a virtue exemplified by St. Francis. His simpler lifestyle freed him from the tyranny of striving to be affluent. His solitude fostered a simplicity of heart.

Perhaps prayer has been difficult for me because I enter into it in an agitated state, distracted by thoughts, desires, fears, and anxieties. I find it hard to "let go" and be still, be silent. I'm learning that it is in the silence of the heart that distractions are diffused and the artificiality of modern life crumbles. In order to grow spiritually, I need to feed on a steady diet of silence.

ACTION AND CONTEMPLATION

I still struggle with the question of what to do when I encounter a homeless person. St. Francis spent fully half of his adult life in prayer, in order to find out what God wanted him to do. He left the busy, noisy marketplaces of Assisi and ascended the mountains in search of silence and solitude, where he could better hear the voice of God by deepening the vast reservoir of his prayer life. Nothing distracted St. Francis from prayer; nothing diverted his love from God. Francis emptied his heart, leaving it undivided and available for God alone. "I have done what was mine to do," the saint said near the end of his life, urging his followers to "pray that God shows you what is yours to do."

I don't have the ability or the freedom to help every homeless person I encounter on the streets. However, if my life is sufficiently grounded in prayer, then—and only then—I'll be receptive to promptings from the Lord on how best to respond to a particular situation. Perhaps it might be to give a little money. Perhaps it might be to offer a silent prayer or a reassuring smile. Perhaps God might ask me to volunteer at a soup kitchen. Only in prayer will I find—as St. Francis did—what is mine to do in relationship to the poor and everything else in my life.

St. Francis was unique. He was a mystic and a person of action. His actions flowed out of his contemplation, out of his longing glance at what is real. The word "contemplation" actually means to witness and respond. Thomas Merton, in *Bread in the Wilderness*, reminds us that "the secret of contemplation is the gift of ourselves to God." And when we give ourselves to God in prayer, we begin to experience the richness of divine love and mercy and are better able to share that love and mercy with others. In prayer, St. Francis was free from the complexities of thought (and figuring out what to do), and he discovered the simplicity of his own heart.

St. Francis doesn't let us off the hook. He urges us to pray persistently and indefatigably. But we want an easy spirituality, one that does not demand too much of us. We want to pray, but not for too long or not very hard. Francis did his utmost to follow the scriptural dictum that we pray without ceasing; we dismiss this as impossible or rationalize that it should not be taken literally. For Francis, life without prayer was impossible. Prayer lifted Francis' entire life to a point where his senses and imagination no longer sought external stimulation; his entire being was centered on God. And the light of God chased away all of his inner darkness.

We need to establish constancy and persistence in our prayer life. Unceasing prayer is an essential attribute of the Christian spirit. It helps us live in God continuously, with alertness and affection. We need to exert ourselves in prayer, so our whole life is permeated with prayer. With perseverance, we shall become alive to God, even when walking the dog or taking out the garbage. Prayer is the breath of life. Without prayer, God dies in our hearts. When feelings about God well up within us, we are, in fact, praying. These moments are gifts from God. Words are unimportant.

Our prayer life needs to move from being mechanical and extrinsic to being mystical and intrinsic. Prayer is the natural expression of the friendship that exists between myself and God, a friendship initiated in love by God. A simple heart is a heart where God is. A simple heart is a pure heart, a heart willing to surrender itself to the will of God. The only thing standing between me and God is me. To pray is to humbly surrender your own power. When you enter into prayer, you must leave your self behind. As you diminish, grace will increase.

Contemplation cultivates a spirit of receptivity and a listening heart. To enter fully into silence, we need to drop all preoccupations, being awake only to the presence of the moment.

WHY FRANCIS?

"He lifted the curtain on a human horizon even vaster than Christianity itself, on a universal brotherhood, at once human and cosmic. Francis was one of those men by whom the Gospel suddenly becomes, once more, the Good News for all, the word that establishes humanity." ❋ **ELOI LECLERC, OFM,**
FRANCIS OF ASSISI: RETURN TO THE GOSPEL

In time, we all come to know that the world is often an ugly place, filled with violence and all forms of evil. We far too easily and far too often place personal or national gain above the good of the whole. The beauty and innocence of childhood quickly fade, and we are left with isolation and loneliness. Life is hard, packed with painful experiences and dashed hopes. Suffering visits every life. Some lives know nothing else but suffering.

It is all very confusing, and in the womb of darkness that surrounds so much of life, dreams of another world, a better world, are born. We dream of a world of justice and peace, a utopian world where people live in harmony as brothers and sisters. But this dream, which is common among all people, is not new. In fact, it is a faint memory of something lost long ago. The Old Testament tells us of a paradise known as Eden, where Adam and Eve had everything they needed. Abundance was theirs. But it was not enough. Reaching for more was their original sin. And ours also. In overreaching, paradise was lost—for them and for all of us.

But there was a man so filled with a longing for God that he showed us that Eden was not lost forever, that Eden was simply a way of living. That man was, of course, Francis of Assisi.

But why Francis?

Because in his innocence, Francis talked with birds. We've lost all sense of innocence, replaced by scepticism and doubt. In taming the wolf, Francis confronted the ferocity of evil that was within him and around him. The peace that was within Francis was so real, so genuine, that people believed him when he preached of the importance of personal, social, and political peace. We accept the violence of war as a normal and needed part of life. Sometimes we just need to kill, even though Jesus told us to put down the sword and to love our enemies.

Francis looked at the world we all look at, but he saw it differently. He saw the beauty of creation and the hand of the Creator. Where we might see a sunflower, if we are not too busy, Francis saw not only the flower, but also the love that created the flower, a love that grows best in the divinely fertile soil of harmony and community. And the flower became his sister.

In his new way of seeing and living, Francis overcame his fear of death. With God in his heart as a presence as real as the sun rising above Assisi, Francis rose above all fear, all anxiety. He lived in the moment, as each moment was filled with transformational grace. Francis demonstrated with his life that to be truly free he needed nothing except God. In poverty, he found richness. In his self-emptying of all that was not God, Francis became truly naked, as unashamedly naked as were Adam and Eve before they succumbed to desires beyond God.

Francis showed how the fullness of life is not just a dream or hopeless desire, but something that can be experienced right here, right now, in this very moment. Francis showed us that those rare moments of our life when we are pure, serene, and peaceful are the most genuine, most truthful moments of life, and that these moments echo the essence of paradise we have lost, but can still regain. Francis showed us that it is possible to see the beauty in everything and see the Creator in the creatures.

Why Francis?

Because he came to trust fully in God. This is where we fail. We lack trust in God; we don't believe God will give us all we need, that God will not withhold any good thing.

Perhaps our pride gets in the way of our trusting. Perhaps our love of God has been supplanted by our love of self. Francis takes us back to Eden, back to a time of purity and innocence, a time when beauty and harmony grew in a garden of love.

Why Francis?

Because he followed his heart and his passion for God. He was willing to surrender everything and to become nothing in order to embrace the fullness of God. In doing so, Francis discovered, in his weakness, something truly powerful. This poor man, this humble beggar, changed the course of Christian life and helped us to see the good in everything.

Why Francis?

Why not us? Why not you? Why not me?

THIS UNTUTORED MAN

Thomas à Kempis claimed that "humble self-knowledge is a surer way to God than searching the depths of learning." I think St. Francis would agree. A few years before his death, Francis was preaching in Bologna, and among the crowd gathered to hear him was a man named Thomas, who was an archdeacon from Spoleto. Later, Thomas recorded his impression of Francis and his sermon.

> In that year (1222), on the feast of the Assumption, I saw Francis preach in the public square in front of the public palace...He spoke so well and with such sterling clarity... that the way in which this untutored man developed his subject aroused even among the scholars in the audience an admiration that knew no bounds. Yet, his discourses did not belong to the great genre of sacred eloquence: rather they were harangues. In reality, throughout his

discourse he spoke of the duty of putting an end to hatred and arranging a new treaty of peace.

He was wearing a ragged habit; his whole person seemed insignificant; he did not have an attractive face. But God conferred so much power on his words that they brought back peace in many a Seignorial family torn apart until then by old, cruel, and furious hatreds even to the point of assassinations. The people showed so much respect as they did devotion; men and women flocked to him; it was a question of who would at least touch the fringe of his clothing or who would tear off a piece of his poor habit.

[FROM *THE OMNIBUS OF SOURCES FOR THE LIFE OF ST. FRANCIS*]

There is a lot of information packed into those two paragraphs. I was struck by the physical description of Francis. He looked insignificant. His face was far from attractive. He wore a ragged habit. Slight, ugly, poorly dressed: it sounds as if poor Francis didn't have much going for him. Yet he drew a large crowd and many, including the educated, were moved by his words. In fact, they were so moved, they were compelled to change their behavior. Why? It wasn't his eloquence. In fact, his address was peppered with caustic comments that scorned the failures of the academic community to right society's wrongs. Yet his words were warmly received even by the educated.

When Francis spoke, people listened, because he spoke from experience and he spoke straight from the heart. Contemplation increased the intensity and simplicity of Francis' love for God and all humanity and creation, and this intensity and simplicity infused his preaching. Francis did not present theological formulas. He presented himself, a life changed by a deeply personal encounter with the living God. The people listening to Francis in the public square in Bologna that day in 1222 heard someone real, someone fully alive.

THE GENTLE EXTREMIST

The word that most quickly springs to mind when thinking about St. Francis is *gentle.* Yet such a mild-mannered word is ill-suited to describe a saint who was above all else a hard-nosed extremist. Every major event in Francis' life reveals an extreme interpretation of either the gospel or what he believed was God's will for his life. The middle ground was unknown territory for Francis; for him, it was all or nothing when it came to God. No middle-of-the-road "Golden-mean" Aristotle for Francis. This posture is hard for us, for we strive for moderation, for the middle of the road, and look at the extremists on the far right and far left as crackpots. How was Francis able to be an extremist and still appear reasonable? And gentle, too. This is one of the many riddles of his life.

St. Francis' life was peppered with startling para-doxes, some of which were nicely summarized by Marie Dennis, Joseph Nangle, OFM, Cynthia Moe-Lobeda, and Stuart Taylor in their thoughtful book *St. Francis and the Foolishness of God*: "An enormously free and spontaneous person, he nevertheless adhered faithfully to the institution-al Church; a fully alive human being, he embraced suffering; a true lover, he chose celibacy; born into relative affluence, he practiced a literal poverty." Francis was also passionate, impulsive, extroverted, fun-loving, and poetic; yet, he was also at times moody, mystical, demanding, introspective, and at times even fearful. Yet we think of him as gentle.

When it came to applying the lessons he learned from his literal interpretation of the gospel to his own life, Francis did so with scrupulous exactitude. Consider Jesus' instruction from the Sermon on the Mount that we should "take no care for the morrow." Knowing the importance of planning ahead, a reasonable person, wishing to follow Christ, would look for the underlying principle in Christ's advice and perhaps come to the conclusion that Christ felt it was important to live in the present moment—that "now" was more important than "tomorrow." Different people, different cultures even, could interpret "take no care for the morrow" in different ways, reflecting the richness of the gospel. But no one would come to the conclusion that Christ really meant "take no thought for the morrow" and make a concerted effort not to take any thought for the morrow. No one but Francis, that is. For him, Christ's advice to take no thought for the morrow literally meant just that: take no thought for the morrow, period. With Christ's instruction in mind, Francis told Brother Cook never to put the next day's vegetables or beans or dried peas in water to soak overnight as was the custom, because that simple and practical action was in effect thinking about the morrow.

Is soaking beans for the next day's meal giving too much thought for the morrow? Was Francis just trying, through exaggeration, to make a point? Can anyone today match Francis' unswerving passion for the ideal as expressed in the gospels, or is he just an example for us to try to emulate as best we can? What would happen if the entire world, for just one day, took no thought for the morrow? Francis is not the patron saint of calendar manufacturers.

Francis was a man of immense courage and profound determination. And it took all the courage and determination he could muster to follow the extremely difficult path he had chosen for himself, and he was very harsh with anyone who tried to persuade him to take an easier way. He wasn't content to just follow Christ; he wanted to be, as Celano observed, "conformed in every act with that of the Blessed Lord." It certainly was not easy to accept every recorded word of Christ at face value and scrupulously follow every command, completely disregarding the cost to himself. I know I have neither the courage nor the determination to so literally and completely follow Christ. Just stop for a second and think about the kind of courage and determination it would take to "set out upon the way of total perfection." That was Francis' goal, and nothing short of it would do.

THE SECOND RULE OF ST. FRANCIS

Francis spent a great deal of time and anguish on the writing and ratification of a new rule for the Order. Every serious biography of the saint devotes a significant number of pages to the painful evolution of the new rule. Volumes upon volumes have been written in which the differences between the rule Francis wrote in 1220/1221 and the one that was eventually approved in 1223 are examined and debated. I even devoted five and a half pages of *The Sun & Moon Over Assisi* to the subject, because it illustrated how difficult it was for his followers to live out the ideals of St. Francis and how much anguish he endured over the softening of those ideals. The full story of the process of evolution from the early form of life to the final rule was riddled with politics (often dirty politics).

All religious orders have rules that govern them, and they generally reflect the charism of their founder. In the beginning, the only rule the followers of Francis had—or needed—was the actual life of Francis. But as more and more men joined the little brothers, a need for a more definitive rule increased also. The first rule, which was orally sanctioned by Pope Innocent III, consisted of little more than quotations from Scripture and a few basic regulations deemed necessary for living a holy life. The rule did not survive in its primitive form. In his will (or Testament) written near the end of his life, Francis said the Lord revealed to him the way he and his followers should live: "I had it written in a few words and simply; and the Lord Pope confirmed it for me."

Over the course of the next dozen years, additions to the original rule were made in response to the needs of a rapidly growing Order. For instance, the establishment of fixed residences, the institution of chapter meetings, the formation of provinces and the appointment of provincial ministers, and regulations governing the reading of the Divine Office, the reception of the sacraments, and fasting were all codified. These and other changes eventually crystallized by 1221 into a rule that abounded in scriptural citations and long, pious admonitions. In a chapter meeting in 1220, Francis announced his intentions of writing a new rule, and he held conferences in which the ministers were given a chance to voice their opinions. For instance, Francis wanted the new rule to state that the Holy Spirit was the minister general of the Order, but the motion didn't pass. The chapter agreed on the essential points of the new rule, but left the form and the details to be worked out by Francis at his leisure. But the rule Francis wrote (known as the Rule of 1221 or Regula Prima), which still exists, was never officially recognized because many felt it didn't adequately meet their needs. The ministers of the Order, along with officials at the papal curia, wanted a rule that would present a clear pattern of thought and contain very definite statutes and regulations.

The Rule of 1221 contained 24 chapters, many of which consisted of a series of sweet yet urgent exhortations, such as a call to love all and to have hatred only for one's own vices and failings. The rule lacked precise articles of a code of law. In the rule, which is more pastoral than legislative, Francis sounded like a father urging his children to live a life in perfect conformity with the crucified life of Christ. Chapter 23 amounts to a long prayer of praise and thanksgiving. The prayer mirrors Francis' enthusiasm and fervor for the glory of God and Christ. The rule reveals Francis' belief that disciplinary rules are not needed if a friar has given his heart to God. And Francis can't imagine a friar not doing so; therefore he was quite incapable of incorporating a rigorous code that accounted for the faults and perversity of human weakness. Francis didn't want a detailed code aimed at enforcing his ideal on weaker people, for that ideal is without meaning unless it is openly embraced with love and enthusiasm. The rule didn't meet with universal acceptance. It had too many loopholes and it lacked precision; moreover, its organizational provisions were primitive.

The rift grew deeper between the ministers and brothers who wanted a softening of the primitive rigor of the rule and the partisans of Francis. The meetings were marked with bitterness, anxiety, and even anger. Francis felt some of the followers were being unfaithful to their vocation. He decried the ministers whom he felt were stealing the Order from him.

As the need intensified for a clear, definitive rule officially sanctioned by the Church, Francis began to work on a new rule, one that would take into consideration an order consisting of men who had strong and frequently differing ideas on how they should live. Francis knew that not all the brothers had the same tender attachment to absolute poverty that he clung to so tightly. Seeking solitude, Francis went to the hermitage at Fonte Columbo in the Rieti Valley with Brother Leo and Brother Bonizio, where, after a period of fasting and prayer, he wrote the new rule, which was shorter and better organized than his rule of 1221.

Francis returned to the Porziuncula and submitted his modified rule to Brother Elias, the new minister general. Elias, who had his own plans for the Order, was not pleased with the paucity of concessions Francis had incorporated into his new rule and so he promptly "lost" the manuscript. Without uttering a word of reproach upon hearing that Elias had lost the rule through carelessness, Francis, exercising great patience, returned to the serenity of Fonte Columbo and dictated the rule to Brother Leo for a second time. The new rule was presented at the next chapter meeting, where anguished discussions between Francis and the assembled ministers resulted in a number of modifications. The rule was endorsed by Pope Honorius III in a bull dated November 29, 1223. The Rule of 1223 (also known as "Regula Bullata") has remained in effect ever since.

There is a considerable stylistic difference between the unapproved Rule of 1221 and the approved Rule of 1223, which has led scholars to believe Francis didn't write it. Absent from the new rule was the saint's "simple and sometime awkward and even repetitious style." Instead, we find "an unusual smoothness and even elegance of style." Clearly Cardinal Ugolino, protector of the Order, and Brother Elias had a hand in softening and modifying the uncompromising and intuitive rule composed by Francis. They cleverly left just enough of Francis' spirit in it, but emphasis had shifted to authority and organization. Francis' admonitions to literally follow the gospel were watered down. For instance, the principle of taking nothing for the journey morphed into living as strangers and pilgrims. The rule reflects the belief that Christ's injunctions are just too hard for most people to follow. A full list of the difference between the two rules would go on for pages. Gone are most of the saint's warnings, exhortations, and counsels. Francis had no alternative but to go along with the alterations. After the approval of the Rule of 1223 in Rome, Francis headed for Greccio. It was time for Francis to celebrate Christmas.

CHRISTMAS AT GRECCIO

During the Christmas season in 1223, Francis journeyed to the little village of Greccio in the Rieti Valley, where he spent time alone in a hermit's cave high on a mountain owned by a noble and pious friend. Below the cave was a level space. Francis asked his friend if he could use the space for a midnight Mass, adding that the Mass would be preceded by a pageant he hoped would evoke a vivid memory of the child born in Bethlehem. With his friend's help, Francis mobilized the whole village, and they set to work, clearing the site, cutting torches, making candles, and building a manger scene. A family was chosen to play the roles of Mary, Joseph, and the baby Jesus. Reflecting on the fact that a manger is an animal feed-box, someone suggested that the birth of Jesus must have been witnessed by the oxen, horses, and mules housed in the stable. Mention of animals caused Francis to recall a verse from the prophet Isaiah: "The ox knows its owner, and the donkey knows the manger of its master." And so he procured an ox and an ass to be part of the scene. Because Matthew's gospel mentions soothsayers were in attendance, and Luke's gospel proclaims the presence of shepherds, Francis enlisted the help of some people from the village to represent them.

On Christmas Eve, great crowds of people came, the forest echoed with their voices raised in song, and the night was lit up by hundreds of torches. St. Francis stood before the crib, his heart overflowing with love and compassion, and preached to the people about the birth of the poor king, whom he called the Babe of Bethlehem. Thomas of Celano, in his *First Life of St. Francis*, said that Francis was "filled with a wonderful happiness." He also writes that the priest celebrating the Mass was filled with "such consolation as he had never before known." Thomas of Celano goes on to report:

> The saint of God was clothed with the vestments of the deacon...and he sang the holy Gospel in a sonorous voice. And his voice was a strong voice, a sweet voice, a clear voice....Then he preached to the people standing about, and he spoke charming words concerning the nativity of the poor king and the little town of Bethlehem....His mouth was filled more with sweet affection than sweet words....At length the solemn night celebration was brought to a close, and each one returned to his home with holy joy.

The moving ceremony, designed to rouse the hearts of those weak in faith, clearly demonstrated Francis' creative imagination and helped to popularize the use of a crèche or Christmas crib in the Christian world. But of greater importance, Francis' experience in Greccio tells us something about the depth and resiliency of Francis' faith. He came to Greccio in defeat. The rule he had written, imbued with the gospel, had been "lost" and replaced by a canonically "arranged" rule. Francis knew he had reached the end of the road. Using his imagination instead of words, he wanted to demonstrate the hardships that Jesus endured from his birth just for us. No matter how canonically astute the new rule was, it could not circumvent the fact that God was born poor among the poor. That fact could not be erased. And Francis had no intention of erasing it; he desired only to magnify it.

DOWNWARDLY MOBILE

The gospels gave us the narrative, each adding different details of that night of nights, but it was Francis' devout spirit that gave birth to the picturesque iconography that has come to symbolize the birth of Christ. But over the centuries, the humble Franciscan crib has been supplanted by a comforting, greeting-card sweetness that conceals the true and revolutionary message of the gospels.

On that first Christmas night, in silence and simplicity, God became downwardly mobile, embracing humanity and entering into its suffering with boundless love. The very substance of humanity was placed in an animal feeder-box at birth. A king who would never claim any worldly authority was presented to the outcasts of society. Greeting cards erroneously depict the shepherds as gentle, pastoral men. But, in truth, shepherds were ostracized in that time and place because they were considered to be common thieves who stole animals and illegally allowed their flock to graze on land they did not own. Shepherds were despised in Jewish circles, yet they responded to the birth of Jesus with piety and adoration. The message was clear: God incarnate came to embrace, forgive, and save all people. Francis wanted to fully embrace that message.

From the very beginning, Jesus identified himself with the poor and the rejected, showing us that divine truth and power lies waiting where the world never thinks to look. Seeking the compassionate response of God is the only path to peace.

THE HEART OF ALL REALITY

It's impossible to imagine the creator of the universe voluntarily reducing himself to the helplessness of an infant. It's hard to wrap one's mind around the deep and magnificent meaning of the Incarnation: that God, in a supreme act of self-emptying love, became poor for us, entering fully into our flawed humanity in order that we could have the chance to enter more fully into God's perfect divinity.

Franciscan theology claims that the primary motivation for God's incarnation is God's goodness, not human sinfulness. Francis understood that the Incarnation was a dynamic expression of God's overflowing love and mercy, as well as a revelation of God's poverty and humility. Through the Incarnation we find redemption and completion, making it the heart of all reality. Christmas is a time for us to see more clearly our own poverty and weakness in order to better receive the gift of God's transforming love. Christmas is a time for us to emulate, as best we can, God's love and goodness by sharing the mercy and compassion we have experienced through our lived experience of Christ's birth in the stable of our humble hearts.

MY STUFF

St. Francis compels me to look at my relationship to all the material things in my life. I moved not too long ago, and as I packed I was dumbfounded by just how many possessions I had. I enjoy most of the stuff I own. Some things, such as books, may actually own me, because I can't imagine living without them. Francis makes me take a second look at the very concept of "ownership," suggesting that, in truth, everything belongs to God, who in his infinite love allows me to use them. Adopting that attitude prevents me from guarding what is "mine" and, instead, fills me with a sense of gratitude for the generosity of God who has loaned to me all the things I need. That shift in consciousness lifts a tremendous burden from my heart. Rather than clutching what I own, I enjoy what has been temporarily loaned to me. The books that surround me are God's, not mine. I'm free to enjoy them, and, more important, I'm free to give them away.

Everything is gift. Everything is God's. Francis taught me that I'm to gently hold things in trust, enjoying God's bounty without becoming attached to anything. But it is not always an easy lesson to put into practice. I still do clutch some things tightly, especially my numerous van Gogh prints. A priest friend of mine from Albany, New York, Fr. Peter Young, despite his advanced years, often worked up to sixteen hours a day serving convicts and drug addicts. I was in his home one day, and I mentioned to him how much I loved a beautifully framed icon of the Blessed Mother hanging on his wall. He took it off the wall and handed it to me, saying, "Take it." I hung it back on his wall but I took with me a valuable lesson in love and freedom.

A mutual friend told me a similar story. One day, Fr. Young was driving a drug addict to a counseling session, and the young man complimented him on his hat. The guy was just making conversation. Still, Fr. Young took the hat off and gave it to him. "Gerry," my friend said, "don't ever tell Fr. Young you like anything of his, unless you want it. I've seen him give away coats and gloves he had been wearing. One night, he met a man who was unable to find a job because he had no shoes and was too embarrassed to go for an interview. Fr. Young took off his shoes and gave them to the guy, and then he walked to his car in his stocking feet—and it was snowing at the time, the temperature hovering around zero. Another ex-convict had no car to go to work in, and Fr. Young gave him his car, and then spent the next month driving an old school bus around town until he got another car."

Fr. Young is the freest man I know. He knows everything is a gift, freely given and freely given away. I can only dream of such a spirit of detachment. Today, in his mid-80s, he is still working on behalf of the addicted and homeless, a tireless servant of love. I'm still nowhere near as free as Fr. Young is. Fr. Young exemplifies the beauty of simplicity.

In his book *Thoughts in Solitude,* Thomas Merton writes: "Poverty is the door to freedom...because, finding nothing in ourselves that is a source of hope, we know there is nothing in ourselves worth defending. There is nothing special in ourselves to love. We go out of ourselves therefore to rest in Him in Whom alone is our hope."

After spending nearly twenty years thinking and writing about St. Francis of Assisi, I am still puzzled by poverty. Francis considered poverty to be a basic component of the Christian life. He urged his early followers to "empty" their hearts of all attachment to earthly goods. He saw poverty as a road a person must walk down if he or she is to become transparent to the Lord, to neighbor, and to self. I've got to work out my own response to Francis' ideal of poverty, a vision that has been severely narrowed over the centuries.

Francis was a man of passionate impulses, which was part of his charm. But his simple, unsophisticated approach to life and his literal interpretation of the gospel also caused him to make illogical conclusions that gave birth to questionable obsessions, such as the extremes of self-deprecation, bodily abuse, and the strict observance of poverty. As the fight over the rule indicated, Francis' ideal of poverty didn't last long within the Franciscan Order; the ideal was far too severe and impractical for anyone to follow in its fullness. Even though Francis implored his followers to avoid the temptations of laxity and to preserve the spirit and truth of complete and radical poverty, it wouldn't be fair to say the friars betrayed the ideal, because it was impossible for the fragile idealism of the saint to survive the harsh realities of daily life.

In the pristine and uncompromising absolutism of his ideal of poverty, the saint was able to fully strip himself of all proprietary ambitions. But who else, in either his day or ours, could follow his example, fully and without reservation? Very, very few persons, if any. The standard Francis set was inhuman, far surpassing the limits of sound sense; it even exceeded the poverty that Christ lived. And so, after Francis' death, modification of the ideal was a natural and inevitable consequence, even though some factions refused to compromise and insisted on strict observance of absolute poverty. Still, attempts to reconcile deviations from the ideal caused, and continue to cause, mental strife and distress within the Franciscan family of priests, brothers, sisters, and lay people who have vowed to follow Francis. It distresses me. I wrestle with the implications of Francis' ideal of poverty almost every day. I think Dorothy Day got it exactly right when she wrote: "The mystery of the poor is this: They are Jesus, and what you do for them you do for Him. It is the only way we have of knowing and believing in our love. The mystery of poverty is that by sharing in it, making ourselves poor in giving to others, we increase our knowledge of and belief in love."

THE COLLECTION BASKET

Most of the poor at Santa Catarina de Sena Church in Manaus, Brazil, located in the heart of the Amazon region, don't have any money to place in the collection basket during Mass. But they are still able to give something. While making my film *Embracing the Leper*, I attended Mass at the church on Friday, April 12, 2002. Rather than passing a plate or basket down each pew, two altar servers, both young girls, stood in front of the altar, each holding a wicker basket. The congregation walked up and placed their offering in the basket. A friend whispered to me that those who have no money to give are invited to come to the altar servers and offer themselves in silent prayer. Many did.

I had no money with me. Still, I walked up to one of the little girls who was holding a nearly empty basket. I placed my hands, palms down, over the basket and offered myself to Jesus. The symbolic gesture so moved me, I began to cry as I walked back to my seat. It felt better offering myself than it would have if I had been able to put a $1,000 bill into the basket. I loved the symbolism of the poor being able to offer something of great value—themselves—when they have no money. I later learned that when persons do offer themselves, they pray that God will give them an opportunity to perform an act of kindness after the liturgy has ended.

The poor around the world have taught me a great deal. Over and over again I have been astounded by their generosity, kindness, and mercy to others, more often than not rendered while they themselves were in a state of absolute insufficiency. It is so easy for me to give from my excess, from what I really don't need. But Christ desires that we do much more than simply share our "leftovers." I think Christ truly rejoices when he sees a poor woman in Manaus offering herself when she has no money to give. Even those who drop a small coin in the basket are giving out of their want, and perhaps the coin they drop in the basket is the only coin they have. And yet they give it, or give themselves.

The longer I walk with the poor—and with Jesus—the more I see the need to put to death the idea of my own self-sufficiency. To think of myself as separate from God and all of creation is an illusion. The truth is, I'm totally dependent on God, no matter how much money I have in my pocket.

NUDGING ME TO GO FURTHER

Over the last hundred years, scholars have analyzed Francis' life and his relationship to poverty from every possible angle and have presented conflicting views about the meaning and importance of poverty in the mind of Francis. I'm not sure Francis had a systematic approach to poverty. I doubt his lofty ideal of poverty sprang to his mind fully developed. He grew into it, through real life experiences. He didn't attempt to articulate a highly developed theology of poverty. I don't think his mind worked that way. His thinking was always spontaneous and immediate. He spoke in personal terms, one-on-one with his followers and to people he met along the road. He didn't deal in abstract ideas; his ideas and responses to problems were always very concrete, very real. He did, however, think in images, and it was easy for him to jump from one image to the next. He spoke about real problems—lepers, run-down churches, money—and offered real responses. He often employed simple parables to express himself.

Francis simply wanted his practice of poverty to be a literal representation of the poverty of the gospel. Francis wanted to live a way of life that was a reproduction of the way

Christ lived. No detail of the gospel was too insignificant for Francis to imitate. He did not care if a literal following of the gospel caused him or his followers discomfort or even placed them in danger. For Francis, the observance of poverty was an essential part of the apostolic life. He could not permit himself to be richer than his Beloved. Francis had nothing and loved nothing in this world, so his soul could be free to love Christ alone.

Francis' ideas about poverty were so extreme, so severe, that it comes as no surprise that they were confronted with great difficulties when he asked his followers to put them into practice, causing deep splits in the brotherhood. Disputes over the nature and degree of poverty raged for centuries, especially between the Spiritual and Conventual branches of the Order. In 1317, Pope John XXII entered the fray, issuing a series of bulls that essentially condemned the doctrine of absolute poverty. The practical needs of the friars' communal life were so overwhelming that the ideal of absolute poverty became more devotional then dogmatic.

Francis had one goal: a total and complete imitation of the life of Christ, with special emphasis on Christ's poverty.

Francis' desire to live a life of absolute poverty seems to be too radical a path for any layperson to follow. However, it would be a grave error to discount his love of poverty as something only he could espouse. We may not be able to embrace Lady Poverty as fully as he did, but we must keep his ideal ever before us. The extremes to which Francis went should challenge us to go further down the path of poverty than we would like to travel. The example of Francis should challenge us, upset us, and compel us to respond. I don't want to become any poorer than I already am. I want poverty to remain symbolic in nature, not a reality. I'm happy to have Lady Poverty point out that I could live with less, that I should share more of what I have with those who have even less. But Francis doses not allow me to be happy with my limited love of Lady Poverty. He gently nudges me to go further, to become poorer—in spirit and in flesh. I may not be able to wed Lady Poverty, but I'm happy to have her as a close friend, a friend who cares enough to tell me the hard truth I may not want to hear.

GLORIFYING BANALITY

The deeper I travel into the life of St. Francis of Assisi, the more concerned I become about the state of what passes for popular entertainment these days, especially in film and television. As a culture, we're becoming obsessed with entertainment, and actors are becoming icons of all we admire and hope for. When I began producing soap operas, I had this lofty idea that I was making art. In time, I came to see that the economic, commercial, and editorial constraints of the soap opera genre stifled individual artistic expression and prevented serious exploration of the important issues of life. I wasn't producing art; I was manufacturing a vehicle that delivered commercials. It was all about ratings.

Today, I watch very little television. I simply can't stomach the near-constant diet of banality and triteness served up by television. So little of it uplifts our souls. All too often, most characters are dysfunctional; sex is casual, gratuitous, and self-serving; violence is excessive; and comedy is mean-spirited. Finding an uplifting show is becoming harder and harder. Still, my non-viewing is not rooted in an elitist attitude that says all TV is garbage. My viewing is decreasing because I've come to realize the importance of silence in the spiritual life. Moreover, I no longer have the same need for escapism, which is what TV primarily peddles.

In a country in which the vast majority of people believe in God, it amazes me how we have been so seduced by the power of entertainment that we no longer have the will to simply turn it off. Day in and day out we are drenched by a torrent of words. Words, words, words, but little silence for the Word to reside. We must be still in order to move into a greater union with Christ. We must give Christ our time regularly, day in, day out, coming before him just as we are, wounded and weak. Without silence there is a deep level of our being that is not contributing to our wholeness. We are incomplete without the fruit of silence and solitude. But withdrawal from the endless possibilities for stimulation modern life offers is painful. It takes faith and hope to give God time.

ST. FRANCIS OF BROOKLYN

St. Francis of Assisi delighted in everything he saw, because he saw God's love in everything. Love exaggerates the good in people. I must say that again: *love magnifies the good in people.* And, conversely, hate magnifies the bad in people.

Perhaps there are two ways of seeing: the normal, everyday way, with our physical eyes, and the more rare way, with spiritual eyes. Our physical eyes see things the way they appear, flat, static, and looked at within the natural dimensions of time and space. Our spiritual eyes do not look at things, but through things, and so their vision is charged with a different reality. Francis saw everything through spiritual eyes; this allowed him to see the innocence woven through all persons and things, as though a shaft of sunlight danced over the most common of people and things and made them look radiant. The electronic gadgets of our consumer society do nothing to bring the beauty of a sunset any closer. I imagine it was easier for Francis to take a bold leap of faith than it is for post-modern humankind.

Throughout human history, most people used a combination of religious faith and their understanding of sacred histories and mythologies to help them make sense of the physical world. Rightly or wrongly, they knew how the world worked and understood their part in it, and this gave them a degree of comfort, along with a sense of belonging and security. We, despite the help of technology that can explore the outer reaches of our galaxy and the availability of a mountain of information at our fingertips, have no such understanding. We live isolated, disjointed, incoherent, and impoverished lives in a superficial, fast-paced, fragmented world where confusion, anguish, anxiety, banality, pessimism, and a sense of lack of order prevail.

The collected wisdom of humanity has been shattered into a million little pieces, all being trampled underfoot by people powerless to put them back together again. Not only can we not find the truth, we've come to believe there is no absolute truth to be found. Everything is as true (or false) as everything else. In our eclectic society, values have become relative, and reason has reached its limits. Life in the postmodern world has become meaningless, and we *tweet* our days away saying nothing to everyone.

During the last century, near the middle of which I was born, rationalism had decidedly won its battle with religion; skepticism had triumphed over mysticism. For a long time, I thought this was a good thing. Religion had wielded its bloody sword for far too long, dividing people and stirring up centuries worth of hatred as countless people were ready to kill over inconsequential religious differences. But has

rationalism, in all its triumphal glory, done anything to re-
duce the level of human misery, or has it simply just shifted
the misery around?

Had St. Francis been born in Brooklyn, New York, in
1950, could he have scaled the heights of faith as he did?
Or would it have been impossible for him to let go of that
rational, critical, analytical side of the modern "self" and
simply live as spontaneously and unreflectively as he did
in thirteenth-century Assisi? Would Francis of Brooklyn
have possessed a sadly too sophisticated realization of the
mythical metaphor as a metaphor, making full participation
in the metaphor virtually impossible? Could he have taken
the words he read in the Bible to be the literal truth? I think
each of those questions would have to be answered in the
negative. Our Western, scientific worldview diminishes the
existence of non-physical realities, thereby making it impossible to examine something that isn't real, isn't able to be
quantified, poked, and probed. That, I think, is a tragedy:
the stillborn child of rationalism.

St. Francis' awareness of God came from his deep awareness of himself, where he discovered that God was the very
ground of his being. This awareness of his true self fostered
a greater awareness of God within others, including all of
nature, which in turn filled him with a profound sense of
reverence for all he saw. St. Francis personalized and sanctified all of creation, including inanimate creation, and so he
could no longer treat things as things. The sun, the moon,
the stars, the trees, the birds all became his brothers and
sisters, members of his family, and as such he was able to
speak to them lovingly. From a rationalist point of view, this
was very foolish. From a spiritual or mystical point of view,
it was profoundly wise.

In the midst of his solidarity with the poor, St. Francis of Assisi made time for solitude in order to pay attention to his inner life. The health of our interior life rests upon our attentiveness. We need to be able to truly pay attention in order to hear the wordless voice of God that is continually drawing us into Oneness. To be attentive, we need to be awake and alert to the boundless grace of the present moment, the eternal now. Our lives have become so splintered, divided among so many responsibilities, so many demands upon our time, that most of us feel frazzled and fatigued. So much of modern technology, designed to make things easier for us, has in fact increased the things that tug for our attention. The Internet, cell phones, laptop computers, Blackberries, iPods, iPads, and the ever-expanding world of cable television all squeeze every ounce of stillness and silence out of life. Life has become a blur, a whirling dervish of enticements and anxieties. Entering into our interior life, where we can encounter the love and mercy of God, is becoming increasingly more difficult.

For me, writing has become a sacramental avenue into that interior empty space where the fullness of God resides. The very act of writing demands attentiveness. Simone Weil claimed that all study and serious reading, with its required concentrated focus, was in essence an excellent preparation for prayer. The Buddhist road to enlightenment is paved with attentiveness. Thomas Merton's dance with Buddhism helped him embrace a freer, more experimental form of writing. His thoughts flowed out onto the page in clear, simple words that expressed the openness of his heart and spirit. It also helped him see the entire world in a more positive light. It seems that Buddhist meditation practices drew him into a deeper silence, which helped him to be more aware of his true self. Merton's interior journey helped him affirm and deepen his Christian understanding that (as he wrote) "Christ alone is the way." And the way of Christ is all-embracing love and peace.

The human heart is drawn to God. The language of the heart is love. Not soft, wimpy, fleeting, Hollywood-style love, but a bold, deep, penetrating love that requires openness and transformation, a love that perpetually gives itself away. We live in a world of hearts. Sadly, most hearts are broken, unloved, and unable to love. God wants to give us new hearts, mystical hearts throbbing to love and to be loved. If you can imagine a world of divinely transformed hearts, you will see a world at peace, a world of plenty where no one goes hungry. Such a world begins within each of us, if we are able to shake off the countless distractions of modern life and pay attention to the silent voice of God.

Prayer is the only weapon we need. Prayer helps us flee from the storm of inner thoughts and the noise that engulfs modern life. Prayer slows down the frenzied pace of life. Prayer quiets negative passions. Prayer helps restore our awareness of God. Prayer is an act of humility, stemming from a mindfulness of our inadequacy. Prayer and humility go hand in hand: prayer deepens humility and humility deepens prayer. Prayer creates the unruffled calmness required to encounter God. To neglect prayer is to neglect God. Prayer helps you see the extraordinary hidden in the ordinary. Prayer should lead us to wholeness and simplicity. Prayer prompts us to reach out in compassion to the suffering and weak, and helps us embrace all of humanity. Prayer is the breath of life, the sunrise of the soul.

WAS THAT JESUS?

"When you see a poor person, you are looking at a mirror of the Lord and his poor mother. So, too, in the sick you are contemplating the kind of infirmities he took upon himself for us." ❊ **ST. FRANCIS OF ASSISI**

In September 1998, I was in Rome to teach a short course on film writing and directing at the Pontifical Gregorian University. One day, in the midst of a pleasant stroll through the heart of Rome, I witnessed a startling and very distressing sight.

The incident took place a few blocks from the Franciscan friary of Sant' Isidoro where I was staying. I had just purchased a train ticket to Assisi and was walking back to the friary. As I reached the corner of via L. Bissolati and via S. Basilio, I looked to the right and was jarred by the sight of an old, homeless woman defecating on the sidewalk. It was obvious that she was suffering from diarrhea. Not to mention embarrassment. She was holding her worn, tattered skirt tightly around her waist, leaving her exposed—totally naked—from the waist down. Her legs were slightly spread apart, helplessly waiting for the attack of diarrhea to end. I took in this sickening sight in a flash, then quickly turned my head away and crossed the street.

When I reached the opposite curb, I stopped and looked back. It was beyond sad. I didn't know what to think or feel. The situation was made worse by three young men who walked by and taunted her, laughing at her deplorable situation. Within two minutes, she was able to move on. But before doing so, she gingerly walked to a nearby trash can, still clutching her skirt about her waist, and rummaged through the can for a piece of newspaper, which she used to awkwardly wipe herself off.

I was totally overwhelmed and confused by what I had seen. I stood motionless as she walked away and slowly disappeared in the urban landscape.

Was that Jesus?

Later in the day, I was sitting alone in the Basilica dei Santi Dodici Apostoli (a church run by Conventual friars) wondering, thinking, and praying. Oh, how we long to find God in some moment of spiritual ecstasy, looking for the divine in some spectacular or extraordinary event. Yet God comes to us, if we are to believe—fully believe—what Scripture says, in a humble disguise, in unexpected places. God comes to us poor, hungry, thirsty, diseased, imprisoned, alone, and lonely. God comes to us in an old woman forced to use a public street for a toilet. God comes to us in people, places, and ways that make it difficult for us to see him or receive him. We don't find God where we expect or want to find him. A few days later, I composed this heartfelt prayer:

Lord, I have often prayed to be able to see you, hear you, touch you, and know you where you really are, yet when I do see you in a lowly, dirty, perhaps crazy person living on the street, I don't know how to respond. Teach me, I beg you, what to do. Knowing you are in the poor is one thing; knowing how to embrace you in the poor is a much more difficult matter. Open my heart to know how to respond the next time I see you defecating or urinating on the street. Help me share the wonders of your love... in the squalor of life.

The words of Raniero Cantalamessa, OFM, Cap, who was

the preacher to the papal household, echo in my head: "We do not fully welcome Christ if we are not ready to welcome the poor person with whom He identified Himself." This is really the core message of Pope Francis.

AN UNCLUTTERED HEART

Francis was no stranger to the suffering Messiah, but as you will read in Part V, for him the wounds of Christ became portals to the unfathomable love of God. Francis' love of God embodied the principle of unity that embraces the multiplicity of creation. Love of the Creator made Francis love all creation and creatures. Francis had a purity of heart that allowed him to embrace chastely the entire universe. In contrast, the impure (of whom I count myself) embrace things lustfully. Purity of heart, for Francis, had nothing to do with sex; it was simply a manifestation of an uncluttered heart. Jesus alone was enough for Francis, and this reality in his life freed him from all the complications that entangle most humans; and the fruit of this freedom was true simplicity. Everything that Francis did flowed from the purity of his heart, which strived only to give glory to and be in union with Jesus.

In his wonderful book *The Ladder of the Beatitudes*, Jim Forest keenly observes: "Mercy is inseparable from purity of heart. What is purity of heart? A heart free of possessiveness, a heart capable of mourning, a loving heart, an undivided heart." Francis' heart was eventually free from all distractions, worries, and ambitions; this freedom allowed him to see the good in everyone and everything. In his mystical eyes, nothing was impure.

PART V

The Stigmata

LAVERNA

In May 1213, Francis and Brother Leo were preaching in
the Marches when they came across a small village that
was busy preparing a banquet celebration to honor a
count who had been made a knight. Francis and Leo entered the courtyard of the castle of Montefeltro and climbed
on a low wall and began to preach. Slowly, Francis' eloquence
began to draw a crowd, who listened and were spellbound by
his words. His effusive tenderness so touched their hearts that
it must have felt as if Christ was in their presence. One of the
guests at the castle was a rich count who was deeply moved
by the impromptu sermon. He asked to speak privately with
Francis. After their conversation the count told Francis he

owned a mountain called La Verna, which was located just over the Tuscan border, and that it was a perfect spot for a hermitage; he wanted to give Francis the mountain.

Today, La Verna stands next only to Assisi as a Franciscan shrine. Even to the skeptical, its history seems directed by destiny. It is an Apennine summit, a heap of tumbled rock standing 4,160 feet above the Casentino Valley. It has been called an altar raised in the very heart of central Italy. St. Teresa of Ávila called it a great castle of the soul. It was at La Verna, on September 14, 1224, on the feast day of the Exaltation of the Cross, that Francis lay in one of the rocky interstices of the mountain caves and received the stigmata.

According to tradition (or more accurately, according to local folklore), the deep, dramatic rifts and chasms in the mountain at La Verna are the result of an earthquake that took place at the time of the death of Jesus. At the place formed (even if only poetically or piously) by Calvary, Francis was going to endure the sufferings of Calvary. For Francis, the road to Christ began with a crucifix speaking to him, and it ended with his being embraced by the cross.

THE WOUNDS OF CHRIST

Francis had great devotion for Mary, Queen of Heaven, and for the Archangel Michael. In his day, many people observed a special fast in honor of Mary and Michael. The fast, known as Angel's Lent, lasted from the feast of the Assumption on August 15 until the feast of St. Michael on September 29. As fall 1224 approached, Francis wanted to spend Angel's Lent on Mount La Verna, and so he and seven brothers (Leo, Angelo, Masseo, Rufino, Silvestro, Illuminato, and Bonizio) traveled to the remote hermitage. They walked north across Umbria and Tuscany through valleys bursting with grapes.

They walked through villages and forests, over hills, and along the banks of the Tiber River. They traveled in their usual manner, keeping silence and stopping only to say the Divine Office at the prescribed hours. At day's end, hungry and thirsty, they begged for scraps of bread while seeking the lodging the Lord had prepared for them, sometimes sleeping in abandoned churches. It was a lengthy trip, covering more than 75 miles, and by the time they reached the foot of the mountain, Francis was far too weak for the steep climb to the summit.

Seeing how exhausted Francis was, the brothers borrowed a donkey from a peasant farmer. The farmer came out to meet Francis and warned him to take care to be as good in reality as he was in the stories people told of him, because so many had put their trust in his preaching. It was a bold, almost insulting admonishment. Francis loved it. Being told by a peasant to be what people thought he was moved the saint to get down on his knees and kiss the poor farmer's feet. Francis humbly thanked the man for reminding him of his responsibility to live as he preached.

Francis mounted the donkey, and the brothers began their trek up the mountain. The farmer walked with them, but he soon grew weary because of the stifling heat. He told Francis he was dying of thirst. Francis got off the donkey, knelt down, and prayed. As he prayed, the brothers saw a spring of water bubbling up near a rock. After refreshing themselves, they continued their tortuous ascent. Upon reaching the hermitage, Francis told the brothers that he believed his death was approaching. He wished to be alone with God so he could lament his sins. He said Brother Leo could bring him a little bread and water, when he felt prompted to do so, but he wanted no other disturbances. It's a good thing he didn't have a cell phone. He blessed them and retreated to his hut, apart from the other huts, under a beech tree.

As Francis entered deeply into the solitude of the mountain, he was troubled about the future direction of the Order. Many in the community disagreed with him. They wanted buildings and complex rules. Many brothers no longer loved Lady Poverty; some openly questioned his efforts at peacemaking. Francis believed he had failed and the Order would not survive. He wanted to be alone. As he prayed in a rocky crevice under a great overhanging stone, he committed his fraternity into the hands of God, in essence giving back to God what God had given to him.

When Brother Leo visited his hut to give him some bread and water, Francis asked his friend to randomly open the gospel in three places and read whatever passages his eyes fell upon. All three times, Leo opened to accounts of Christ's passion on the cross. Francis took this as an indication that his remaining days on earth would be filled with suffering, and he resigned himself to fully accepting God's will.

That night Francis was unable to sleep. As he lay on his hard bed, an angel appeared to him in a vision, saying he would soothe Francis' restless spirit by playing the violin the way it was played before the throne of God in heaven. The angel gently moved the bow across the strings just once, but that was enough to fill Francis with unimaginable joy and sweetness. Francis was approaching a kind of all-transforming union with God that only a few mystics have experienced. He was being submerged in a fathomless fountain of happiness.

Francis moved to a secluded spot on the far side of a deep ravine by crawling across a large, fallen tree. He spent the next few days in almost continual prayer, becoming fully absorbed in God. He begged God to show him the way in which God desired him to walk for the remainder of his life. He declared himself entirely submissive and ready to endure any anguish of mind or any bodily torture; one thing only he asked, that the divine will might be manifested to him.

The days and nights of deep solitude rolled by in a haze of prayer. Before dawn on the feast of the Exaltation of the Holy Cross, Francis surrendered himself to the fading darkness of night. He pleaded with God to allow him to experience the suffering of the crucified Christ. He prayed, "Lord God, I beg you to give me the grace to feel within my being the same love for all of humanity that your Son felt. But also, Lord, grant me the additional grace to feel in my own body the same dreadful pain and passion Jesus felt when he died for my sins."

Francis knelt silently in prayer, his gaze fixed upon the night sky. He was never more alone and never closer to God. The wind whistled through the mountains and the branches of the trees quivered as an inner flame began to transform him into the likeness of the crucified Christ. While Francis was lost in ecstasy, his hands began to bleed. At first just a trickle, then more forcefully. His feet also began to bleed. Francis remained motionless. Finally, blood gushed from his side, soaking his frayed habit.

The next morning, out of humility, Francis tried to hide the wounds from the brothers, but the blood had soaked through his habit, and his wounded feet made it impossible for him to walk, so Francis could not conceal what had happened. The brothers took turns nursing him and washing his clothes. But only Brother Leo was permitted to see and swathe the saint's wounds. The brothers knew something wonderful and mysterious had happened. The stigmatization caused great joy to spread across the hermitage. On the feast of St. Michael the Archangel, Francis asked Leo to bring him some parchment and a pen. Francis wrote a litany of praise to God. When Francis handed the parchment back to Leo, the brother feared that Francis loved God so much now that he would no longer love him. Francis sensed what Leo was feeling, and so he took the parchment back, turned it over and wrote the blessing of Aaron from the Book of Numbers for Leo: "The Lord bless you and keep you. The Lord show his face to you and have mercy on you. May the Lord turn his countenance to you and give you peace."

On September 30, Francis rode a donkey down Mount La Verna for the last time. He slowly made his way back to Assisi. Along the way, as he passed through many towns, crowds rushed to greet him, hoping to kiss his hand. They chanted *Ecco il Santo*—"Here comes the saint." But Francis was oblivious to their veneration. As they traveled, they encountered early snows, but even the bitter cold that penetrated his threadbare habit did not seem to disturb the saint, whose heart and soul were still transfixed by the beauty and pain he experienced on Mount La Verna. And amazingly, after a short rest in the town of his birth, the merchant's son set out on yet another missionary trip to the surrounding towns.

EMBRACED BY THE CROSS

For me, the issue of the stigmata was a thorny one at first. I was surprised to learn that some Franciscan friars actually doubted that Francis received the physical wounds of the crucified Christ on his own body. I went to La Verna the first time as a skeptic. I left fully believing that it happened.

Francis was the first person in history to experience the

phenomenon of the stigmata, but we know very little of his experience because of his silence on the subject. Today, some accept the miracle of the stigmata; some don't. And there is no use trying to intellectualize or explain one's belief or skepticism.

Francis desired nothing else but to follow Christ, and Christ ended up being nailed to a cross. The great Spanish mystic St. John of the Cross said: "One who does not seek the Cross of Jesus is not seeking the glory of Jesus." Francis wanted nothing else, and because of his faithfulness it seems truly possible that God granted him the desire of his heart. Regardless of the veracity of the incident, should we not all be desirous of sharing in the suffering of Christ, even if we are too frightened of the pain to ask for the wounds to be visited upon us the way Francis did? Entering into the experience of the stigmata forces me to more closely look at the passion and death of Christ. In doing so, I better understand the depth of Christ's love—and the shallowness of mine.

The stigmata of St. Francis forces us to look at the unity between the sensory world of creation and the unseen world of the spirit. The stigmata was an external, physical manifestation of Francis' interior spiritual harmony with Christ. Francis' inner identification with Christ was made visible through the stigmata, and his body itself became a prophetic statement that humans can truly become like Christ through total immersion into his suffering. Francis so completely entered into the humanity of Christ that the wounds of Christ became the best and most natural way for God to sanction his experience.

For Francis, the road to Christ began with a crucifix speaking to him, and it ended with his being embraced in an experience of the cross. Francis experienced the immanence of God in his flesh. The stigmata says the Incarnation is not only a divine event that broke through history, but a human possibility that can break through our lives. Francis always takes us further than we want to go. Further in poverty and further in love. With the stigmata, he takes us further into the mystery of salvation. Don't try to understand the stigmata of St. Francis; simply enter into it and allow it to deepen your faith.

For Francis, the stigmata seemed inevitable, even if it had never happened before during the history of Christianity. Francis had the simplicity and originality to want what no one ever dreamed of: to experience the pain and suffering of Christ in order to better feel the depths of the Savior's love. At La Verna, Francis was crucified and transformed. It was his destiny.

The stigmata lifts Francis out of the birdbath by shattering our romantic notions about him being a gentle, warm friend of the birds. Of course, this animal-loving image of Francis is the one we hold dearest because that Francis helps us think we can be happy without giving of ourselves; that love demands no sacrifice. The image of Francis bleeding from the wounds imprinted in his flesh tells us a different story: the story of salvation won through the agony of the cross. Francis did not spend his time avoiding suffering; rather, he embraced it fully because by the suffering and death of Jesus, we have won the promise of the resurrection.

Talking to birds is easy; dying to self is hard. Francis did both.

THE LIVING DEATH OF THE CROSS

St. Francis came to realize that an unrestrained appetite for power, money, and pleasure fragments the soul, causing our lives to be too divided and cluttered to find the true peace and joy that can only be found in loving and serving God above all else. Francis understood that—on the cross, through grace—reconciliation and union with God became possible. He would urge us to live the paschal mystery—to enter the living death of the cross.

But we have a way of getting in our own way. We give in to pride, avarice, lust, anger, and envy all too easily. Francis—poor, simple Francis—told us how to get out of our own way: "Do not look to life outside, for that of the spirit is better."

Francis listened to the word of God, and the light of grace penetrated to the incandescent center of his being. His spirit responded to the word's freedom by a corresponding readiness to not only continue to listen but also accept and follow.

The life of St. Francis of Assisi dramatically illustrates how the detached heart knows the fullness of peace, joy, and freedom, and sees the face of God illuminated in all of creation. Those who struggle for their daily bread can offer great insight to those of us who struggle to go deeper into our spiritual lives. The road to mystical consciousness is paved with an acceptance of our natural state of exodus, acceptance of the reality of human misery, and acceptance of our limitations and fragility. The poor know about these things. And the humanity of Christ illuminated the vulnerable character of human nature.

Over the last dozen years as I made my poverty films, I've came to see that an awareness of oppression and a struggle for justice are integral to genuine mysticism. The all-embracing Christ invites us to be with him, so that he, through us, can be with all people.

We are all migrants. As people of faith, we are migrants going from sin to grace, from earth to heaven, from death to life. Our migration is grounded in our belief that God first migrated to us in the person of Jesus and that, through Jesus, we are called to migrate to God. If migration worked itself into the self-definition of all human beings, we would not be as threatened by migrants as we often are; instead, we would see in them not only a reflection of ourselves but of Christ, who loves us.

POOR, SIMPLE FRANCIS

The deeper I dig into Francis' life, the richer it becomes. But it also becomes more complex. No, that's not right. It becomes more simple, and in that simplicity it becomes more complicated. Not for Francis, but for those who follow him. Francis is not easy to follow, because he goes places we would prefer not visiting. Places such as poverty and penance. Which raises the issues of how poor and how much penance.

From the time Francis handed over the leadership of the Order to Peter Cantani, there has been a great debate over the Order's direction and charism. The debate wasn't always courteous or even orderly. In fact, it rarely was. There was shouting and name-calling, deep rifts and division. After Francis' death, the Order splintered into various factions. The divisions still exist. The First Order of Friars Minor consists of three separate groups: The Friars Minor (OFM), the Conventuals (OFM, Conv), and the Capuchins (OFM, Cap).

The history of the Order is as messy as all histories of human endeavor are wont to be. As I read about the debates over the rule, the role of poverty, and the Order's mission, I began to lose sight of Francis. He was simple—or rather, his way of following the Christ was simple: do what the gospel says. And he did. Literally, exuberantly, and totally.

When I first read a history of the Order covering the period just before the saint's death to the splintering of the Order in the years after his death, I often felt confused and a bit overwhelmed by all the arguments on how to follow Francis, how best to live a Franciscan life. Is "poverty" poverty or a metaphor? Should friars teach or preach? Serve or study? How do you blend contemplation and action?

I thought about my struggles with faith, the battles between belief and unbelief that raged within me for so many years. Religion was riddled with absurdities. Atheism was laced with desperation. I found no answer to the problem of evil and suffering in the world. I alternated between belief that the world was created by God and the belief that the world was nothing more than a chemical accident. At times, the model of self offered by Christ, namely, self-abnegation, charity before anger, passivity before action, and not caring about tomorrow, seemed desirable but impossible to follow. At other times, the way of Christ, the way of the cross, seemed like a disgusting ritual of self-punishing sacrifice demanded by a masochistic God. Yet, without the support of some kind of metaphysical hydraulics, life seemed hopeless.

Somehow poor, simple Francis knew that study, education, and the pursuit of knowledge, if pursued to a greater degree than prayer and piety, would eventually lead to nothing but confusion and doubt.

Francis—poor, simple Francis—understood: the cross was all the education he needed. Thanks to St. Francis of Assisi and God's unmerited grace, today I know peace.

A LIFE OF ONENESS

In January 2012, I spent two weeks in Kenya making a film for Jesuit Refugee Service, a world-wide ministry serving both refugees living isolated lives in remote, massive refugee camps, and refugees living marginalized lives in the bleak, lonely shadows of urban centers. JRS is a ministry of being with refugees rather than doing for refugees. In the eyes of JRS, refugees are all God in exile. Their sole mission is to accompany and serve refugees and to advocate on their behalf.

In Eastern Africa, countless refugees are left outside the circle of life; they are shunned, disempowered, ignored, and forgotten. They are desperate people fleeing hunger and violence in such drought-stricken and conflict-riddled nations as Somalia. They live in huge, secluded, overcrowded refugee camps. The film, titled *We Anoint Their Wounds*, featured the Kakuma Refugee Camp in northwest Kenya. Surrounded by endless miles of harsh, unforgiving desert, the camp is home to 95,000 refugees.

Under the burning heat in Kakuma, life is direct and raw. To be a refugee means to live on the edge of society, socially and politically ostracized. Around the world there are more than fifty million people who have been forcibly displaced, and eighty percent of them are women and children. Like all humans, refugees want to live productive lives, and life in refugee camps is very stifling. Moreover, life in the camps is very harsh and can be intimidating and unsafe. Some camps are rife with instances of sexual and gender-based violence, as well as tribal violence. Some camps lack adequate health care and educational opportunities. Life in the camps can also mean prolonged periods of unproductive, enforced idleness that can trigger a host of social problems such as violence, crime, substance abuse, and depression.

The film also explored the harsh, hidden, and solitary lives of refugees who fled the camps and are living in the shadows of Nairobi, the capital of Kenya. Many refugees live in massive slums. I filmed in a dismal and dispiriting slum known as Kibera, which is considered to be one of the largest, and perhaps most wretched, slums in all of Africa. Estimates vary, but perhaps as many as a half-million people live in the massive Kibera slum. It has been estimated that the total number of people living in all of the slums of Nairobi might be as high as two million.

The extremely high rate of unemployment in Kibera often leads men into crime, which often lands them in prison. After a frustrating and unproductive day of looking for work, or, if they are lucky, after a long day of hard work, usually earning under two dollars a day, many men end up in illegal drinking dens consuming a potent, home-brewed alcohol. Most of the kids in the Kibera slum depend upon their mothers for survival. Many babies are born in unsanitary mud huts without any medical assistance. It's a rare day when there is enough food for a mother and her children. Most children rarely advance beyond a grammar-school education. Many uneducated teenage girls face the dreadful choice between an early, unwanted marriage or working in the sex trade. And if all of that wasn't bad enough, virtually no one in Kibera has a toilet in their home. There are so few public toilets in the slum that each privately owned toilet is used by at least a hundred people.

In order to survive, some refugees have no other option than picking through the rotting waste of garbage dumps, desperately searching for food to eat and recyclable items they can sell. To be a refugee is to live a life of fatigue and long journeys. It's a draining, dreary life, filled with fear and anxiety. For many it can be a life of constant uncertainty and unbearable physical and emotional suffering. For the most part, it's a life of being ignored and scorned. Refugees are often greeted with deaf ears and hard hearts, forced to face a wall of indifference. To be a refugee is to endure a life of mental anguish, a life of being unwanted and unloved.

As I pondered the hardships of the life of a refugee during my time in Kenya, I began to put their experience into a clearer perspective and to connect their pain to my vastly different American life. In America, I sense that within many people there is a great spiritual hunger. Even in our perilously seductive culture and despite the apparent abundance that surrounds so much of modern life, many people sense that something vital is missing. But this hunger for something deeper is often temporarily satiated by superficial nourishment, often in the form of mindless entertainment and exotic vacations that are merely distractions from our true hunger. We avoid pain and we either numb or stimulate ourselves with nonsense. Television is a weapon of mass distraction.

The mystics of all religions have this spiritual ability to live with the darkness and not knowing that surrounds so much of life in all its complex uncertainty and swirling chaos. But more important, within that darkness they live in an unshakeable joy that can only come from a deep and profound encounter with the living God. This great encounter quiets them in a manner beyond even their understanding.

The true joy we all seek is always present, and the source of that joy is not separate from us but is within us, a very part of our being. That source, of course, is God. And God is always offering the grace we need to become aware that we already possess all that we need and that God wishes nothing else than for us to realize that what we think is the gap between humanity and divinity does not actually exist.

When we connect with the oneness of God, we will know

joy even in the darkness. This is the new life that Christ wants us to embrace, a life of Oneness and true joy, a life that embraces all of creation, even the leper, and sees everything as a brother and sister, even the sun and the moon. We are all brothers and sisters. We are all connected. The ideal of compassion is based on a keen awareness of the interdependence of all living things. God wills the fullness of life and love for everyone, not just a select few. Jesus came to give good news to the poor and to offer a communion of love to every human being. God wants our help in creating social and economic justice, ensuring food, shelter, jobs, and humane living conditions for all.

Around the world, poverty is choking people to death. Jesus established the kingdom of God based on the Jubilee principles of the Old Testament. These principles called for a political, economic, and spiritual revolution in response to human need. Jesus intended nothing less than an actual revolution, with debts forgiven, slaves set free, and land returned to the poor. Of course, this revolution threatened the vested interests of the powerful and therefore put Jesus on the road to Calvary.

Human need—be it physical, emotional, spiritual, or social—was Jesus' reason for being—and it should be ours as well. Christ wants us to respond to the suffering that torments the poor. Jesus wants a new social order where human lives are dignified with justice, uplifted in compassion, and nurtured by peace. The ever-increasing world of violence that threatens us all can only be defeated by love, by the reaching out of a hand in a moment of darkness. Compassion is the most effective response to hatred and violence.

Because of the birth, life, death, and resurrection of Jesus Christ, we know that every birth, every life, and every death matters to God, and must matter to us. In the face and presence of the poor we can learn to see the face and presence of Christ. God is at home among the poor. Jesus was born in the midst of their poverty and rejection.

Like the poor and oppressed, Jesus was despised and rejected. Like the poor and oppressed, Jesus was hungry and discouraged. Jesus did not come as a royal ruler, as king of the universe. He was born into poverty and lived among the poor. He was an outcast, living among outcasts, living among people with no privilege or rights. His message was so radical, so unsettling, he was quickly put to death for threatening to turn the established power structure upside down.

Poverty gives birth to hunger and despair. Poverty means one bad thing after another. Worse, poverty often also means death. Francis would tell us that death by poverty blasphemes the reign of life proclaimed by Christ. Nowhere in the gospels do we hear Jesus ranting about a person's moral behavior; his focus was solely on liberating people from all forms of oppression. And that is precisely what Jesuit Refugee Service is devoted to doing: to liberate refugees from the oppression that forced them into exile.

THE PAIN OF REJECTION

One the deepest pains humans experience is the pain of rejection, the pain of feeling nobody wants you. Rejection gives rise to tension, fear, isolation, and a terrible anguish. This inner pain destroys inner peace. One of the most effective ways of beginning to see beauty within the pain of rejection is through genuine communion. To be in communion with someone means to be with them. In communion we discover we actually belong together, and truly need each other. Communion means accepting another just as they are, with all their warts and baggage, all their imperfections and weaknesses, in all their pain and need.

Communion does not mean doing something for someone. It means being with someone; it means showing someone their own beauty and value. In communion, we give each other the gift of the freedom to grow. Communion's main enemy is elitism, and seeds of elitism are within all of us. Elitism is at the heart of apartheid and every form of racism.

St. Francis would encourage us to bring the beautiful gift of communion to the refugees and the poor of the world. He would urge us to work to create a society that is founded on welcome and respect, embracing the most vulnerable among us, a society free of frontiers, divisions, and forced displacement, a world where the value of hospitality is extended to everyone.

POVERTY AND PRAYER

"God waits like a beggar who stands motionless and silent before someone who will perhaps give him a piece of bread. Time is that waiting. Time is God's waiting for us as a beggar for our love." ✱ **SIMONE WEIL**

In modern-day, consumer-driven America, we continually feel the need for the accumulation of goods and security. We have ignored what God has put in our hearts to do: love one another. Instead, we are being consumed by consuming, reaching the point where there is no way out. We have deceived ourselves into thinking we can follow Christ without becoming one with the poor, that we can know and love God without loving others, and not just friends and family and those who love us back! Jesus says that's easy; even unbelievers do that. Christ calls us to a different, deeper kind of love: a love for the unlovable, for those who cannot give back, even for our enemies. Christ said that at the end of our lives that is the litmus test we all will face.

When it comes to those living in dire poverty, we seem to tinker around the edges in our efforts to relieve their suffering, offering little more than speculative comments from afar. We might be willing to give some spare change, but we are not willing to change how we live, to live more simply. I sense within people a fatigue of compassion. The need is so great that our humble efforts to help seem woefully inadequate. It's easy to think one person can't make a difference.

I know, deep down and with conviction, that one person can make a difference in the lives of many. I've seen it and filmed it, over and over again—in Peru, Brazil, Mexico, El Salvador, the Philippines, Kenya, Uganda, Jamaica, Haiti and in Detroit, Philadelphia, Los Angeles, and San Francisco. But the levels of poverty and suffering I've seen, especially in the war-torn north of Uganda and the earthquake-ravaged city of Port-au-Prince, Haiti, distresses me so much that I struggle to resist becoming depressed, of feeling that it is all hopeless, that the unthinkable suffering endured by countless millions will never end because of our stunning and callous indifference.

One of my films has this very tough, demanding thought: "Consuming more than you need is stealing from those in need." My films are known for those types of challenging statements, such as this one, which is even harder: "Christ is not asking for your spare change (in response to the poor); he is asking for your very life." I wrote those lines; living them is another story. Even though it is still a struggle at times, I must be on guard not to confuse the necessities of life with what is luxurious. The humble simplicity that embodies poverty of spirit stands in stark contrast with the frenetic pursuit of comfort, power, pleasure, and riches that permeate a society that prizes possessions as a good in itself.

The emptiness we feel stems from not realizing we are made for communion with God. If we are not growing toward unity with God, then we are growing apart from God. We need to bring to Christ what we are so that in time we become what he is. I believe personal wholeness is attained when we achieve freedom from the greedy tendencies of the ego and its insatiable hunger for possessiveness. Yet I struggle with how to be empty, how to be willing to lose myself in order to enter into a deep and rich communion with others.

Each of us needs to escape from the distorting influences of society by checkering our lives with periodic periods of solitude. Again, only solitude allows us to reconnect with the truth of our own nature and our relationship with God. This is where true, fulfilling joy lies. In the book of Genesis we read the story of creation—how God took six days to create the universe and then rested on the seventh day. The metaphorical point of the story is that we need to rest, to literally stop, every seventh day in order to fully appreciate creation and connect with the loving force that brought us and the entire universe into existence. Likewise, the Islamic proverb states: "The hen does not lay eggs in the marketplace." We can't connect with God, ourselves, or others if we are in perpetual motion.

No one can see the depths of their own poverty. Without words or thoughts, I must force myself to stand naked before God. Only then can I learn to say truthfully: "Blessed are those who know that they are poor." Coming face-to-face with my own total poverty is the only way to come face-to-face with God and find true enlightenment. We are all beggars. None of us is sufficient unto herself or himself. All of us are plagued by unending doubts and restless, unsatisfied hearts. By ourselves, we are incomplete. Our needs are always beyond our capacities, and we only find ourselves when we lose ourselves. Prayer and contemplation free us from our self-serving tendencies and prepare us to lead lives of service to others without unconsciously desiring our own success.

We live in a world of stark inequality and injustice. So did Jesus. Jesus had a deep concern for those who suffered and were marginalized. So should we. For followers of Jesus, compassion is not an option; it's an obligation—and a sign our lives have been transformed into the healing presence of Christ.

As I studied the lives of the saints, I was drawn more to those saints whose lives reflected a love of both prayer and the poor. Poverty and prayer, for me, are the perfect match, and the perfect path to God. On his life's journey, St. Francis of Assisi took his own path. He made mistakes; and some of his actions were rather irrational. Some of his ideas were outrageous. One can easily imagine him as difficult to be with, at times being downright ornery. But no matter his mood, no matter what people thought of him, he kept his focus on God. This is our challenge.

St. Francis said the road to God is straight and narrow: the road is poverty and prayer. Far too often, I go to God with my hands full and ask for more. Francis was willing to go to God with empty hands. For him, the only thing that really mattered was utter trust in God; his adult life was a continual witness to the realization that total trust cannot exist until we have lost all self-trust and are rooted in poverty. The deepest levels of self-denial that St. Francis reached present us with a huge gap in comparison to our feeble efforts at approaching perfect trust in God. What is it that keeps me from total surrender into the loving embrace of God? I know what God seeks, yet I hesitate. I know God loves me, and this love, I realize, does not spring from a reluctant heart; God stands always willing and waiting to love us even more deeply...yet we hesitate in accepting God's love out of fear of losing ourselves and being buried in God.

The only way to overcome this fear and grow in trust in and love of God is through a serious commitment to prayer. In poverty, St. Francis found a way into prayer. Nothing was more important to him than spending time in prayer. Prayer is about building a relationship with the source of love. For St. Francis, prayer was the way to learn how to live love.

I've been walking in the footsteps of St. Francis for nearly twenty years, and I'm only now beginning to see, albeit dimly, the connection Francis made between poverty and prayer. Contemplation leads to communion: communion with God, communion with each other and all creation. Contemplation leads to action, action that manifests and makes real God's mercy and compassion. Contemplation and poverty are natural partners. Contemplation helps us to see both inside us and around us. Our contemplative vision improves as our lives become more simplified. Our lives are cluttered with so much stuff, and we are so easily distracted by so many things, that our spiritual vision is severely diminished.

We live in a thick fog of materialism and escapism. Poverty and simplicity help us see what is important; they help us see another's need; they help us see injustice and suffering; they help us see the need to be free from all attachments that limit our freedom and ability to love. We strive to amass wealth, but true wealth resides in creating fraternity. The world is divided into two camps: the rich and the poor. And between those two camps there is no communication, no shared life, no communion. The rich and the poor are strangers, and their mutual isolation gives birth to misunderstanding and mistrust. And the gap between the rich and the poor grows wider and deeper by the hour. Jesus condemned the unnatural and unjust division between the rich and the poor, because the division causes pride, envy, jealousy, self-centeredness, and loneliness. The kingdom of God, Jesus tells us, is about unity, reconciliation, harmony, peace, and love.

Contemplation and communion lead to action; they call us to the margins of society, to the American urban jungles of deprivation, crime, and violence, to the dark corners around the world where people live in massive slums of overwhelming need, clinging to life without clean water or electricity and barely enough food for survival. In these deprived places, we not only give life, but life is also given to us. It is here we see for the first time the oneness that has always been there, though obscured by our blindness.

Through contemplation we learn to see. Through communion we learn to share. Through action we learn to love. Be still. Know God. Live love.

LOOKING FOR JESUS

If you are looking for Jesus, you'll find him everywhere, because he is at home with all of creation and all of humanity. But you'll most certainly find him in the midst of those who are being crucified, rejected, alienated, and oppressed. He is in the dark corners of your neighborhood, waiting for you to help him. When you stand shoulder-to-shoulder with the poorest of the poor, you will certainly encounter Christ, and you might even begin to experience the richness of his resurrection.

Francis chose poverty as his bride because he wanted to imitate Christ. And Christ himself not only embraced poverty by becoming human, being born in the poverty of a stable as the son of a poor woman, but Christ also embodied God's love of the poor, a love that is reflected in countless Old Testament verses. God transformed poverty—willingly chosen for the sake of others—into a thing of splendor. Poverty taught Francis how to love more perfectly. Lady Poverty is a real flesh-and-blood person, living within the destitute and rejected, bestowing royal dignity upon the poorest of the poor. Francis passionately embraced that which Christ embraced. In a stable in Bethlehem and on a cross at Calvary, Jesus freely embraced poverty, freely endured humiliation and suffering. Francis constantly reminded his brothers that Jesus gave up the riches of heaven and became poor for us, and out of a love of Christ the friars have chosen the path of poverty.

INTIMACY WITH JESUS

While Francis respected the ecclesiastical hierarchy, as well as the priesthood, he harbored no hint of clericalism. Nor did he engage any moralizing claims. Francis believed that to point a finger at others would put him in a position of superiority, which was in direct opposition to his path of *minoritas* and humility. Francis never received any clerical education, nor did he study any theology. He was unfamiliar with the world of scholastic study and university culture; he had no idea of hermeneutical principles of biblical study. He simply read Scripture with his entire being, his mind, heart, and soul. Without a Bible of his own, he only heard the words of Scripture that were proclaimed during Mass. Francis probably had access to various collections of psalms and Scripture passages, but probably never the entire Bible. He loved the psalms and the New Testament, especially the three synoptic gospels. Francis had a kind of patchwork knowledge of Scripture that he effectively used to communicate his own internal experience of God and his own life of poverty. Francis rejected any form of intellectual advancement. Francis preferred the simplicity of living in fidelity to the Spirit that he believed was animating him. He aspired to living in a relationship of intimacy with Jesus and nothing more. He did so through a dynamic and joyful asceticism that recognized God within everyone. Failures and humiliations did not bother him in the least; in fact, they were direct channels to God. He desired to unite himself with the suffering and most despised members of society. Compassion became his trademark. Penance, peace, and reconciliation were his top priorities. Francis was a prophet who still speaks to our day and age.

PART VI

The Canticle

THE POETIC SUMMATION

After that momentous day at La Verna when the wounds of Christ were manifested on his own flesh, St. Francis' strength continued to diminish. From then until his death, his life became increasingly more interior. In the spring of 1225 Francis was in the midst of the most painful period of his life. He had been very sick for months, forced to live in a hut hastily constructed in the garden at San Damiano, where St. Clare and her sisters cared for him. He was back where it all began, just a few feet from where he first heard Christ invite him to restore the church that was in ruin. Now, it was poor Francis laying in ruin. He was completely blind, and his body was so racked with pain that he had hardly slept for nearly two months. The wounds from the stigmata bled constantly.

Almost twenty years after his conversion, Francis was in the eventide of his life; exhausted by fasting and illness, he was in the twilight of his final agony. His suffering must have pushed him to the limits of his endurance. Worse than his physical suffering must have been the suffering of his soul. Eloi Leclerc, modern son of Francis, a Franciscan friar and priest who suffered greatly at the hands of the Nazis, writes, "The evangelical values of pure simplicity, poverty, and peace that were, in his eyes, so essential to the revelation of divine Love, had been shunted aside in a Christendom engrossed by power and ruled by the idea of crusades. They were even questioned by his own followers."

Rather than curse the darkness that enveloped him, Francis cried out to God, pleading for mercy. He cried out, "Lord, help me in my infirmities, so that I may have the strength to bear them patiently." In his poverty and pain, Francis heard good news, a voice proclaiming that he should be glad because his sufferings could not compare to the immeasurable treasure awaiting him in heaven. Francis was instantly filled with joy, as if a brilliantly bright sun had risen in the darkness of his soul. Being a poet and a lover of song, Francis responded to the vision trumpeted by the voice with a poem that was meant to be sung. He knew his time and mission on earth were nearing an end, and now he was reassured that his lifelong dream of seeing his Creator in paradise was going to be fulfilled, that his way of suffering with Christ on earth was truly a way to the resurrected and risen Christ in heaven, and he wanted to sing for joy a poem of gladness for all the world to hear. Here is that poem, an inspired prayer of thanksgiving from the tender heart that continually thanked God for all living things.

THE CANTICLE OF BROTHER SUN

Most high, all-powerful, all-good, Lord!
     All praise is yours, all glory, all honor
     And all Blessing
To you alone, Most High, do they belong.
     No mortal lips are worthy
To pronounce your name.
All praise be yours, my Lord,
     through all that you have made,
And first my lord Brother Sun
Who brings the day; and light you give through him.
     How beautiful is he, how radiant in all his splendor!
     Of you, Most High, he bears the likeness.
All praise be yours, my Lord,
     through Sister Moon and Stars;
In the heavens you have made them,
     bright and precious and fair.

All praise be yours, my Lord, through Brothers Wind
     and Air, And fair and stormy,
     all the weather's moods,
By which you cherish all that you have made.
All praise be yours, my Lord, through Sister Water,
     So useful, lowly, precious and pure.
All praise be yours, my Lord, through Brother Fire,
     Through whom you brighten up the night.
How beautiful is he, how gay!
     Full of power and strength.
All praise be yours, my Lord, through Sister Earth, our
     mother, Who feeds us in her sovereignty

and produces
Various fruits with colored flowers and herbs.
All praise be yours, my Lord, through those who grant
    pardon For love of you; through those who endure
Sickness and trial.
Happy those who endure in peace,
By you, Most High, they will be crowned.
All praise be yours, my Lord, through Sister Death,
    From whose embrace no mortal can escape.
Woe to those who die in mortal sin!
    Happy those She finds doing your will!
    The second death can do no harm to them.
Praise and bless my Lord, and give him thanks,
    And serve him with great humility.

Francis composed the portion of *The Canticle* up to the verses about pardon and peace in the garden of the Poor Clares' convent at San Damiano. His body was disintegrating. He was blind and unable to enjoy the beauty of nature. Though his spirit was housed in a broken, dying body, it was able to sing a hymn of adoration to all of creation. He later added the last portion of *The Canticle*, which stresses forgiveness, suffering, and endurance, after learning about the bitter feud between the bishop and mayor of Assisi. He then had two friars sing the longer version of *The Canticle* at a meeting he arranged between the bishop and the mayor. During the meeting the two men set aside their grievances and peace was restored.

By means of his inner purity, Francis had evolved into a being who could see the goodness of God in every person he met. In Francis' eyes God's goodness shimmered through all of creation and inspired him to compose a great symphony of praise to the Creator.

It has taken humanity many centuries just to feebly see how we are threatening to destroy the world through our careless and often violent acts stemming from our total disregard of the sacred nature of all of creation. We thoughtlessly pollute our air and water; moreover, many of us, blinded by thirst for power, deny that we are hurting the very environment that sustains all of us. But at long last, Francis' penetrating love for all of creation is beginning to be emulated by more and more people, and they worry that the natural world is slowly being destroyed by the greed of people who are blind to the connectedness of all of creation.

Francis was not some tree-hugging guy dripping with Hallmark greeting card sentimentality. In creation, he saw the hand of the Creator. He knew that humanity was dependent upon the splendor of the world, and therefore it should cause us to give praise to God for gifting us with what we needed for our physical, emotional, and spiritual survival. The world was created by God, therefore it is good and deserves to be honored and protected. When we see the divinity within creation and within each other, we have no other choice but to turn away from our selfishness and reject all forms of violence. *The Canticle* sings of Francis' love for God, whose beauty is reflected in all of creation.

In *The Way of St. Francis*, my friend Murray Bodo, OFM, writes:

> *The Canticle of Brother Sun* is a sublime articulation of the secret of Francis' life: you integrate the depths of the self by leaving self and entering into what you can see and hear and touch and feel and smell. God dwells "deep down in things" [Gerard Manley Hopkins] and you find

Him when He finds you loving the world He has created and redeemed.

In *The Canticle of Brother Sun*, which today has come to be called *The Canticle of the Creatures*, Francis is telling us that all of creation is united with God the creator of all, and that the essence of that union is best expressed and fully realized in a spirit of fraternity in which all of creation forms an unseen oneness.

The Canticle reveals Francis' dexterity as a poet. Out of his silent contemplation flowed skillfully composed works that shimmered with creativity and color. Written in the dialect of the Umbrian people, *The Canticle* is generally considered to be the earliest example of lyric poetry in the Italian language; some even claim it to be the true historical source of Western nature poetry. His heart had become so immersed in prayer that even in the darkness of intense physical suffering Francis was nonetheless able to express extraordinary joy and profound gratitude for the limitless love of God. *The Canticle* is an inspired hymn of praise and thanksgiving. As Paul M. Allen and Joan deRis Allen wrote in their book *Francis of Assisi's Canticle of the Creatures:*

> In the text of the Italian original, the word "per" (through) is repeated frequently, but is often overlooked by translators of the canticle into the English language, when in a number of instances the word "for" is used instead of "through." This, however, alters a most fundamental point which Francis wished to express in the canticle—namely, that all creation is the means through which God himself is "praised and glorified"—not that God is to be praised and thanked "for" all things created by him. Therefore

not only the sun, moon, stars, and the four elements, but even forgiveness, suffering, and death are shown to be the means by which the creator is "honored and blessed."

In his silent contemplation of the beauties of nature during his solitary walks through the fields of the valley below Assisi...and in the Umbrian forests on the slopes of Mount Subasio, Francis' heart opened again and again to behold all that surrounded him in the sky above, the creations of nature around him, and the ground beneath his feet. In all this he experienced the tones of a true symphony of gratitude to God, the creator of all.

Thus it was abundantly clear to Francis that the whole of nature is the means "through" which God is eternally being glorified.

Simone Weil, who besides being attracted to both Buddhism and mystical Christianity, spoke out against injustice and sided with the oppressed prior to her death at 34 in 1943. She admired the sheer beauty of St. Francis' *Canticle* because it so eloquently expressed his attitude of grateful dependency on all things as gifts of God. In her book *Waiting for God,* Weil writes:

> The example of St. Francis shows how great a place the beauty of the world can have in Christian thought. Not only is his actual poem perfect poetry, but his life was perfect poetry in action. His very choice of places for solitary retreats or for the foundations of his convents was in itself the most beautiful poetry in action. Vagabondage and poverty were poetry for him; he stripped himself naked in order to have immediate contact with the beauty of the world. [NEW YORK: G.P. PUTNAM'S SONS, 1951]

In his book *A Window on the Mystery of Faith: Mystical Umbria Enlivened by the Eucharist,* Fr. Michael L. Gaudoin-Parker offers the following observation on Simone Weil's thoughts on St. Francis:

> Such a phrase as "immediate contact with the beauty of the world," that Weil exalts, catches the sublime symbolism of Francis' own imagery of a bride or spouse to express the Christian value he discovered in poverty. Only by experiencing and acknowledging his nakedness before God—in every sense of "being naked"—did this man know himself: not only as vulnerable, defenseless, and ridiculous in his pride, but as great too. For in his nakedness, and in no other condition, did he see that every human being is great because he is sought by God—as is brought out again and again in the Scriptures.

Francis' poetry, as well as his life, grew out of his love of poverty, which helped him penetrate the mystery of God-incarnate.

In his book *The Canticle of the Creatures: Symbols of Union,* Fr. Eloi Leclerc, OFM, says it is impossible to understand *The Canticle* properly "unless we directly relate it to Francis' innermost experience, his bitter suffering, his heroic patience, his daily struggle for evangelical values, and his supernatural joy, or in a word, to his life of intimacy with Christ. *The Canticle* springs from existential depths. It is the end result and surely the supreme expression of a whole life."

Even though Francis could no longer see or enjoy the beauty of creation, even though he could no longer see other creatures, even though his eyes were so diseased that they couldn't even be exposed to the light of a fire let alone the glorious light of the sun, he was still able to express his innermost joy through material things, through the sun, the moon, and the stars, through the wind and air, through water and fire, through the flowers and herbs and all of earth, and he could do so only because all of nature was being illuminated from within. For Francis, the sacred had electrified the cosmos and the cosmos was manifested within him. For Francis, there could never be a separation between the Creator and the creation. His deep experience of God in creation enabled the saint to enter into communion with all of creation, including the lonely and lost souls struggling for survival and self-worth on the margins of the social life of Assisi. In Christ, Francis saw God's humility and willingness to become lowly. Francis' interior life and external life slowly became a synthesis of love. *The Canticle* is both his praise of the cosmos and a hymn to his inner depths.

Paul's epistle to the Ephesians states: "God has given us the wisdom to understand fully the mystery." The key to that wisdom has eluded me. Perhaps Francis, with his ability to embrace all of creation as the glory of God, combined with his ability to let go of everything within himself that allowed him to simultaneously discover his true self and to experience the presence of God, found the key to that wisdom.

I hunger for that kind of wisdom.

If St. Francis could walk among us today, I think he would be horrified at what he would see. He would tell us, in a firm but gentle prophetic voice, that if we wanted to truly love our neighbor, we would have to curtail consuming so much for ourselves. He would be shocked to see how so many things that we accept as a normal part of life—everything from cars, to air travel, to our excessive use of plastics and accepted use of genetically modified food—are in effect destroying creation and in the process betraying God. He would point out that our self-centered ways of life are endangering the Earth's regenerative capacities. He would be mystified by how we have banished God from the public square, how we have so casually accepted the reality of widespread, crippling poverty, and how we see nothing wrong with the unbridled accumulation of private wealth. He would point out our moral imperative to resist structural evil. He would urge us to sing in harmony his *Canticle* and to live the wisdom it contains.

THE BEAUTY OF ALL LIFE

Francis knew that God's love is universal. It is for all. We need to recognize the inalienable dignity of every human being, regardless of race, religion, or nationality. The inclusivity of the gospel requires us to love everyone, especially those living on the margins of society, the poor, the outcasts, the neglected, and the abandoned. We need to make ourselves poor with the poor, to identify with their misery, their grief, their sickness, and even their death. Only then will the poor feel loved and, as a result, strengthened. Only when we enter into this kind of relationship with the poor is it possible for them and others to detect the divine-human solidarity of the God-Man, Christ, with all men and women. Our lives need to reflect the reality that God gave us as gifts to each other. As we grow in compassion, we are able to see more clearly the beauty of all life, and we also increase our desire to transform everything ugly into something beautiful.

Love of God requires us to take a stance of gentleness, reverence, and respect in our attitude toward all other beings. We especially need to cultivate respectful and gentle mindfulness of the needs of the poor. Prayer and charity are soulmates. Charity is the art of knowing how to do the will of God. In prayer, we learn what to do, how to respond to the poor, the persecuted, and the suffering. And it is prayer that sustains and guides what we do for them. Action is as important as prayer; each of us must take responsibility for meeting the world's need, for we are the accomplices of evil if we do nothing to prevent it.

MEMBERS OF HIS FAMILY

Francis gradually developed an ever-deepening attitude of reverence and respect for all of creation. He personalized the whole of creation, seeing the sun, the moon, the trees, the birds, the animals as his brothers and sisters. They were members of his family, and he spoke with them in the most intimate and lovely fashion.

Of course, from our rationalist point of view, it seems, at first blush, to be silly to preach to birds. But from the point of view of a mystic, Francis' dialogue with all of creation was profoundly wise and sanctifying at the same time. By personalizing creation, Francis was able to put aside his adult prejudices and he became like a little child; in the process he discovered a little sliver of the kingdom of heaven.

Spacious, sweeping landscapes have a spiritual dimension to them. They are open-air cathedrals. Vast, unspoiled landscapes are sacred places, spiritual spaces. They are sacramental, healing, unifying—and very real. They echo the landscape within. Christ is radically present in the entire universe as its ultimate fulfillment. In creation we contemplate a manifestation of God's face, of God's presence—and our souls are set afire with charity for all of creation, leading us to embrace the whole world, a world deformed by sin yet transfigured by grace.

Nature has the power to awaken the soul. On the wings of a hummingbird my spirit flies to an awareness of the sacred. An incredibly beautiful world lies silently all around us all of the time, and it remains unseen, a lost paradise, until some quiet miracle opens our eyes and we see everything afresh. By grace, seeing deeply into a flower or a weather-beaten old barn or even the tormented face of a homeless person, we catch a glimpse of Paradise, a vestige of God. Through creation we can pick up the footprint of God. Beauty is a vestige of God. God made the flower, and your reaction to it picks up a vestige of God. Listen to the silence of nature and you will hear a symphony singing the praises of God. We do not need to run and catch God; we need to stop running and be caught by God.

The One who has always been is always present. We are the ones too busy to be present to God's presence. The frenzied pace of life today easily leaves us feeling disoriented and unbalanced. The crush of time and competition has nearly squeezed contemplation out of existence. Without regular periods of stillness and contemplation, we are doomed. Simplicity is the key to unraveling the complexities of modern life.

In the sea of dysfunction and destruction that engulfs so much of modern life, there is an island where hope abounds, a sacred space that nurtures the soul. That island has a name: prayer. Intimacy with God grows freely on this island. Because so much of life distracts us from Life, we must guard against the onslaught of distractions our culture hurls at us each day. We need to incorporate structured time for spiritual reading and reflection.

SUNFLOWERS AND GRASSHOPPERS

"The beauty of the world is Christ's tender smile for us, coming through matter." ❋ **SIMONE WEIL**

By any honest measure, planet Earth is in trouble, perhaps even in peril. Many think the fate of humanity is precarious. The Earth can't sustain the unbridled greed and misguided philosophy of individualism by so many. At the root of our common problem is a rampant spirit of disconnectedness. The survival of our fragile planet, our home, depends upon our ability to rediscover the connectedness of all life. Every particle of nature is attached to the rest of creation. Even the least thing affects everything. When one part of creation is hurting, all of creation is hurting.

We are abusing creation, plundering its resources; the earth is crying and dying, because of our failure to see the solidarity of all life. Our spirit of individualism separates us from each other and all of creation. We have become the center of the universe. It is all about "me." And that self-centered attitude gave us our current economic disaster.

St. Francis of Assisi was not self-centered. He was God-centered, which means he was also creation-centered, seeing all life as his brother or sister, seeing all life as connected by virtue of the fact that God created everything, permeates everything, is the Father and Mother of all, of the sunflower and the grasshopper. In Chapter 40 of the Book of Isaiah we read: "Who measured the waters in the hallow of his hand and marked off the heavens with a span, enclosed the dust of the earth in a measure and weighed the mountains in scales and the hills in balance?" The sixth-century BC Jewish prophet Isaiah saw God as a supreme landscape artist, carefully designing a garden of delights to support, sustain, and entertain all of life. By God's divine hand a mountain rose here and a lake formed there. With dirt below and sky above our home sprung from nothing and contained everything.

But it was not enough for us. We wanted more. Much more. We wanted to rule—ourselves, each other, all of creation. We wanted to be God. In the scope of the massive and magnificent creation, the poet-prophet Isaiah saw us mighty, all-powerful humans as mere grasshoppers. Funny, yet insightful. If only we had acted like grasshoppers, as little slivers of life, instead of acting like lords, dominating all of life. St. Francis saw himself with humble eyes, no better than a lowly worm. He also saw himself with exalted eyes as a son of God and hence connected to and equal with all of creation, a delicately interwoven tapestry of wonder and awe, lovingly stitched together by the Master Weaver.

If we don't recapture our original connectedness, if we don't return to the garden of paradise, we are doomed. We are slowly killing the poor and the weak. We are slowly destroying planet Earth. We need to recapture a sense of awe and wonder; we need to look at the night sky in all its vastness and beauty and say with the poet who penned Psalm 8: "I see your handiwork in the heavens: the moon and stars you set in place. What is humankind that you remember them, the human race that you care for them?" The psalmist knew that God entrusted the beauty and bounty of creation to us, to sustain us. God laid all of creation at our feet and gave us dominion over it. But instead of safeguarding this priceless treasure, we choose to dominate and abuse it.

St. Francis of Assisi understood that the earth belongs to God and that God let us be temporarily in charge of creation. We betrayed that trust. Lord have mercy. St. Francis would say it is not too late. God is a God of hope, a God of mercy.

Turn back. Love life, all of life. Give praise and thanksgiving to the author and sustainer of life—God our Father and Mother—by embracing and protecting all of life, even the lives of our enemies. St. Francis knew we are one, and he wished we would sing in unison a song of praise.

There was a holy fire that burned within Francis that transformed every encounter he had into a living experience of spirit and life. Francis so cleansed the window of his own perception that everything he saw appeared as it truly is— infinite. He saw things in their native purity. The windows of our perceptions are dirtied by our own self-interest. I'm guilty of not seeing things as they are, but how they affect me. Mystics like Francis, schooled in self-simplification, humility, contemplation, and detachment, are able to brush aside all obstacles blocking their ability to see the hidden reality of the invisible in all things visible. For them, there is no separation between heaven and earth, between the sacred and the profane, and the whole of creation is holy and open to God.

PART VII

The
Transitus

THE LAST DAYS

In summer 1225, Francis, suffering from a severe eye ailment, traveled on foot from Assisi to Reiti. He had been ordered by a cardinal to be treated there by the pope's ophthalmologist. He wore special shoes the nuns at San Damiano had made for him to walk more comfortably on his stigmatized feet. Before arriving in Reiti, Francis stopped at the home of a poor priest near Poggio Bustone. News of his presence at the priest's home caused a crowd of people to surround the priest's humble residence. In the field next to the church was a small vineyard that was the tiny parish's main source of income. The crush of people trying to catch a glimpse of Francis trampled on the grapes, destroying most of them.

And the grapes they didn't destroy, they ate. Francis knew the priest was upset because the vineyard's normal yield of thirteen barrels of wine was lost. Francis told the priest to allow the people to eat the grapes out of the love of God, and that God would reward him with a harvest greater than normal. The priest put his trust in Francis' promise of divine help and allowed the people to remain in the vineyard and eat the grapes. When it was time to harvest the grapes, they produced twenty barrels of wine.

By the time Francis reached Reiti, his eyes had deteriorated to the point where he could hardly distinguish light from dark. The physicians decided his condition was so bad that they had to resort to a very drastic method of treatment. At the time, it was believed that applying red-hot irons to the temples surrounding the eyes could relieve problems such as ophthalmia, a condition causing a severe inflammation of the eyeball. The procedure was performed without an anesthetic at the hermitage of Fontecolombo, not far from Rieti. The doctors placed the cauteries into a fire until they glowed. It was a moment of sheer terror. As the incandescent iron drew near his eyes, Francis said, "Brother Fire, God has given you a splendor that has made you the envy of all creation. You are the most noble and useful of all creatures. Be kind and courteous to me, and temper your heat so that I am able to endure your burning caress." With that prayer, the terror Francis had felt riddling his body melted away. The brothers gathered in the room could not endure the awful sound of his flesh hissing as it was touched by the burning irons. They fled the room. Francis did not even flinch. When the physicians completed the treatment, Francis told them they could do it again—"cook it more"—if they needed to, because he had not felt a thing. The treatment no doubt increased the faith of the doctor, but it had no effect on Francis' eyesight.

From then on, Francis' life was a painful, downhill road to death. He spent the following winter in a hermitage north of Siena, where the milder weather and companionship made his pain more bearable. In spring 1226, following a night when he hemorrhaged badly, Francis was transported to the hermitage of Le Celle outside of Cortona. The brothers took two habits and two cloaks for the dying saint, which they continually changed and cleaned to conceal the flow of blood from the stigmata, which Francis wanted hidden from the world. His condition was deteriorating rapidly. His legs and feet were now swelling, and he was unable to retain food. He endured pains in his spleen and liver. His stomach was swollen. He vomited blood.

Francis was wasting away from tuberculosis. The end was near, and Francis had only one wish: to see Assisi before he died. Before leaving, he told the friars to always love Lady Poverty.

SISTER DEATH

Because of the increasing esteem for Francis' holiness, the friars transporting him back to Assisi feared that the people of Perugia might try to seize the dying saint (who was a living relic), in order to lay claim to his bodily remains after his death, and so they took a rather circuitous route, walking beneath a scorching summer sun. For Francis, the road became his *via dolorosa*. He was in unbearable pain. Sister Death was waiting to embrace him.

Fearing the Porziuncula was too unprotected, they elected to bring Francis to the bishop's residence. As they approached the city walls, news of the dying saint's return spread through Assisi like a wild fire. As evening approached, they processed slowly into the city. People lined the streets to see Francis. But Francis' eyes were so bad that he was practically blind, barely able to distinguish shadows.

Once inside the bishop's palace, Francis was surrounded by the brothers and some doctors. One doctor told Francis his disease was incurable and that he would not live longer than another month. Francis stretched out his arms and said he welcomed Sister Death. He asked the brothers to sing *The Canticle of the Sun,* which of course they were happy to do. But they were unable to control their tears and emotions. While sobbing, they made beautiful music for Francis. And Francis added a new verse to the poem:

> Praised be thou, O Lord, for our Sister Bodily Death,
> from whom no living man can escape.
> Woe to those who die in mortal sin.
> Blessed those who have discovered thy most holy will,
> for to them the second death can do no harm.

Francis said he didn't want to die in a palace, and asked to be taken to the little field chapel in the valley, a place he loved dearly. Accompanied by a great throng of people, the brothers carried Francis down the hill to the valley below. At a leper hospital halfway between Assisi and the Porziuncula, Francis asked the brothers to stop and turn him around so he could face his beloved city one more time and bless it. Through his blind eyes, Francis looked long and hard at the city, whose image must have been emblazoned on his mind. It was a moment of profound silence. Francis slowly raised his hands, and, while making a sign of the cross over the city, said, "Blessed be you, holy city, for the Lord had chosen you to be a home and abode for all those who in truth will give glory to him and give honor to his name. And through you, holy city, many souls will be saved, and in you many servants of God will dwell."

Francis, lying prostrate on a cot, was perilously close to death. As the moment of death approached, Francis asked to be stripped naked and placed on the bare ground. His wish was granted. Lying naked on the ground, Francis was still preaching without words, showing the brothers his fragility and his closeness to Mother Earth. He was without any defenses, without any pretenses. He was an artist of his own life, and his last dramatic gesture was a symbol of his life, a life of vulnerability and humility, waiting for the final encounter with God. Welcoming death as his dear sister and ready to embrace her, Francis told the brothers, "My work is done. May Christ teach you what is yours to do."

Francis began to softly recite Psalm 141, his weakened voice barely audible: "my prayers rise like incense, my hands like the evening offering...to you, my Lord, I turn my eyes...." As the brothers chanted a psalm, Francis quietly died, naked on the ground, faithful to Lady Poverty until his final breath, which came late Saturday night on October 3, 1226. The larks flying over the little chapel sang their final farewell to their friend as his spirit ascended to heaven. Right up until his final breath, the chant of the resurrection, the chant that expresses the fullness of life, of peace, and of love, never ceased to be on Francis' lips.

The brothers carried Francis' body on a stretcher for one last trip to Assisi. They were followed by a procession of townspeople and clergy carrying olive branches and lighted candles and singing hymns. They stopped at San Damiano, so the Poor Clares could say farewell.

His life and heart had been completely transformed, going from a man of war to a man of peace. As he embraced Sister Death, Francis was at peace with God, with himself, and with all of creation.

Francis let God change his heart. God let Francis change the world. God wants to change our hearts so we can change our world.

Francis experienced God through the recognition of the supernatural within himself. He wasn't converted by theological ideas. Once he had awakened to the reality of God, he simply followed the gospel in purity and wholeness, transforming it from an ideal into a way of life. And he gave the gift he was given to others. It was all so simple for Francis: repent and live the gospel in simplicity and fullness, period. No need for embellishments or refinements, and certainly no need for altering or discounting anything that Christ asks. His idealism was uncompromising. Francis wanted for himself nothing but complete compliance to the gospel, giving his highest and utmost to God and eliminating everything else from his life.

WOVEN INTO THE MUNDANE

St. Francis of Assisi was truly a vessel of spiritual renewal within the Catholic Church. He had set Christian thinking on a new course. He opened windows that had been long closed; he let in fresh air and bright sunlight. Francis uprooted the gloom that pervaded Christianity and supplanted it with joy. When Francis was a child, the faithful were taught that their time on earth was brief and an insignificant prelude to eternity, and as they made their inexorable march toward this final reality, they did so alone. St. Francis didn't believe the prospect of the next world should cloud humanity's vision of this world. He saw an inherent harmony between the realm of the spirit and the realm of physical reality.

For many in his time, spirituality was other-worldly. But not for Francis. His spirituality was rooted right here on earth, and he never forgot that God humbly came to the earth he created. For Francis, spirituality was found in relationships, work, attitudes, illness, and dreams. Simply put, spirituality is an essential part of ordinary everyday life, fully embracing our emotional, physical, and mental states of being. The difficulty lies in achieving the concentrated attention needed to observe what is going on, moment by moment, in ourselves and around us, to uncover that spiritual dimension. Spiritual growth hinges on our ability to see the divine woven into mundane human reality—a feat that will take a lifetime.

Francis loved nature and saw all creation as a gift from God that was meant to be enjoyed. Moreover, because God animates all creation, all of creation is in relationship. We are all brothers and sisters bound together by love and therefore all equal in the eyes of God. For Francis, Christ wasn't a cosmic ruler and judge to be feared and worshipped. For Francis, Christ lives in you and in your neighbor. Christ literally dwells in your flesh. Francis loved the cross because the cross is a symbol of God's humility, poverty, and love. In meditating on the cross, Francis saw that God's love lacked nothing and that nothing was held back.

To come to Assisi and to walk in the footsteps of St. Francis is, ultimately, to walk in the footsteps of Christ. In his own time and for all time, St. Francis is the tireless messenger of love, continuously singing Incarnation's song. St. Francis is a towering figure because of his simplicity, which reduced the entire Christian faith to one word: love. As he neared the end of his earthly pilgrimage, St. Francis of Assisi did not judge, reject, hate, or condemn anyone or anything. He merely loved all, equally and passionately.

"Merely"...as if it were that simple.

A FOUNTAIN IN A PIAZZA

There is a line spoken by one of the characters in Alice Walker's book *The Color Purple* that I really love: "People think pleasing God is all God cares about. But any fool in the world can see [God is] always trying to please us back... always making little surprises and springing them on us when we least expect them." St. Francis always expected little surprises, little unexpected and pleasing gifts from God. He was always looking with open eyes. Francis had a profound reverence for the holiness of all created things. He looked at the visible things before him—a bright, yellow sunflower, a shimmering cypress tree, a lazy lizard on the path to the Carceri, a glistening fountain in a piazza—and was able to see the glory and perfection of his invisible God. Francis saw the essence of things and how they mirrored the essence of God.

God was always within his sight. Everything the saint saw was a sacrament. The Incarnation was a daily event for Francis, as God spoke through all the material things in the world God so lovingly created for us. What joy! Francis praised and thanked God every day for the simple things that revealed the grandeur of God. Teilhard de Chardin, the great French Jesuit philosopher and paleontologist, who was deeply influenced by St. Francis of Assisi, writes in *The Divine Milieu*: "God, in all that is most living and incarnate in Him, is not withdrawn from us beyond the tangible sphere; He is waiting for us at every moment in our action, in our work of the moment. He is in some sort at the tip of my pen, my spade, my brush, my needle—of my heart and of my thought."

Francis kissed the earth because he was keenly aware of the wonder of creation, and he was telling us we must respect all of creation. Francis praised Brother Sun and Sister Moon because they were created by God and are reflections of God's love and beauty. When Francis praises all of creation, he is not doing so as a high priest of ecology; rather, he is making a mystical statement that claims we can have an experience of God through creation, because God is present in all of created matter, energizing it.

St. Francis, help me see what is right in front of me. I too often see past things to the next thing, not allowing time for my eyes to really see and my mind to be truly mindful. I continue to pray: "Help me, Saint Francis, to see God in everything."

THE PERFECT ANTIDOTE

For a world that is currently searching for a spirituality that isn't encased in rigid or lifeless religions, Francis serves as a model of someone who went beyond religious dogma and into the realm of pure spirituality without condemning his Church. In the end, he renewed it. Francis was a man of contemplation and action, which is a rare combination. He loved greatly and he suffered greatly. Pope Pius XI wrote, "In no man, we think, was the likeness of Christ our Lord or the Gospel's ideal more perfectly reproduced than in St. Francis." Francis took his inner loneliness into the caves above Assisi, where in deep solitude he discovered the truth about his one true inner necessity, which became his authentic and unique vocation.

Francis, the wandering minstrel, became both a nature

mystic and what we would call today an environmental activist, perhaps the first in history. He pleaded with political authorities to ban the trapping of larks. He convinced one young boy to free some doves. He urged people to feed the birds, especially on Christmas Day. But the hallmark of his ministry was peacemaking and reconciliation. He was always willing to do whatever he could to resolve disputes, be they within families, between cites, among religions or private citizens. When it came to preaching, his approach was truly innovative in that he preached outdoors, in piazzas and open fields, which was unheard of before Francis. In his preaching, Francis spoke in the vernacular and avoided theological arguments or polemics. He spoke spontaneously from his heart about his personal experience, offering the possibility and promise of transformation rather than mere information. He said he simply wanted to "heal wounds and unite what had fallen apart." He wanted people to find peace within themselves, with God, with each other, and with all of creation.

To understand St. Francis and to fully appreciate him, you must penetrate the mystery of his deep devotion to the humanity of Jesus, a devotion not born of a learned tradition but which sprang directly from his heart and his personal experience of God's love. His devotion is appealing because it was not satisfied with merely imitating or following Christ, but it transformed Jesus into a friend whom Francis could embrace and be comforted by within the brotherhood of his own heart.

It's important to realize that this was a revolutionary concept; it toppled the stern, majestic, Byzantine Christ who sat on a mighty, heavenly throne as the supreme ruler and judge of humankind, and in its place offered the tender infant Jesus, born to share our human weakness and suffering and to endure the bitter, brutal passion of the cross for us. St. Francis took the enshrined Jesus out of the cathedrals and monasteries and let him walk among the people, touching them with his mercy, kindness, and compassion.

Dante, in *Paradiso*, his poetic tribute to Francis, praises the saint's capacity for wonder, love, joy, and the appreciation of beauty, and exalts Francis over all the learned doctors of the Church and holy founders of monastic orders as the most perfect imitator of Christ. St. Francis was a simple man who was enthralled by the mysterious beauty of creation. He delighted in everything he saw, for he saw the resplendent love of God in everything, and so he praised God for all of creation. Francis did not shun the world nor try to escape it; he embraced it, fully and without reservation.

So many people today feel they must be able to express their religious beliefs in Hegelian or Heideggerian terms. They miss the point. In contrast, St. Francis' life illustrates the power of total self-surrender to the kingdom of God, giving up everything for the fullness of life in communion with the Creator, Sustainer, and Fulfillment of all things. What do we not enjoy who enjoy God, who enjoys all things? What do we not have who have communion and friendship with God, who is lord of all things?

Francis is the higher wisdom of those who know how to hold on to all things with open hands. All our great scientific and technological advances have somehow stripped us of our innocence and simplicity, leaving us feeling alone and disquieted. St. Francis can help us recapture the pure simplicity and gentle innocence that are the cornerstones of human happiness. St. Francis can still be a teacher and a guide for the modern follower of Christ.

The words Francis heard while kneeling before the cross in San Damiano—"repair my church"—entered so deeply into his heart that he was profoundly changed. While he reached heights of unimaginable joy, he also frequently plunged into deep suffering—a dark night of the soul mixed with physical sickness and mental dismay of bickering among the brothers, many of whom had no zeal for his mystical vision. But his love of God was so great, nothing could diminish or extinguish it. In the midst of great suffering and darkness he composed a brilliantly beautiful poem that shimmered with sparkling insight into the mystery of creation. The smaller he became, the bigger God became. Francis is the perfect antidote for all the ills that plague modern life.

THE HEARTBEAT OF GOD

After each trip I made to places of crushing suffering, such as Uganda and Haiti, coming home was always a difficult transition. Going from extreme need to stunning abundance is jarring. In a land of plenty we hunger for more. We have turned greed into a virtue. Our lives are fragmented and disconnected. How sad, how tragically sad, that we allow ourselves to be ruled and controlled by our illusions and fears. And so we live much of our lives in a prison of falsity. This is not God's plan for any of us. God wants us to know true peace and freedom. We were created in the image of God, which is to say we were created to mirror the love of the Trinity by giving ourselves away, for life to give life, for mercy to give mercy, for compassion to give compassion, for peace to give peace, for love to give love.

Because we don't know our real self, our true nature, we live in darkness and doubt. Conflicts haunt us. We feel threatened. And so we build walls around ourselves for protection. In the depths of our being we feel isolated, alone, naked. Joy is fleeting. Bitterness grows in our uncultivated garden starving for sunlight. The goodness and creativity of God is unknown, hidden, in part, by our own brokenness, our own weakness.

In the slums of the world, I saw more clearly my own weaknesses, and subsequently I slowly began to see the importance of humility. Only through humble eyes can God be seen. I am nothing; God is everything. But, in my nothingness, God gives me everything. Humility helps shatter illusions. Humility is the truest form of honesty. It sees our weaknesses and vulnerabilities. Humility allows God to transform our weaknesses into strengths. As the opposite of pride, humility reflects honesty, a holistic sense of reality, and a keen awareness of the awesomeness of the universe and the profound mystery of God. Growth in humility is a sign of maturing holiness. One of my dearest friends is an Orthodox monk and priest. He said, "Humility is honesty, is holiness. And it is only in humility that we can authentically meet God, on God's terms. Humility is not a giving up, but rather, a giving in."

Humility is also a pathway to prayer. Prayer is the doorway to the heart, the center of our being, the place where we can let go, let go of pretense, pride, ego, and a host of things blocking us from the true source of life, the true source of love, God. In the innermost chamber of the heart we see the dissonance between the Spirit of God and our spirit; it is here we struggle to dissolve that disharmony. In the safety of the heart, we can let go of fear and we can risk change. In the heart, conflict gives way to harmony. In the heart, what's mine becomes God's. In the heart, humility becomes holiness.

St. Francis clearly understood that God became vulnerable for us. And God's vulnerability is a supreme expression of divine love. A psalmist once said that God's love is better than life itself. More to the point: God's love is life. Without God, I am nothing; I have no life. With God, I lack nothing; I have the fullness of life. Love is life. Jesus is a lover. Love cannot be conditional. Love cannot be purchased. Love cannot be used for our gain, cannot be self-centered. Love is liberating. Love is self-emptying. Love is to be given away. Love is only known from within, as an experience that changes everything—even changes bread and wine into the very substance of God. Love is all-powerful, all-merciful, all-compassionate, all-forgiving, always giving. The source of love is God the Creator and Sustainer of everything. Love animates all life. And through love all life is connected.

Love does not throw stones. Love tosses bouquets of kindness. Love does not judge or condemn others. Love only gives and shares, everything, always. Our incapacity to love is rooted in pride and our false notion that everything must have a tangible benefit toward increasing our status and security. "What's in it for me?" is not a question love asks. Love seeks no remuneration, knows nothing about the market economy or credit cards or tax deductions or cost-benefit analysis. Love is a gift to be freely given and freely received. We do not merit nor can we earn God's love. Yet in every moment, in every place, in every situation, God's love is there reaching out to us, calling us by name. But most of the time we're deaf and don't hear the silent voice of God. The wordless voice of God can only be heard in the heart. God's heart speaks to our hearts. But our hearts are a tangle of contradictions, fragmented and overwhelmed by disappointments, struggles, worries, and doubts; in the noise and chaos of our cluttered hearts we cannot hear God, know God, or feel God's love.

Sadly, our hearts are broken, wounded by a thousand little cuts and bruises, wounded by betrayal and rejection. Jesus came to heal our hearts. Through his Sacred Heart, the heart of God is revealed. To contemplate and imitate the Sacred Heart of Jesus is to contemplate and imitate the love of God. Through Jesus' heart, God loves us and shows us how to relate to the divine and to all of humanity.

Jesus is the heartbeat of God. The heart is the center, the core of our bodies, spirits, and souls. The heart is the home of our deepest thoughts, our deepest desires, our deepest longings. It is in and through our hearts that we come to understand ourselves and learn how to relate to others. The heart is fundamental to physical and spiritual life. In the physical heart of Jesus, the spiritual heart of God was incarnated and made flesh. Jesus loves with a human heart, a human heart that beats with divine love. Our human hearts need to be transformed into sacred hearts, divine hearts that beat with human love. We were created for relationship. Love is the doorway to authentic, life-giving relationships.

Each day brings its share of sweetness and bitterness, of joy and misery, of comfort and pain, of laughter and tears, of hopes and disappointments. Each day brings rejection and acceptance, loneliness and communion. Each day brings moments of fear and despair, courage and delight. Each day brings a flood of words and a desert of silence. Each day we have moments of transparency and deception, moments of faithfulness and infidelity, moments of strength and weakness, moments of purity and lust, moments of beauty and cruelty, moments of abundance and famine, moments of peace and turmoil. And each day God is present in all these things, in all the ups and downs, in the heartache and elation, in the victories and the defeats. But God's presence is hidden and silent. It is only through faith that we can see and hear God, even though our seeing and hearing are gravely impaired and far from perfect. We really don't know God, yet we do know God. Our not knowing is the beginning of our knowing. But the fullness of knowing will always be beyond us, yet hidden within us.

To see God in all things each day is the mysticism of everyday life, the ordinary mysticism that sees the extraordinary work of God even in the mundane events of everyday life. With everyday mystical eyes we are able to see God in both the cries of the poor and the laughter of a child, in both a tender kiss and in a deadly disease.

God doesn't bomb us in order to get us to change our behavior. God whispers words of love to our hearts. We may resort to "shock and awe" to show our power in order to get others to bend to our will, but that's not God's way. God gives us space and freedom to accept or reject his gentle overtures of love. God seeks a deep emotional response from us that emerges from a transformed inner life that allows us to acknowledge God's power and our need for God. And it is our response to God that allows us to subdue our ego and permits our true self to emerge. This transformational change leads to a radical reorientation of our outlook on life. We will see the world and all of creation with new eyes and we will love with new hearts. Badness shall be transformed into goodness. Grace changes everything, makes everything beautiful. We simply need stillness and silence...and ears to hear.

A NEW HEART

On the morning of July 26, 1997, during the communal recital of morning prayers from the Liturgy of the Hours at Collegio Sant' Isidoro, we read five verses from Ezekiel. I heard the middle three verses in a way I had never heard them before. The words rang out in clarity:

> I will sprinkle clean water upon you,
> and you shall be clean from all your uncleannesses,
>   and from all your idols I will cleanse you.
>
> A new heart I will give you,
> and a new spirit I will put in you;
> and I will take out of your flesh the heart of stone
>   and give you a heart of flesh.
>
> And I will put my spirit within you, and cause you to
>   walk in my statutes and be careful to observe
>   my ordinances.

The pilgrimage helped me to see more clearly the abundance of God's goodness, and in the light of that awareness I could better see my own shortcomings and insignificance. Often while studying the life of St. Francis, his words sound harsh when he expresses his attitude about his own sinfulness and need for penance. Murray Bodo, OFM, explains why:

> The main reason why the words of St. Francis sound at times rather negative, rather deprecatory of what is earthly, even what is human. He is not saying that the body, the world, the human person are evil. He is only saying that apart from God, without God, in comparison

to God, we and everything else that exists are really nothing. Of ourselves we are worthless and vile. Of *ourselves*, on our own, as it were.

During that first pilgrimage I realized that I was still a sinner who stumbled all too frequently. I was not "clean of all my uncleanness." I still harbored a few false idols. My heart of flesh was still all too easily hardened into stone. But I also realized that my life was no longer about falling...it was about getting up, about accepting God's love and grace. Despite its weaknesses, my heart had been changed, and was growing stronger. *(Confession: 17 years later, I still stumble far too often.)*

During the pilgrimage, I came to see that conversion is a continuing process rather than a single moment or event in my life. Francis' life was filled with conversion moments. The process of conversion includes a constant need for repentance and renewal. Conversion, at its root, is a change of heart; it turns us away from the notion that we are the center of the universe. Conversion often means listening to the events in our lives that change our perspective. The fruit of conversion is a release from the burden of self-groundedness so that we can enter into the freedom of being grounded in God, which will create a complete recentering of our passion and a complete realignment of our affections. But it takes time and effort. Each day, I need to be cleansed, to be given a new heart and a new spirit. On the morning of July 26, 1997, I felt, ever so briefly, that cleansing, that new heart, that new spirit. Incarnation is a daily event.

St. Francis of Assisi is a saint of incarnation. There was a visible manifestation of the conversion process that was going on inside of him. He preached by the witness of his life.

His life was his sermon. And that sermon still has something to say to us today.

FAR AND NEAR

There is a loneliness to the past and the future. I am not there; I am here in the present. I am far from whom I was in the past and far from whom I will be in the future. I am only near myself in this present moment. God too is far and near. Far in the sense that God leaves us to ourselves in order for us to discover our own hearts and the heart of God; yet God is as near as the next breath we take, as near as our very heartbeat. Because we do not see or know God, who is so far and so near, we have the anguish of loneliness at the core of our being. We know emptiness not plenitude. Sadness is always around the corner; joy occasionally comes and quickly goes.

To discover God in your heart you must journey beyond all self-consciousness to an awareness of a reality greater than yourself. It is a long journey and a short journey. And on the journey we must drop all notions of God and all notions of self. Only then can God reveal God to you and reveal you to yourself.

In loneliness and longing, we begin our journey to God. Stripped of everything, we have nothing; we take nothing. Yet our very loneliness is graced with the possibility to discover the transcendent. Even the silence of God is graced and speaks of the mystery of God and God's forgiving nearness, God's hidden intimacy. In stillness and silence we learn about a love that shares itself, an overflowing love that dissolves all alienation and fills the empty space within us.

God is here in this moment, waiting with open and outstretched arms, waiting to embrace and caress you with endless love. Kiss this moment, for in it is perfect joy and all good. Love is the symphony of life. It needs to be practiced and played every day. God is the composer, Christ is the conductor, and we are the performers.

John O'Donohue, a deeply sensitive Irish writer, said: "If we could but find a rhythm of being which could balance a contemplative grace, a poetry of motion and an accompanying stillness and silence, our pilgrimage through this world would flow in beauty through the most ragged and forsaken heartlands of confusion and dishevelment." St. Francis found that way of being.

As our journey in the footsteps of St. Francis comes to an end, I leave you with a prayer penned by St. Francis that gives us a glimpse of the ascetic theology that emerges from his interior life. Near the end of his life, Francis was too ill to attend a chapter meeting. Instead, he sent a letter to the chapter general and all the friars in attendance. In it, he wrote:

> Almighty, eternal, just, and merciful God,
>> have us poor wretches for your sake do
>> what we know you want,
> and have us always want whatever is pleasing to you;
>> so that cleansed interiorly,
>> and interiorly enlightened
> and aglow with the fire of the Holy Spirit,
>> we may be able to follow
> in the footsteps of your Son, our Lord Jesus Christ.
> Aided by your soul-saving grace,
>> may we be able to get to you, who in perfect Trinity
> and simple Unity
> live and reign and triumph
> as God almighty world without end. Amen.

THE HOLY, LITTLE CITY THAT SITS ON A HILL

Pope John XXIII was in Assisi on October 4, 1962, in order to celebrate the feast of St. Francis. On that occasion, he said:

> It may be asked: why has God lavished on Assisi such enchanting surroundings, such a wealth of art, such a fascination for holiness which seems to hover in the air and which pilgrims subconsciously sense? The answer is simple: so that we, through a common, universal language, might learn to know our Creator and to feel ourselves in solidarity with one another...

In Assisi, I came to know the Creator and truly did feel in solidarity with all of humanity. And that knowledge and feeling stayed with me after I left the holy, little city that sits on a hill. It burns within me. But I must keep it burning. Each day, as best I can, I try to stoke the flames within me, the flames of the spirit of the eternal shrine that is Assisi.

All praise be yours, my Lord, through all that you have made...

Pax et Bonum Communications

"Every act of mercy and kindness brings us closer to the reality of God."

Founded by Gerry Straub, *Pax et Bonum Communications* is a nonprofit charitable organization whose primary purpose is to proclaim through image and word that care for the chronically poor is an essential component of the spiritual life, especially for the followers of Christ. Rooted in Franciscan spiritually, along with the mystical traditions of all faiths, *Pax et Bonum Communications* produces films that foster compassion for those who suffer from hunger and injustice while also inspiring genuine and respectful community among all people, no matter one's faith or lack of faith.

Pax et Bonum Communications champions the importance of contemplation and action. In addition to our films, we offer free educational presentations to churches and schools that focus on two major themes: poverty and prayer. No matter our faith, we believe the best way to love God is through acts of love, mercy, compassion, and kindness for those who are suffering in cruel prisons of unjust poverty. We believe everyone is called to a life of sharing, caring, and giving. We believe in the importance of genuine interfaith dialogue. We believe violence is always wrong, that war is never a solution. Our goal is stress the necessity of prayer, peace, harmony, humility, and social justice. In the spirit of St. Francis of Assisi, we hope to show the connectedness of all of creation, which will promote a deeper understanding and appreciation of the common good and our essential need to become nurturers, healers, and consolers. We will not shy away from confronting the injustice of global poverty where more than 10,000 children a day die of starvation; we will be a strong, consistent, and prophetic voice speaking out on behalf of the poor and encouraging people to enter more deeply into prayer and to be more compassionate to those in dire need.

Our name comes from the salutation always used by St. Francis: peace and good. Pax et Bonum is the Latin translation of the saint's wish for everyone he encountered. In his native Italian, Francis would have said, "pace e bene"...which we prefer to translate as "peace and blessing."

And peace and blessing is what we hope and pray *Pax et Bonum Communications* offers to a world sorely in need of peace and blessing.

Pax et Bonum Communications, Inc.

827 N. Hollywood Way # 555 ⁑ Burbank, CA 91505

Please visit our website: http://www.paxetbonumcomm.org/

Pax et Bonum Communications is a 501(c)3 Public Charity

Other Books by Gerard Thomas Straub

SALVATION FOR SALE

DEAR KATE (A NOVEL)

THE SUN & MOON OVER ASSISI*

WHEN DID I SEE YOU HUNGRY? (PHOTO/ESSAY)

THOUGHTS OF A BLIND BEGGAR

HIDDEN IN THE RUBBLE

❋

Films by Gerard Thomas Straub

WE HAVE A TABLE FOR FOUR READY

ROOM ENOUGH FOR JOY

GLIDEPATH TO RECOVERY

WHEN DID I SEE YOU HUNGRY?

EMBRACING THE LEPER

HOLY PICTURES

RESCUE ME

ENDLESS EXODUS

POVERTY AND PRAYER

THE PATIENCE OF A SAINT

WHERE LOVE IS

THE FACES OF POVERTY

ROOM AT THE INN

THE NARROW PATH

THE FRAGRANT SPIRIT OF LIFE

POVERTY AND PRAYER II

A DISTRESSING DISGUISE

CATHEDRALS OF THE POOR

MUD PIES AND KITES

WE ANOINT THEIR WOUNDS

THE WINGS OF LOVE

THE SMILE OF A SICK CHILD

named best spirituality hardcover book of 2001 by the Catholic Press Association